CONGRESS IN REVERSE

CONGRESS IN REVERSE

Repeals from Reconstruction to the Present

JORDAN M. RAGUSA AND
NATHANIEL A. BIRKHEAD

THE UNIVERSITY OF CHICAGO PRESS
CHICAGO AND LONDON

The University of Chicago Press, Chicago 60637
The University of Chicago Press, Ltd., London
© 2020 by The University of Chicago
All rights reserved. No part of this book may be used or reproduced in any manner whatsoever without written permission, except in the case of brief quotations in critical articles and reviews. For more information, contact the University of Chicago Press, 1427 E. 60th St., Chicago, IL 60637.
Published 2020

29 28 27 26 25 24 23 22 21 20   1 2 3 4 5

ISBN-13: 978-0-226-71733-3 (cloth)
ISBN-13: 978-0-226-71747-0 (paper)
ISBN-13: 978-0-226-71750-0 (e-book)
DOI: https://doi.org/10.7208/chicago/9780226717500.001.0001

Library of Congress Cataloging-in-Publication Data

Names: Ragusa, Jordan M., author. | Birkhead, Nathaniel, author.
Title: Congress in reverse : repeals from Reconstruction to the present / Jordan M. Ragusa and Nathaniel A. Birkhead.
Description: Chicago ; London : The University of Chicago Press, 2020. | Includes bibliographical references and index.
Identifiers: LCCN 2019052055 | ISBN 9780226717333 (cloth) | ISBN 9780226717470 (paperback) | ISBN 9780226717500 (ebook)
Subjects: LCSH: Repeal of legislation—United States. | Repeal of legislation—United States—History. | United States. Congress.
Classification: LCC KF4945 .R34 2020 | DDC 328.73/077—dc23
LC record available at https://lccn.loc.gov/2019052055

CONTENTS

1.	When and Why Repeals Occur	1
2.	Significant Repeals, Killer Congresses, and Doomed Statutes	25
3.	Problem-Solving Efforts	50
4.	Partisan Motivations	69
5.	Preferences of Lawmakers	100
6.	Conclusions and Discussion	126
	Acknowledgments	149
	Appendix A	153
	Appendix B	159
	Appendix C	161
	Appendix D	165
	Notes	185
	References	197
	Index	215

CHAPTER ONE

When and Why Repeals Occur

In the 2008 campaign, candidate Barack Obama promised to deliver "affordable, accessible health care for every single American." Upon taking office, Obama invited his Democratic allies in Congress to take the lead in creating the new law. After all, Democratic lawmakers had begun work on health care reform long before Obama took office. With a first-term president, majorities in both chambers, and the ability to circumvent a Republican filibuster via reconciliation in the Senate, health care reform could be achieved in the 111th Congress (2009–11) with Democratic votes alone.

Democrats ultimately succeeded in their effort to expand national health insurance coverage in March of 2010. At the White House signing ceremony, Vice Present Joe Biden was caught on camera saying "This is a big f**king deal." Yet lost in celebration that day was the fact that the Affordable Care Act's (ACA's) fate was far from certain. In fact, the day *before* the law was enacted, with Democrats still in control of both chambers, Republicans introduced three repeal bills in the House and one repeal bill in the Senate. Needless to say, these bills had no chance of passing either chamber. Later, after winning control of the House in the 2010 midterm, Republicans in the 112th and 113th Congresses (2011–15) passed dozens of ACA repeal bills in the lower chamber. Predictably, these bills died in the Senate, which remained under Democratic control. But once the GOP gained control of the Senate in the 114th Congress (2015–17), Republicans employed the same reconciliation procedure Democrats used to circumvent a filibuster in 2010 and, for the first time, passed a single repeal bill in both chambers. Although Obama's veto was inevitable, the bill's passage represented a significant milestone because it demonstrated the viability of the GOP's repeal efforts under the right institutional conditions. As Speaker of the House Paul Ryan explained, "Now, is someone named

Obama going to sign a bill into law repealing Obamacare? Of course not. But we have now demonstrated that, if we elect a Republican president, we can use this same path to repeal Obamacare without 60 votes in the Senate."[1]

In the 2016 campaign, candidate Donald Trump promised, "When we win on November 8th and elect a Republican Congress, we will be able to immediately repeal and replace Obamacare." Upon taking office, Trump invited his Republican allies in Congress to take the lead in repealing the law. After all, Republican lawmakers had begun work on repealing the ACA long before Trump took office. With a first-term president, majorities in both chambers, and the ability to circumvent a Democratic filibuster via reconciliation in the Senate, an ACA repeal could be achieved in the 115th Congress (2017–19) with Republican votes alone.

In September of 2017, following a seven-year effort—consisting of countless campaign pledges, dozens of proposals, and approximately one hundred votes—the Republican Party *failed* in their effort to repeal the ACA despite the same institutional conditions that saw Democrats successfully enact the law. In this respect, unified party control was not sufficient for Republicans to repeal the health care reform law, despite the predictions of countless observers, including Donald Trump and many GOP lawmakers. However, Republicans did succeed in repealing a portion of the ACA—the individual mandate—when they enacted a sweeping tax reform bill in December of that year.

Given the ACA's passage and postpassage history, it seems safe to conclude that repeals defy easy explanation. It is difficult to overstate: the GOP's inability to repeal the ACA despite an intense multiyear effort is one of the most notable political events in recent political history. Further complicating matters is the fact that in the 1990s, the Republican Party succeeded in repealing a number of major statutes—the Glass-Steagall Act, Aid to Families with Dependent Children (AFDC), and the National Maximum Speed Law—even with Bill Clinton, a Democrat, opposing their repeal in the White House. In this book, we hope to make sense of the puzzle described above and understand when and why repeals occur. In doing so, we seek to answer the following questions:

(1) *Are law creation and law repeal mirror opposites of one another?* Given the GOP's failure to repeal the bulk of the ACA, despite the same institutional conditions as at the time of the law's enactment, the answer may be no even though law creation and law

repeal are subject to the same legislative procedures and constitutional requirements.

(2) *What factors make repeal more likely in some Congresses?* Because the Republican Party succeeded in passing a number of notable repeals in the 1990s, under divided government, but repealed few laws in the 2000s, with unified control, it would seem that the majority's capacity to repeal legislation waxes and wanes over time.

(3) *Why are some statutes more likely to be repealed?* Given the repeal of the ACA's individual mandate—a tax provision—despite the failure to repeal the law's health care provisions, some statutes seem to be more durable than others.

(4) *Can existing theories of the legislative process make sense of when and why repeals occur?* Although legislative scholars focus almost exclusively on the factors that lead to the creation of new laws, perhaps one or more of the literature's leading theories explain repeals as well.

FUNDAMENTAL QUESTIONS

Why Study Repeals?

Studying repeals is worthwhile for two primary reasons. First, repeals are substantively important. As a policy matter, repeals often represent decades-long efforts to reshape the nation's laws, and when they succeed, repeals make dramatic changes to the nation's policies and programs. As a political matter, repeal efforts often hinge on the key issues of the day and are usually, though not always, contentious. Readers familiar with American political history will recognize many of the successful repeals that we discuss in this book, including the Tenure of Office Act in 1887; multiple monetary statutes in the 1890s; the gold standard in 1933; the Chinese Exclusion Acts in 1943; the Gulf of Tonkin Resolution in 1970; multiple New Deal statutes, including AFDC and Glass-Steagall, in the 1990s; and Don't Ask, Don't Tell in 2010.

Secondly, studying repeals is theoretically valuable, because they provide a different lens through which observers can assess Congress's performance. Although academics and nonacademics alike focus on the creation of new laws, repeals may have their own dynamics that require more nuanced theories of legislative politics. In this way, studying repeals may provide fresh insights on Congress's operation. Repeals also allow researchers to compare congressional activity across time in a longitudinal manner. Not only can we compare the initial creation of the law to its subsequent repeal, but we can also relate the enactment period to every subsequent period where repeal does not occur. Finally, repeals have normative importance. On the one hand, repeals are part of the normal process of revising the nation's laws, and when defective laws are passed, the public interest is served by repealing them. On the other hand, a number of prominent thinkers, including James Madison and Alexis de Tocqueville, warned of the dangers of too much repealing activity and the "capricious tendencies" of the American political system.

Despite the value of studying repeals, research on the topic is surprisingly limited. Instead, since the Founding era, legislative scholars have focused their attention on the politics of law creation. When asked to explain lawmaking under the new Constitution, James Madison is said to have cited three key principles: "compromise, compromise, and compromise." Woodrow Wilson in his doctoral dissertation (1885) lamented the slow nature of law creation in Madison's system of government, favoring instead a British-style parliamentary system. A host of mid-twentieth-century scholars proposed strengthening political parties as a solution to the challenges of enacting new laws (Burns 1963; Schattschneider 1942), while in the last quarter century, several notable political scientists have explored the determinants of legislative productivity (Binder 1999; Mayhew 1991; Rohde 1991). In the most recent work in this tradition, researchers explore nuanced factors that explain legislative productivity such as the importance of bill cosponsors (Woon 2008), how the House and Senate resolve policy disagreements (Ryan 2018), how legislative procedures affect lawmakers' capacity to forge compromises (Koger 2010), the effectiveness of individual lawmakers (Volden and Wiseman 2014), and how policy type affects legislative productivity (Lapinski 2008), among other topics.

Yet many of the authors who have contributed to our understanding of the policy process, including some of those listed above, cite repeal as an important legislative action. In "Vices of the Political System of the United States," James Madison lamented that some legislatures hastily undo legislation, writing: "We daily see laws repealed or superseded, before any trial can have been made of their merits: and even before a knowledge of them can have reached the remoter districts within which they were to operate." In describing how laws enacted in one era spawn legislative action in subsequent eras, Woodrow Wilson (1885) remarked that "once you begin the dance of legislation, you must struggle through its mazes as best you can to its breathless end—if any end there be" (297).

Lastly, in discussing possible extensions of his pioneering work, David Mayhew (2005) asked, rhetorically, "What ever became of . . . repeal of the right-to-work clause (14b) of the Taft-Hartley Act?" (94).

Nonetheless, in political science and economics, a small but growing group of scholars have studied efforts to reverse prior enactments and decisions. Researchers have written on the survivability of federal programs and reauthorization efforts (Adler and Wilkerson 2012; Berry, Burden, and Howell 2010; Carpenter and Lewis 2004; Corder 2004), the longevity of executive orders (Thrower 2017), the maintenance of general interest reforms (Leighton and López 2012; Patashnik 2008), and the passage of amendments (Adler and Wilkerson 2012; Maltzman and Shipan 2008). In this group, we are the only authors to focus on repeals exclusively, having published two articles and one book chapter on the topic (Ragusa 2010; Ragusa and Birkhead 2015; Ragusa 2017). No book has yet conducted an in-depth examination of what we believe to be a theoretically interesting and practically important topic.

What Is a Repeal?

Despite the heightened focus on repeals in some key eras in US history, including the current one, we lack a clear understanding of what repeals are. As a starting point, figure 1.1 tracks how often the word "repeal" appears in national news coverage of Congress from 1877 to 2017.[2] We can see that the media's interest in the topic of repeals, and presumably that of lawmakers and the American public as well, is not constant throughout history: repeals garner more attention in some eras than others. Likewise, while the contemporary focus on repeals is high, due in large part to the GOP's effort to repeal the Affordable Care Act, it is not unprecedented.

As shown in the figure, the three biannual periods from January 1932 to June 1933—during the Great Depression, with multiple repeal efforts focused on monetary and macroeconomic policy—had the greatest repeal coverage in history. Similarly, popular attention on the repeal of bimetallism was high in the latter months of 1893. Attention was also high throughout the year 2017 as a consequence the GOP's effort to repeal the ACA and exact a sweeping tax reform bill. A number of other historically notable spikes in repeal coverage exist as well. From left to right, the figure shows spikes in repeal coverage in 1879 with debates over the Reconstruction-era Force Acts and bimetallism; in 1926 when lawmakers repealed a range of taxes, including the gift tax and capital-stock tax; in 1930 in debates over repealing Volstead Act and the Eighteenth

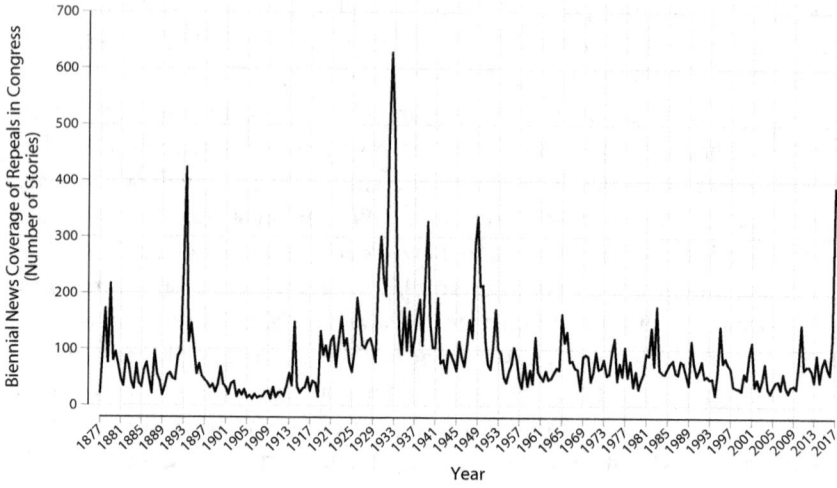

Fig. 1.1. Historical News Coverage of Repeal Efforts (1877–2017)

Amendment; in 1939 when Congress repealed the Neutrality Act's arms embargo; in 1949 with a failed effort to repeal Taft-Hartley; in 1965 during another failed effort to repeal Taft-Hartley and successful repeal of a series of excise taxes; in 1983 when Congress repealed the withholding tax on interest and dividends; in 1995 with efforts to repeal the assault weapons ban, pesticides regulation, and the national speed law and to enact sweeping welfare reform; and in 2010 during debates over repealing Don't Ask, Don't Tell.

In an effort to better understand what repeals are, a necessary first step toward understanding when and why they happen, in the paragraphs below we discuss what *counts* as a repeal, for analytical purposes, and *how* laws are repealed, from both a legislative and legal standpoint. We explain that repeal has both a legal and a substantive definition—with each having trade-offs as to how repeals are measured—and that repeals can be classified as either full or partial, with one more common than the other.

From a strictly legal standpoint, a repeal is an action that removes text from a statutory volume. At the federal level, when Congress enacts a new law, the various provisions are rearranged according to their policy content and added to the US Code. As a legal reference volume, the US Code makes it easy to catalog repealed statutes, yet this approach suffers from a few limitations. First and foremost, it is not possible to discern whether the repeal was substantively meaningful without strong assumptions or post hoc calculations. Most new laws contain some repeals, and many existing laws have had at least one provision repealed, raising questions about which repeal, if any, was a notable change in national policy. Likewise, repeals in the US Code can be relatively mundane actions that simply reorganize the nation's statutes and/or update old laws to include new text. Second, there are methodological limitations to cataloging repeals in this manner. A statute can be repealed "by implication," without the express intent of lawmakers, if a new law is simply inconsistent with an existing statute. At the same time, because the unit of analysis is an individual statute, not a full law, it can be difficult if not impossible to identify variables that explain repeal at the same measurement level.

An alternative approach—which we adopt in this book—is to focus on historically notable repeal efforts cited by journalists, policy experts, and academics. Cataloging repeals in this way prioritizes substantive value over ease of measurement. First, by relying on the judgment of experts, it is easier to isolate substantively important changes in the nation's laws and ignore mundane or technical statutory revisions. Second, researchers can be sure that the action was consistent with the concept of a repeal as an effort to "nullify," "annul," or "undo" a previously enacted law. And third, because the unit of analysis is a law rather than a tiny portion of a law, it is possible to identify covariates at the same measurement level including characteristics of the roll-call vote, the sponsor of the law, etc. An obvious downside is that we lack objective criteria for what makes a given repeal notable, significant, important, etc. We note, however, that this approach is consistent with how legislative scholars have typically measured legislative productivity. For example, in 1991 David Mayhew challenged researchers to move beyond simple law counts in their analyses of legislative productivity and focus instead on the handful of substantively important laws enacted during a legislative session.[3]

Legislatively, repeals may occur in several ways, including through bills that directly target prior laws, as a rider in a bill with other statutory content, or as one element in a broader set of reform efforts. As an example of a law expressly targeting a prior law, consider the Neutrality Act of 1939—establishing the direction of American foreign policy during the build-up to World War II—which included specific language that repealed the arms embargo passed in the Neutrality Act of 1937. By contrast, the "Risk Rule" statute—which the Pentagon had utilized in an attempt to prevent women from serving on combat ships or aircraft—was repealed as one element of the much larger National Defense Authorization Act of 1994. Lastly, in the case of welfare reform in the 1990s, Temporary Assistance for Needy Families (TANF) repealed and replaced the AFDC program by amending the Social Security Act enacted in 1935. All in all, repeals can take on several forms.

Adding yet another layer of complexity, a particular legislative act may face multiple repeals over many years. As an example, consider efforts to repeal the Affordable Care Act. It may come as a surprise to some, but the fact is that a number of ACA provisions have, in fact, been repealed. Among the dozen or so repeals, three stand out. First, in 2011, just a year after enactment, 40% of Democrats joined with every Republican in repealing the ACA's 1099 tax reporting requirement. In his signing statement, Obama said he was glad to "work with Congress to improve [the ACA]."[4] Second, in 2013 lawmakers repealed a set of ACA provisions dealing with community living assistance. In this case, the Obama administration asked Congress to repeal the Community Living Assistance Services and Supports (CLASS) Act, saying the policy did not have "a viable path forward" to implementation.[5] Notably, these two repeals—and more than a dozen others—are contained in the US Code, yet we do not consider them in this book on the following grounds. First, neither made substantively important changes to the ACA's basic structure. Second, it would be a stretch to say they "nullified" the ACA given that they likely strengthened the law. And third, the CLASS Act repeal is best described as a technical revision given administrative challenges. Simply put, we think these repeals do not accurately reflect what is most important about the seven-year effort to repeal the ACA.

A third notable ACA repeal—no doubt the most consequential—is the repeal of the individual mandate in 2017. In this case, the challenge arose due to the fact that Republican lawmakers *amended* the individual mandate to make the penalty for not purchasing health care $0 without formally repealing the corresponding statutes. As President Trump noted in his State of the Union address in 2018, "We repealed the core of disastrous Obamacare—the individual mandate is now gone."[6] Nevertheless, this action, which most observers agree constitutes a historically notable effort to undo a landmark law, does not appear in the US Code as such.[7] In each of these cases, our approach of relying on the judgment of experts helps ensure the database we compile ignores routine or technical forms of repeals while also capturing what counts as a repeal on substantive grounds.

We also note that repeals can also be classified as full or partial. A full repeal is an action that reverses an entire law or the entirety of the law's central components. A partial repeal, by comparison, is an action that reverses a key aspect of the original law while leaving other major statutes unchanged. It is important to note that, while lawmakers frequently talk of full repeals, campaigning on promises to "repeal law x," partial repeals are the norm by a very wide margin. Simply put, there is a wide gulf between how repeals are spoken about in the popular understanding and how repeals actually occur from a technical standpoint. Likewise, there may be little difference in the policy implications of a full or partial repeal, as there are dozens of partial repeals that represent some of the most important in history even though they revise a smaller portion of a law's original content. For this reason, in this book we count both full and partial repeals, focusing on the substantive importance of the action rather than its raw statutory size.

Another landmark health care law provides a clear illustration of the distinction between full and partial repeals. Enacted in 1988, the Medicare Catastrophic Coverage Act (MCCA) was the largest increase in Medicare benefits since the program's creation in 1965. Unfortunately for those who crafted and helped enact the law—and in particular House Ways and Means Chair Dan Rostenkowski (D-IL), who had to flee a group of angry seniors on foot—the MCCA caused a sudden backlash among many elderly Medicare recipients. In a stunning turn of events, Congress repealed a number of central elements of the law just one year later. Yet even in this seemingly straightforward case, a handful of notable provisions in the 135-page law—in particular the creation of the US Bipartisan Commission on Comprehensive Health Care—remained untouched by the repeal effort (Saldin 2017). As we noted, full repeals are rare even though this is how lawmakers typically discuss them, and despite the fact that partial repeals—that leave some elements of a law untouched—often represent notable cases of statutory revision that deserve the attention of academics (Bianco 1994; Hacker 2004; Himelfarb 1995; Patashnik and Zelizer 2013; Skocpol 2010).

Are Repeals a Unique Form of Statutory Revision?

Having established what repeals are and how they occur, it is worth discussing how repeals differ from other common forms of statutory revision. Consider, first, sunset provisions, in which language included in a bill authorizes a program, regulation, or funding level, but only for a fixed period. If that item is not renewed by the end of the period—that is, if Congress fails to act—the program expires. In colloquial terms, the "sun sets" on the statute. As Adler and Wilkerson (2012) show, these sunset provisions are a common and important aspect to understanding policy change and can be one of the most common ways of stimulating congressional action.

The perspective we take here is that a sunset and a repeal differ primarily in what Congress has to do to reverse a particular policy. Opponents of a statute that has a sunset provision need only wait out the clock and prevent a reauthorization from going forward. While preventing a reauthorization is not assured, checking (or negative) powers are common in the political system and thus constitute a relatively easy pathway to kill a program. By contrast, opponents of a statute that has no end date cannot just wait out the clock and utilize negative powers to prevent reauthorizations. Rather, opponents must actively repeal the legislation by bringing bills forward in the House and Senate—a much higher bar to clear.

A second form of statutory revision is for opponents to adjust the program's funding in an appropriations bill. From the perspective of lawmakers, the advantage with an appropriation is that killing a particular aspect of a program is feasible given that appropriations bills are considered "must pass" and often bundled with other such bills. In this respect, opponents to a program only have to gain enough support to allow their adjusted funding level to go through, and the program will cease. As Patashnik (2003) and Berry, Burden, and Howell (2010) show, while programs are rarely killed outright, it is common to find a program's opponents consistently ratcheting down its funding.

Lastly, a program may simply be unraveled by a series of smaller, discrete changes—most notably via amendments—that are independently modest but cumulatively dramatic. On this process Maltzman and Shipan (2008) argue that the stronger and more unified the enacting coalition, the better able they are to protect their policy from future amendment. Nevertheless, Patashnik (2008) points out that the actual impact of reforms can be quite unstable: while the 1986 Tax Reform Act closed old loopholes in the tax code, new loopholes emerged in the following years. Similarly, agricultural subsidies have persisted despite reforms like "Freedom to Farm."

Although these scholars explore the topic of statutory reversal in a number of ways—from declining to reauthorize a bill and changing funding levels to failing to maintain the goals of reform efforts—we contend that repeals stand out as a distinct way to undo a law. In particular, we believe repeals are unique because of what they require: a dramatic, positive action by a legislature that is often deeply contentious and uniquely difficult. While other forms of revision can occur piecemeal over time, or occur without any action whatsoever, repeals require lawmakers to allocate scarce resources to reversing a previous enactment. We develop these points in greater detail in the next section.

As a final matter, why would opponents of a law choose to repeal its core components rather than taking one of these alternative approaches? We suggest there are three reasons. First, some policies simply require a repeal rather than any of the alternatives mentioned above. For example, the shift from bimetallism to the gold standard required repealing statutes that authorized silver as an alternative. No silver sunset existed, and amendments would be less definitive on the important topic of the nation's monetary basis, which requires certainty. Second, repeals are more permanent than cutting agency funding levels, as the program's supporters can restore funding later. In this way repeal may be favored by those with the strongest objections to a law. And third, repeals are more dramatic, and better for party brands, than unwinding a policy piecemeal. Namely, the ability to claim credit for definitively ending a particular program, or the ability to magnify the differences with political rivals, can be achieved more easily with a repeal effort.

A THEORY OF REPEALS

As we noted above, volumes have been written about the politics of law creation, while precious little exists on efforts to repeal rather than enact legislation. Yet scholars may have legitimate reasons for overlooking repeals. A repeal, after all, is "just another law." We cannot deny the simple fact that law creation and law repeal are governed by the same constitutional requirements, institutional structures, and legislative procedures. As a theoretical matter, a distinct possibility is that our general understanding of legislatures and the legislative process is sufficient to understand when and why repeals occur.

We, of course, challenge this view. While the prevailing theories of Congress and legislative productivity have much to offer as far as explaining when and why repeals occur, the processes of law creation and law repeal *differ* in fundamental ways. Our argument as to why repeals are different from the politics of law creation may seem counterintuitive, but we detail our reasoning on both normative and empirical grounds.

As a matter of first principles, a number of thinkers, including the chief architect of the Constitution, have claimed that too much repealing activity runs the risk of undermining the rule of law itself. James Madison argued that repeals can "poison the blessings of liberty," and he elaborates on the negative effects of legal instability in Federalist No. 62:

> It will be of little avail to the people, that the laws are made by men of their own choice, if the laws be so voluminous that they cannot be read, or so incoherent that they cannot be understood; if they be repealed or revised before they are promulgated, or undergo such incessant changes that no man, who knows what the law is to-day, can guess what it will be to-morrow. Law is defined to be a rule of action; but how can that be a rule, which is little known, and less fixed?

Alexis de Tocqueville (1838) echoed those sentiments nearly fifty years later in *Democracy in America*. In writing about the limitations of American democracy, de Tocqueville criticized lawmakers' "capricious tendencies," citing legal instability and incessant statutory revision as a unique danger in the young republic.[8] De Tocqueville writes: "America is, at the present day, the country in the world where laws last the shortest time . . . a single glance upon the archives of the different States of the Union suffices to convince one that in America the activity of the legislator never slackens." A similar logic applies in writing about judicial decision making, where a common normative belief is that the principle of *stare decisis* should be maintained. As articulated by James Kent's (1826) *Commentaries on American Law*, "When a rule has been once deliberated adopted and declared, it ought not be disturbed . . . except for very cogent reasons, and upon a clear manifestation of error; and if the practice were otherwise, it would be leaving us in a state of perplexing uncertainty as to the law."[9] Such views are echoed in modern game-theory discussions of the "problem" of too much policy cycling (Shepsle 1979; Tullock 1981) and claims about the virtues of legal stability (Fuller 1964; Eskridge and Frickey 1994; Cross and Lindquist 2009). Simply put, law creation and law repeal differ on normative grounds, as the latter runs the risk of violating a democratic ideal, while the former is considered central to democratic practices.

Switching gears, as an empirical matter, we argue that repeals differ from other enactments due to their fundamental nature. Specifically, we believe repeals face a unique set of hurdles compared to other types of legislation. We caution that these are general tendencies rather than cardinal rules—there are certainly exceptions to each case. Nevertheless, we argue the following. From a policy perspective, lawmakers tend to confront a uniquely constrained negotiating environment when they draft and attempt to enact a repeal bill. From a political standpoint, repeals can exacerbate the path-dependent nature of legislation and must overcome the various interest groups that have an interest in maintaining the status quo. And from an institutional perspective, attempts to repeal elements of a party's brand often heighten conflict in a system that empowers those who seek to block legislative action.

Policy Perspective

A common view in the study of organizations is that the wider the range of choices available to members of a group, the more likely they are to find an outcome that satisfies a majority.[10] Unfortunately for members of Congress, their negotiation environment is constrained tightly: by constituents, by the president, by the other legislative chamber, and by the opposition, to name just a few. It is no surprise that in such an environment, bills have a low probability of passing both chambers and being enacted into law. Yet scholars recognize that not all bills are equally difficult to enact (Adler and Wilkerson 2012; Volden and Wiseman 2014). In enacting a new law versus repealing an old law, we argue that new laws often afford lawmakers more flexibility and a wider range of policy choices, while repeals present lawmakers with a narrow choice and thus a more constrained decision-making environment.

We believe this claim is most evident in the literature on legislative responses to external events. As policy problems arise, which create a "window" for legislative action (Kingdon 1984), lawmakers are under pressure to pass *some* legislation that addresses the problem. For virtually any policy problem, various solutions are available, and little consensus may emerge as to which policy outcome is best (Kingdon 1984; Baumgartner and Jones 1993; Cohen, March, and Olsen 1972). Adler and Wilkerson (2012) note that constituents are "more concerned with whether a perceived problem is addressed rather than the specifics of how it is addressed" (6). In creating a new law, lawmakers often have more flexibility in identifying a proposal that addresses the problem in some way that presents opportunities for claiming credit (Mayhew 1974) or engaging in logrolling (Buchanan and Tullock 1962; Weingast and Marshall 1988).

Negotiation on new legislation can be eased further by the fact that lawmakers are often working with imperfect information about the actual effects of their legislation (Krehbiel 1992). In that respect, lawmakers suffer from the same cognitive biases and framing effects that citizens do and may engage in risky behavior or heavily discount the future (Sheffer et al. 2018; Sheffer and Loewen 2019). Although "uncertainty" has a negative connotation in popular discourse, when attempting to reach a legislative bargain, uncertainty can be a benefit, as it may allow various lawmakers to have different visions for the same plan and thus increase their likelihood of reaching consensus (Riddell 1981).

On both points—negotiation over a policy outcome and the extent of uncertainty—repeals often present different legislative challenges. First, the range of policy choices available to lawmakers is commonly constrained in a repeal effort. In the language of the decision-making literature, the outcome of a repeal can be either failed negotiation, thus upholding the status quo, or a known reversion point: the law before the statute in question was enacted.[11] There are of course notable exceptions—namely, the repeal of AFDC with TANF, which we detail more below—but in general, opportunities to bargain, logroll, and claim credit can be more constrained in repeal efforts than in new law creation. Second, the cognitive biases that help facilitate the passage of new laws are reduced in a repeal effort. It may seem counterintuitive, but repeals afford lawmakers greater policy information about the effects of their action, which may decrease rather than increase the likelihood of their reaching agreement. After all, the main purpose of a repeal is to negate the policy effects of a known law. As we note next, this can be especially damaging to a repeal effort when the costs of undoing an existing law are concentrated and the benefits are diffuse.

Political Perspective

A common adage in political science is that "policy creates politics." In this vein, a second reason why repeals are difficult to pass has to do with the underlying politics of repeal. In any effort to enact major policy—whether it be passage of a new law, an amendment, changes in funding levels, a repeal, or some other change—lawmakers confront the path-dependent nature of legislation. While the term "path dependency" refers to numerous processes (Pierson 1994, 2000, 2004), here we focus on the concept of increasing returns, whereby action in one period reinforces the same action in subsequent periods and increases the costs of change. As Margaret Levi (1997) aptly put it: "Once a country or region has started down a track, the costs of reversal are very high" (28).

One explanation for the path-dependent nature of legislation is the fact that new laws often create constituencies and activate interest groups that have a stake in the law's continuation. Voters, not surprisingly, are quite likely to react more strongly to the loss of a tangible benefit more than to its gain (Tversky and Kahneman 1991; Jervis 1992; Weiner 1985). At the same time, interest groups are particularly adept at insulating their preferred policy area from changing democratic forces (Baumgartner and Jones 1991). For example, the tobacco industry was quite successful at preventing state governments from imposing antitobacco regulations in the 1990s, despite the growing pressure from various health advocacy groups (Givel 2006). As E. E. Schattschneider noted in 1935, laws "stimulate the growth of industries dependent on this legislation for their existence, and these industries form the fighting legions behind the policy" (288).

Although this status quo bias can occur in any policy domain, one area where this effect is known to be especially pronounced is social legislation, where repeal might trigger loss aversion in voters, who tend to react far differently than if they never received a social benefit in the first place (Tversky and Kahneman 1991). Dozens of studies have documented that retrenchment—the unraveling of social programs—is especially difficult (Pierson 1994, 2000). In one of his seminal works, Pierson (1994) makes our precise point that statutory creation and reversal are not the same. He claims that his "central thesis is that retrenchment is a distinctive and difficult political enterprise. It is in no sense a simple mirror image of welfare state expansion" (1). As a theoretical matter, while it may be easier to pass laws with "concentrated benefits and diffuse costs," to borrow Olson's (1965) language, reversing this calculation in a repeal can cause a public backlash. As one example, consider the resistance of Fannie Mae to reform, where the government has backstopped the mortgage industry and helped subsidize the now commonplace thirty-year fixed-rate mortgage. Nevertheless, despite numerous calls for reform, from both the left and the right, it has continued to endure in similar form since the 1960s (Landis and McClure 2010; Boyack 2011; Jaffee 2008). Simply put, "concentrated costs and diffuse benefits" is not a recipe for success in politics.[12] Former Speaker of the House Tip O'Neill made this claim more colorfully, often referring to Social Security as the "third rail [of politics]—touch it and you die."

Another axiom in the literature on path dependency holds that incremental policy adjustments are more likely to succeed than major policy changes (Hacker 2004; Pierson 2000). Given that the repeal of a major law often represents a major policy change by its very nature, we would expect repeals to be less likely to succeed compared to less dramatic forms of revision—amendments, changes in funding levels, etc. Likewise, one body of work shows the amount of "friction" involved in any policy change increases the value of incremental adjustment versus major change (Jones and Baumgartner 2005; Jones, Sulkin, and Larsen 2003). Because repeals constrain the negotiating environment, as detailed above, and exacerbate partisan conflict in a system of separation of powers, as detailed below, we believe repeals add extra friction to the legislative process and are therefore unlikely to overcome the path-dependent nature of legislation.

Institutional Perspective

A third reason why repeals are different from other types of legislation lies at the nexus of partisan behavior and institutions that create a status quo bias. A canonical view in the literature on parties is that they work to develop ownership over certain issues and create a favorable "brand" that is electorally beneficial (Petrocik 1996; Cox and McCubbins 2005). As Koger and Lebo (2017) point out, these brand names are cumulative and updated based on politicians' actions (Snyder and Ting 2002; Pope and Woon 2009). As a theoretical matter, a party's brand serves as something of a public good for its members: when a party has successfully gained ownership over an issue, the members of that party all benefit from their collective reputation (Aldrich 1995; Cox and McCubbins 1993, 2005). In other words, a brand is an important byproduct of a party's legislative actions, and there is a considerable body of work linking a lawmaker's party affiliation and her electoral fate (Butler and Powell 2014; Green, Palmquist, and Schickler 2004; Snyder and Ting 2002).

Although there are various ways to create a favorable brand, the main route is through what Cox and McCubbins (2005) refer to as "team production." As they put it, "Achieving their goals—reelection, internal advancement, and majority status—requires passage of legislation" (22). In other words, the brand is formed based on the laws the party enacts (Snyder and Ting 2002; Pope and Woon 2009). Yet there are other strategies to develop a favorable brand. In particular, party leaders will on occasion bring up bills and amendments that separate the parties on important issues, even if they have no chance of passing (Koger and Lebo 2017). Likewise, Lee (2009) notes that partisan strategies can extend beyond genuine policy disagreement and include many legislative matters devoid of clear ideological divisions.

We echo these canonical claims but focus on repeals instead of all kinds of legislation, and ask: What happens when lawmakers attempt to repeal statutes that are part of the other party's brand? We believe the answer to be simple: the party that created the law will resist efforts to undo its signature accomplishments. Naturally, not all repeal efforts target bills that are central to a party's brand, but as we show in chapter 4, most repeal bills are introduced by those in the minority party and are more likely to be messaging bills than earnest attempts at policy change.

Given the super-majoritarian institutions in Congress, such as the filibuster, the presidential veto-override (Brady and Volden 2005; Koger 2010; Krehbiel 1998), and the requirement that both chambers pass legislation in identical form to become law (Binder 1999, 2003), the enacting party often has the capacity to stymie legislative action. Blocking the other party's repeal effort may help maintain the enacting party's ownership of an issue, as research suggests that voters punish lawmakers for shifting positions (Tomz and Van Houweling 2010). At the same time, safeguarding a party's signature accomplishments may reflect the party's sincere commitment to a set of policy goals (Aldrich 1995). Alternatively, blocking a repeal may stem from raw teamsmanship rather than genuine ideological motivations (Lee 2009). Whatever the exact mechanism, it may be easy to *propose* a repeal, but when one party levels its sights on its opponent's signature accomplishments, given the minority party's empowerment in American politics, the party that opposes a repeal is more likely to win, all else being equal.

An Empirical Test

Our theory as to how repeals differ from other legislative activities points us in a few directions for explaining when and why repeals occur. First, however, we conduct an analysis of our claim that repeals are uniquely difficult to enact. In the following discussion, the question is not "What makes a repeal more likely?" but rather "Are repeals truly different from other enactments?"

For the present analysis, we specify a simple model of bill passage. Using the Congressional Bills Project and data on every bill introduced from the 80th to 114th Congress (1947–2017), we recorded three outcomes: whether a House bill passed the House, whether a Senate bill passed the Senate, and whether a bill introduced in either chamber was enacted into law. Additional data came from the Policy Agendas Project database and Keith Poole's VoteView webpage. Our model controls for a range of factors that are known to correlate with the probability of bill passage as well as variables for the bill's underlying policy content.

We acknowledge that members of Congress introduce legislation for a number of reasons, including both "sincere" and "symbolic" reasons, but for this analysis, we are only interested in sincere bills. As such, we restrict our analysis to bills that have a reasonable chance of being passed by dropping those that the Congressional Bills Project deems unimportant, namely private bills, ceremonial or commemorative bills, and bills sponsored by members of the minority party. We also isolate bills with a reasonable chance of passing by focusing on those with a large number of cosponsors in the chamber of origin.[13] We refer to this subset of bills as those with a "high chance of passage" and discuss the results of this subset below. However, we also examined a model without any of these refinements, which we refer to simply as "all bills." Complete results and additional discussion are in appendix A.

Our primary independent variable in this analysis is a bill's type, which is derived from keywords in the bill's title. We consider five bill types: reauthorizations, amendments, appropriations bills, and repeals. Notably, each of these bill types affect existing statutes in one way or another. We created a fifth category for bills that have no explicit bearing on an existing law, which we call a "new law." Although the average bill title contains just twenty-seven words (including preambles such as "A bill to . . ." and plain words such as "the" "and," or "to"), they often contain useful policy information and specify the bill's effects on other laws.[14] Specifically, it is quite common for bills to have summaries such as "A bill to repeal/amend/reauthorize the [ACT] of [YEAR] . . ."

Returning to an example from earlier, in 1988 Congress passed the Medicare Catastrophic Coverage Act, one of the most significant expansions of Medicare since the law's enactment in 1965. However, the law's passage created a public backlash, and just one year later, Congress passed a bill to repeal the bulk of the law. Notably, the repeal bill's title reads simply: "To repeal Medicare provisions in the Medicare Catastrophic Coverage Act of 1988." No doubt, this can aptly be characterized as a "repeal bill," as it did little else besides undo provisions of a prior act.

In this analysis, we test the simple proposition articulated above, that repeals are harder to pass than other kinds of legislation. We expect that reauthorizations and appropriations, which are often considered "must pass" legislation, will be easiest to enact, all else being equal. In the analysis, the distinction between amendments and repeals is most illuminating for our theory, however. Because amendments *also* make critical statutory revisions and can undo key elements of an existing law, we suspect that they, too, are quite difficult to enact. Nevertheless, guided by the theory above, we hypothesize that amendments will be more likely to pass than repeals, as amendments generally modify an existing law rather than representing a full-scale reversal of a law's key provisions. We also include

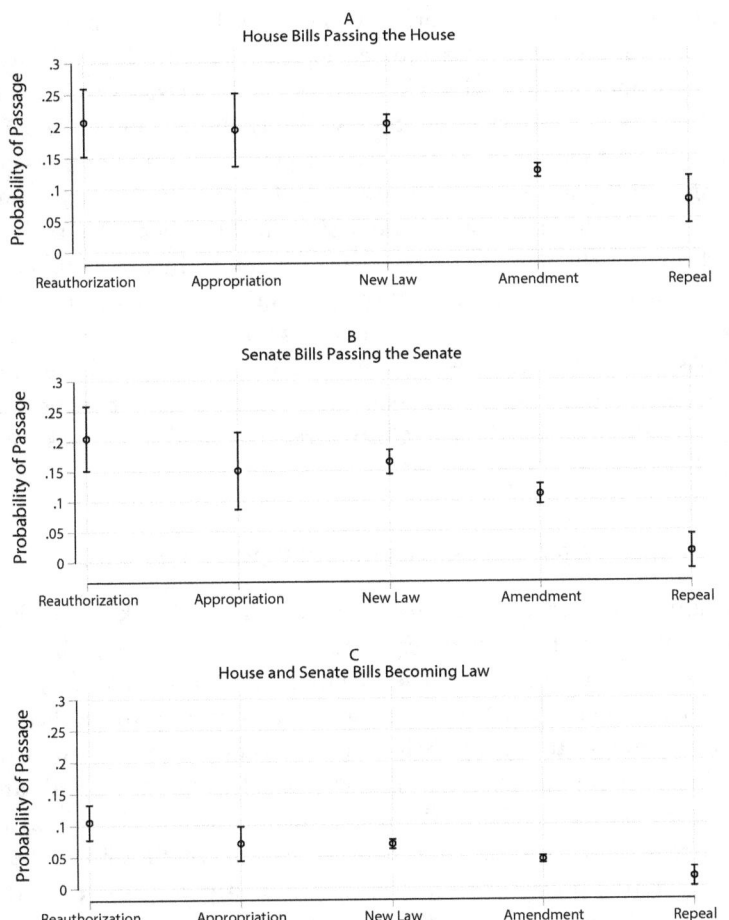

Fig. 1.2. Effect of Bill Type on the Probability of Passage

estimates for the reference category—new laws—which we expect to fall somewhere in the middle in terms of their ease of passage.

Figure 1.2 presents the estimates of three logit models for which the dependent variable is a dichotomous measure of whether the bill was passed by its chamber of origin—either House or Senate—or was passed by both chambers and enacted. Once again, the full details of these models can be found in appendix A in models 1–3. In the figure, each of the bill types are arranged along the x axis, and the y axis indicates each bill's estimated probability of passing, with all other factors in the model held at their mean.

As shown in figure 1.2, the results confirm the intuition above. While no bill is *likely* to pass, reauthorizations fare the best. By contrast, repeals are the least likely to be passed by either chamber and enacted into law. Relative to amendments, which have the second-lowest likelihood of passage, repeals are 37% less likely to pass the House according to panel A, 87% less likely to pass the Senate according to panel B, and 64% less likely to be signed into law according to panel C. Post-estimation tests indicate that these differences are statistically significant: repeals are truly more difficult to pass than any other bill type, even amendments. Finally, given the discussion of party brands and the opposition's tendency to safeguard its signature laws from repeal, we think it is notable that repeals are hardest to pass in the Senate, where the minority party is better able to block legislation. Although this is a cursory analysis, it shows that the success rate of repeals is strikingly low. Clearly, repeals are different, as we have claimed.

WHY REPEALS ARE (MOSTLY) PARTISAN

Our finding that repeals are harder to pass than other kinds of legislation is itself interesting. However, it also gives us clues regarding one of the central questions of this book: What explains when and why repeals occur? In this book's main chapters, we draw from prevailing theories in the congressional literature to help answer this question, what we call the "three Ps" for simplicity. Specifically, we consider whether repeals are the result of legislative *problem solving*, lawmakers' personal *preferences*, or their *partisan motivations*. To be clear: we contend that no single theory—problem solving, preferences, or parties—perfectly explains each repeal. Moreover, disentangling such effects for the purposes of a critical test is a difficult task. Rather, our distinction between the "three Ps" of repeal is intended to impose some intellectual order on the host of interrelated factors that are known to influence the legislative process. Ultimately, we find some evidence for each perspective.

An intuitive answer to the question of when and why repeals occur is that they stem from lawmakers' sincere efforts to craft good policy and their interest in fixing policy errors. Put another way, members of Congress want to solve problems (Adler and Wilkerson 2012), and one way to do so is to repeal problematic laws. We therefore address the problem-solving nature of repeals in one of the empirical chapters. A different perspective leads us to consider whether repeals occur because of legislators' personal preferences (Krehbiel 1993). One possibility is that repeals are a distinctly conservative action (Grossmann and Hopkins 2016). As an example, in his famous *Conscience of a Conservative*, Barry Goldwater (1960) wrote, "My aim is not to pass laws, but to repeal them" (15). Another possibility is that repeals occur with the replacement of pivotal lawmakers who helped enact the law (Krehbiel 1998; Horn and Shepsle 1989). We take up these possibilities in another of the empirical chapters and evaluate if thinking about lawmakers as individuals with particular policy demands helps explain when and why repeals occur.

Although both perspectives have value when it comes to understanding repeals, one of our main arguments in this book is that repeals are uniquely partisan. Specifically, we argue that repeals are most likely to occur when the parties are ideologically cohesive—consistent with the notion of conditional party government (Aldrich and Rohde 2001)—and when the majority party wins control of Congress after a long stint in the minority—consistent with research on the importance of electoral factors in explaining legislative politics (Koger and Lebo 2017; Lee 2016).

On the importance of the majority's ideological cohesion, we focus on the finding that repeals are exceptionally difficult to pass. As we argued, repeals are a particularly narrow policy outcome and exacerbate the already path-dependent nature of legislation. Moreover, undoing a party's signature accomplishments and taking aim at elements of their brand can exacerbate legislative conflict in a system that empowers minorities that seek to stymie action. For those reasons, our belief is that it takes an especially cohesive majority to overcome the special barriers to enacting a repeal. In that respect, the main limitation in repealing a law is not the supply of exogenous policy problems or the range of potential solutions, nor is it the underlying arrangement of preferences in a legislature, though these factors certainly matter. Rather, one of the keys to repeal is the majority's decision to dedicate precious agenda space to undoing an existing law, along with its capacity to bring a repeal bill to the floor and shepherd it through the legislative process and past all the major veto points.

On the importance of the majority's electoral success, we note that time is a scarce resource in Congress, and the legislative agenda often is crammed with program reauthorizations, passing funding bills, responding to crises, and so on (Walker 1977; Adler and Wilkerson 2012). Quite frequently, the legislative calendar is so full with these mandatory items that Congress has very little time to address discretionary matters. Rohde, Stiglitz, and Weingast (2013) argue that, because plenary time is so scarce, members' demands in a particular period shape leaders' decision to exercise positive agenda-setting powers (see also Dodd 1986a, 1986b). In this case, when homogeneous parties have *recently* won control of Congress, they will be more likely to centralize powers, thus bolstering the ability of party leaders to set the agenda and act in a decisive manner. In other instances, such as when the parties do not feel a threat to their majority status, agenda control will be decentralized. Consequently, the party's capacity to repeal will ebb and flow over time depending on the majority's electoral record.

We also argue that when recently "ascendant," having won control after a long time out of power, the rank and file will have a long list of statutes enacted over a decade (or more) while they were out of power that they would like to reverse. Notably, an ascendant majority's time in the minority can also serve to alleviate the party's internal ideological divisions while also affording leaders a crop of new lawmakers interested in policy change rather than power (Dodd 1986a, 1986b). The role of electoral competition has been especially salient since the 1980s, where congressional parties simultaneously cultivate their own reputations while actively undermining the achievements of their opponents (Lee 2016). Nonetheless, we argue that this tendency is not unique to the contemporary context, but similar patterns are evident as far back as the 1890s. In this way, the constant tug-of-war over the nation's statutes is not always ideologically motivated (Lee 2009) and can encompass many items that previously were bipartisan or that constitute successful established policies. We extend this logic to suggest that after suffering a loss on a major policy issue while in the minority, upon ascension to power, the party leadership specifically focuses on the issues that the former majority party had used to beat them.

CHAPTER OUTLINE

Having detailed our book's theoretical claims in this chapter, in chapter 2 we develop a way of measuring the significance of a given repeal, which helps us identify the most notable repeals in history and compare them across time. For illustrative purposes, we describe three repeals in our data set: the Glass-Steagall Act (1933–99), the National Maximum Speed Law (1974–95), and the Tenure of Office Act (1867–87). In the second part of that chapter we examine the occurrence of "doomed" statutes and "killer" Congresses. We find that parties play an important role in explaining when and why repeals occur, as "doomed" statutes (those that ultimately get repealed) are more likely to be passed under unified government, and Congresses that are most likely to repeal legislation ("killer Congresses") are those where partisan conflict is common and the majority is recently ascendant. Finally, we show that patterns of legislative productivity do not automatically correlate with patterns of repeal. Congresses that enact a large volume of new laws are not more likely to be killers, while productive Congresses are no more likely to have statutes doomed to repeal in the future.

In the three chapters that follow, we focus on the "three Ps," or three lenses, that might explain repeals: that they are the result of lawmakers' *problem-solving* motivations, that they are the result of *partisan* battles over policy, and that they are the result of shifts in lawmaker's personal *preferences*.

Chapter 3 examines whether the problem-solving efforts that Adler and Wilkerson (2012) find are behind most of Congress's activity explain repeals as well. While lawmakers often explain their repeal efforts as either a solution to a policy problem or effort to fix defective statutes, we find that these explanations are largely "cheap talk" when it comes to repeals. Utilizing a measure of issue attention—a common indicator of policy problems—we show that legislative attention in a given domain is often unrelated to repeal occurrence. Likewise, we find no evidence that historic changes in the policy environment (wars, recessions, bank failures, and technological advancements) explain repeals in the corresponding issue domain. Overall, we conclude that while problem-solving efforts are central to policy creation, repeals seem to be governed by other forces.

In chapter 4 we test whether repeals are the product of long-term competition between the parties over the majority's prior achievements, as we have claimed. We find substantial evidence that while lawmakers may pass new laws in response to policy problems, their repeal attempts are driven by partisan motivations. First, repeals are more likely to occur during unified government, when one party controls both chambers and the White House (Edwards, Barrett, and Peake 1997; Binder 1999, 2003; Jones 2001). Second, and most importantly, repeals tend to occur when a majority is recently "ascendant," having seized control after a long period out of power (Dodd 1986a, 1986b; Lee 2016; Rohde, Stiglitz, and Weingast 2013) and in eras of high party conflict when the majority is ideologically cohesive (Aldrich 1995; Rohde 1991). Given these findings, the willingness of the party to dedicate scarce agenda space to undoing their rival's signature laws—instead of advancing new legislation—indicates the importance of repeals in the minds of party leaders. Finally, we show that bills passed on a party-line vote are more likely to be targeted for repeal in the future.

As a whole, the evidence that partisan motivations are at work is clear and consistent.

In chapter 5 we examine whether the policy preferences of lawmakers—apart from their party affiliation—explain when and why repeals occur. First, we test whether Goldwater's (1960) conservative credo "My aim is not to pass laws, but to repeal them" (15) extends to his ideological counterparts: Are conservatives more active in repealing legislation? We show that while conservatives do indeed *introduce* a greater volume of repeal bills (Grossmann and Hopkins 2016), those efforts are no more likely to succeed. Second, we test whether shifts in the preferences of Congress's membership explain repeals (Krehbiel 1998). We test this claim by calculating the gridlock interval—a zone in the ideological spectrum where policy change is impossible—for each Congress. We show that repeals are indeed less likely to occur when the enacted policy is within the so-called gridlock interval. And third, we explore whether legislative drift—the gradual replacement of the enacting coalition—explains repealing activity (Horn and Shepsle 1989). Not only does our evidence refute this claim, but the opposite seems to be true, with repeals most likely in the first few Congresses after passage (when many members of the enacting coalition are still in Congress) and less likely decades after passage (when most have exited Congress). Overall, while we do find support for the role of preferences in explaining repeals, the partisan factors in our analysis are still dominant.

In the concluding chapter, we take a holistic look at repeals and their overall dynamics, which helps contextualize the results from each of the empirical chapters while also placing our findings in a broader context. We also summarize the evidence that, on balance, supports our theoretical claims about the partisan nature of repeals, and we place our results in the context of Republican efforts to repeal the Affordable Care Act. We then discuss the implications of our research for various topics, including the "responsible parties" thesis, public approval of Congress, and legislative capacity. Finally, we discuss possible extensions of our work—ranging from the repeal of constitutional amendments to broader theories of statutory revision—and conclude with a discussion of future repeal efforts.

CHAPTER TWO

Significant Repeals, Killer Congresses, and Doomed Statutes

Assessing a legislature's performance is a surprisingly complicated task. On the one hand, even the most unproductive legislature will be quite active. For example, the famous "do nothing" Congress (1947–49) enacted 472 public laws comprising several thousand pages of statutes.[1] On the other hand, many of the laws a legislature enacts—even productive ones—are of modest consequence. For these reasons, political scientists assess legislative performance based on the *significance* of the laws enacted.

As with the creation of new laws, even the most unproductive legislature will repeal a large volume of statutes in a given session. Oftentimes, these repeals are a perfunctory aspect of updating the nation's laws: removing obsolete text from the US Code or resolving inconsistencies between existing statutes and new laws. In this respect, there are dozens or perhaps hundreds of repeals in any session of little consequence. Other times, however, repeals represent pivotal shifts in national policy. As with legislative productivity, our capacity to understand repeals requires that we develop a measure that allows us to compare the importance of one repeal to another.

Consider, for example, three very different laws doomed for repeal: the Glass-Steagall Act, the National Maximum Speed Law, and the Tenure of Office Act. Each existed in a distinct policy area, had different goals, and was enacted in a unique historical era. Glass-Steagall (formally known as the Banking Act of 1933) was a Depression-era statute that limited the cross-ownership of investment firms and commercial banks and was repealed in 1999 by a Republican-controlled Congress. Not only was the Banking Act of 1933 one of the most significant laws of all time (Clinton and Lapinski 2006), but contemporaries debate whether the repeal of Glass-Steagall contributed to the Great Recession of 2007–9 (Stiglitz 2009). The National Maximum Speed Law was enacted during the oil crisis in 1974, creating a uniform national speed limit of fifty-five miles per hour, with the dual goals of reducing oil consumption and lowering traffic fatalities. Although repeal succeeded in devolving power from the federal government to the states, public health experts estimate it caused over ten thousand highway fatalities and over thirty thousand injuries (Friedman, Hedeker, and Richter 2009). Lastly, the Tenure of Office Act of 1867—which restricted President Andrew Johnson's authority to remove Reconstruction-era officials from office—was passed during the period of Radical Reconstruction, and was used as the legal basis for the impeachment of President Johnson. Repeal of the Tenure of Office Act in 1887, during Cleveland's presidency, had dramatic implications for the balance of power between the president and Congress (Foner 2010).

As these examples illustrate, repeals, even major ones, come in varying degrees of importance, both in how the policy change affects the lives of citizens and in terms of when and why they occur. And while each of the above repeals is significant in some way, the reasons for their significance can be multifaceted. One (Glass-Steagall) represented a major change in economic policy, one (the National Maximum Speed Law) affected the balance of power between the federal and state governments, and the third (the Tenure of Office Act) reflected a generation-defining conflict between two branches of government.

We have three goals in this chapter. Our first aim is methodological: to measure the significance of the repeals in our data set. We extend the work of Clinton and Lapinski (2006) and estimate the significance of repeals using an approach borrowed from educational researchers that is akin to an SAT or GRE score: it incorporates various bits of information and arrives at a summary metric of importance. Although each repeal we catalog is notable in some way, we want to put our repeals on a common scale to determine which ones are most significant. Our second aim is to use the corresponding estimates to describe *when* significant repeals have occurred since Reconstruction. In one section, we describe "doomed statutes," the volume of an enacting Congress's statutes that were eventually repealed. In another section, we describe "killer Congresses," the volume of significant statutes repealed by particular Congresses. Combined, these sections identify the Congresses that passed the greatest volume of repealed statutes and which Congresses have been the most active at repealing. Lastly, we consider the timeline of repeal, identifying when in a law's life cycle it is most vulnerable. As we note, the basic timing of repeal has important implications for the question of when and why repeals occur. In the conclusion, we reconcile our results with the theoretical perspectives of lawmaking introduced in the last chapter. As we note, the results of this chapter help us understand the history of repeals but also provide clues about the ways Congress approaches both lawmaking and repealing laws.

CATALOGING REPEALS (1877–2012)

In previous research projects, we adopted two different measurement strategies for identifying repeals: first (Ragusa 2010) by identifying repeals through changes in the US Code and in our second article (Ragusa and Birkhead 2015) by recording repeals noted by academics, policy experts, and journalists. For the reasons outlined in the last chapter, we follow the latter approach in this book in an effort to focus on the most notable political and policy outcomes in the 135-year time span of our study. Simply put, while tracking repeals in the US Code would yield a much larger data set and has considerable merit for those focused on the law itself, our approach emphasizes the most consequential changes in national policy and keeps the theoretical focus on Congress.

Our project benefits from the longest time span (1877–2012) that both theory and data availability permit. As a theoretical matter, this time span coincides with the end of the Reconstruction era and the reemergence of the competitive two-party system in US politics. Likewise, because some repeals take decades to occur, we began coding repeals in 1877 to obtain variation in many of the key factors that may explain repeals. As a pragmatic matter, a number of variables used in our empirical models in later chapters are simply unavailable prior to this year.

At the heart of our data collection effort is a series of "contemporaneous" and "retrospective" sources of legislative activity (see Mayhew 1991). A contemporaneous source is one that summarizes the major events of a given Congress, written at the time and focused on the key issues of the day. A retrospective source has the advantage of hindsight, written decades later and focused on major events of an era. Each offers various advantages: contemporaneous sources offer insight into what issues politicians considered to be consequential, while retrospective sources help contextualize the particular event. Moreover, the breadth of sources helps reduce the likelihood that any estimates we make are influenced by idiosyncrasies from a particular legislative observer. By drawing on multiple kinds of sources we have a comprehensive data set that is also balanced in its perspective.

In total we examined six contemporaneous volumes, compiling hundreds of "session wraps" that summarize the events of a Congress on a yearly or biennial basis. We use the historical *New York Times* and *Washington Post* as our primary contemporaneous sources. From 1877 to 1946, we searched both newspapers for session wraps in this period. From 1947 to 2012, we use the session wraps compiled by David Mayhew. We also cataloged session wraps in four secondary volumes that span specific periods: *Political Science Quarterly* (1887–1925), *American Political Science Review* (1919–29), *Western Political Quarterly* (1949–67), and *Congressional Quarterly* (1949–2012). We have included the extended session wraps from 1877 to 1946 on our personal website.[2] We added to these various contemporaneous sources a total of nineteen retrospective volumes. Specifically, we cataloged eleven period histories in the New American Nation series (see also Clinton and Lapinski 2006) and four public policy reference volumes including Stephen Stathis's *Landmark Legislation* and Brian Landsberg's *Major Acts of Congress*. All twenty-six sources and the time span they cover are listed in table 2.1.

After we identified and digitized the primary source material, each document was scanned for discussion of repealed statutes.[3] We were conservative at this stage, cataloging the literal word "repeal" and its immediate derivations ("repealed," "repealing," etc.) rather than synonyms such as "abrogated," "rescinded," "undid," or "killed" so that we do not inadvertently categorize some alternative form of statutory revision—sunsets, failed reauthorizations, amendments, defunding efforts, etc. While these alternative forms of statutory revision are notable on their own, we have argued that repeals are unique for a host of theoretical reasons. The conservative approach we adopted has one important benefit worth emphasizing here: objectivity. Simply put, there were no judgement calls made by the research team concerning cases to include or exclude, nor were there interrater reliability measures to correct. As we discuss in further detail below, they are not simply a list of all changes to the US Code, nor are they a list of all repeals Congress passes. Rather, they are a list of the most consequential repeals passed by Congress. Finally, we cataloged adopted repeals and ignored mentions of repeal efforts that were unsuccessful. Yet as we discuss later, we created a secondary data set of repeal efforts based on bill sponsorship data.

After finding discussion of a repealed statute, the last step was to

TABLE 2.1. *Contemporaneous and Retrospective Sources of Legislative Activity*

Source	Time Period	Years Covered	Type
New York Times historical	1877–2012	135	Contemporaneous
Washington Post historical	1877–2012	135	Contemporaneous
Political Science Quarterly	1887–1925	38	Contemporaneous
American Political Science Review	1919–1949	30	Contemporaneous
Western Political Quarterly	1949–1967	18	Contemporaneous
Congressional Quarterly key votes	1949–2012	63	Contemporaneous
Oxford Encyclopedia (Critchlow and VanderMeer, 2012)	1877–2011	134	Retrospective
Encyclopedia of U.S. Political History (Robertson et al. 2010)	1877–2010	133	Retrospective
Landmark Legislation (Stathis 2003)	1877–2002	125	Retrospective
Major Acts of Congress (Landsberg 2003)	1877–2002	125	Retrospective
The New Commonwealth (Garraty 1968)	1877–1890	13	Retrospective
The Development of the American Constitution (Beth 1971)	1877–1917	40	Retrospective
The President, Congress, and Legislation (Chamberlain 1967)	1877–1941	64	Retrospective
Politics, Reform, and Expansion (Faulkner 1959)	1890–1900	10	Retrospective
America's Rise to World Power (Dulles 1955)	1898–1954	56	Retrospective
The Era of Theodore Roosevelt (Mowry 1958)	1900–1912	12	Retrospective
Woodrow Wilson and the Progressive Era (Link 1954)	1910–1917	7	Retrospective
Woodrow Wilson and World War I (Ferrell 1985)	1917–1921	4	Retrospective
The Constitution in Crisis Times (Murphy 1972)	1918–1969	51	Retrospective
Republican Ascendancy (Hicks 1960)	1922–1933	11	Retrospective
Franklin D. Roosevelt and the New Deal (Leuchtenburg 1963)	1932–1940	8	Retrospective
The United States and World War II (Buchanan 1964)	1939–1945	6	Retrospective
Government's Greatest Achievements (Light 2002)	1944–2001	57	Retrospective
The Crucial Decade and After (Goldman 1960)	1945–1960	15	Retrospective
Recent America (Grantham and Maxwell-Long 2011)	1945–2010	65	Retrospective
The Unraveling of America (Matusow 1984)	1960–1969	9	Retrospective

identify the specific repealing and repealed laws. Cataloging the repealing law was straightforward, though labor intensive, given that the sources almost always mentioned the second law by name or bill number. Cataloging the repealed law posed a set of challenges, however. First, the primary sources rarely noted the repealed law or bill by name, often using colloquial terms instead. For example, a 1902 *Washington Post* session wrap mentions a bill enacted in the 57th Congress that repealed the "war taxes." In these cases, we had to read additional newspaper articles and other contemporaneous sources—including the *Congressional Record*, Congress.gov, the US Code, and others—to identify the enacting law. In the example above, the enacting law was the aptly titled "War Revenue Bill of 1889." A second challenge was the fact that a repealing law occasionally repealed multiple statutes that had been enacted in varying Congresses. For example, an 1895 *New York Times* session wrap noted that the 53rd Congress repealed "the remaining vestiges of the reconstruction federal election laws." Upon closer inspection, this law was responsible for repealing three separate election laws known collectively as the "Force Acts," which were enacted from 1870 to 1871 in the 41st and 42nd Congresses.

In total we identified 111 notable repeals that occurred between 1877 and 2012. As a substantive matter, we believe these cases represent the universe of landmark repeals for two reasons. First, our data collection follows published studies that catalog significant legislative activity (Howell et al. 2000; Clinton and Lapinski 2006; Mayhew 1991, 2005). Second, while journalists, policy experts, and academics may fail to mention a specific repeal for various reasons, these idiosyncrasies should not plague our list given the broad scope of our primary sources. As table 2.1 shows, our source material covers the 135-year time span with an average of ten sources—both contemporaneous and retrospective—for each year, giving us a total of 1,364 source years.

In this chapter, we examine the most significant repeals in our data set and we make use of all 111 repeals from 1877 to 2012. Additional details are in appendix B. In chapters 3–5, which contain our main analyses, we focus on the most significant 10% of enacted laws in history according to Clinton and Lapinski's 2006 data set. As a result of this focus, fourteen repeals are excluded from the main analysis, as they fall outside the top 10%.[4] Likewise, in chapters 3–5 we can only analyze laws that were enacted *beginning* with the 45th (1877–79) Congress and ending with the 111th Congress (2009–11). Additional details are in appendix D.

ENACTMENT SIGNIFICANCE

An important area of congressional research is the development of sophisticated ways of conceptualizing and measuring the significance of legislation. Nearly a dozen books and articles address this topic (e.g., Binder 1999, 2003; Clinton and Lapinski 2006; Edwards, Barrett, and Peake 1997; Howell et al. 2000; Mayhew 1991), while several thousand have utilized the data developed in the above studies (e.g., Coleman 1999; Erikson, MacKuen, and Stimson 2002; Kelly 1993; Krehbiel 1998). Although the distinction between "landmark" and "routine" legislation is important from a policy standpoint, as major laws affect Americans the most, it is also important from a scholarly perspective. As Cameron (2000) wrote, "The vast bulk of legislation produced by that august body [Congress] is stunningly banal" (36). For this reason, most, if not *all*, books on the legislative process were developed with major enactments in mind (Rohde 1991; Bianco 1994; Krehbiel 1998; Adler and Wilkerson 2012; Curry 2015).

David Mayhew's *Divided We Govern* highlights the importance of this issue. In his book, Mayhew examined whether split party control of Congress and the White House limits the government's capacity to enact important laws. Mayhew noted that an answer to this question hinged on the development of a measure of significant legislation. Famously, Mayhew found that landmark legislation passes in the same proportions during times of divided and unified government, a result that "[stands] a century of scholarship on its head" (Kelly 1993, 476). Given the implications of Mayhew's work, subsequent researchers began developing alternative measures of major enactments. One group focused on the issues that were important but did not become law (Edwards, Barrett, and Peake 1997; Binder 1999, 2003), while a second group developed alternative measures of significance using the number of sources and/or volume of text discussing a law (Clinton and Lapinski 2006; Howell et al. 2000; Jones and Baumgartner 2004).

CONCEPTUALIZING AND MEASURING REPEAL SIGNIFICANCE

As described in chapter 1, our primary data collection effort follows Mayhew's (1991) approach: the provenance of our repeals data set is a host of external raters of Congress's performance. In that sense, *all* of the repeals we identified are important by virtue of the fact a national newspaper, a policy expert, or a historian felt compelled to mention it.[5] Like the subsequent improvements on Mayhew's methodology, however, we recognize that the binary treatment of significance—significant / not significant—ignores that there is enormous variation in the universe of major repeals. Some represent major changes in national policy, have important historical consequences, affect the balance of power across political institutions, or reshape the dynamics of American politics, while others are notable but of less consequence in a comparative sense.

Before describing our methodology, it is appropriate to pause and note that we are sensitive to questions about what "significance" means as a conceptual matter. Quite simply, it is difficult for any researcher to develop a specific set of criteria that can be used to judge the consequence of any legislative act, as there are any number of features that can make a law important. Like Clinton and Lapinski (2006) and others, our measure is best described as that which is "notable." Consistent with many of the studies cited earlier, we view this as a reasonable standard, even if we have no way of knowing what specific criteria motivated a rater to note a given repeal.

Our specific approach utilizes item-response theory, which was developed in educational testing to assess a student's aptitude in a subject area (Lord 1980; Baker 1992). In political science, item-response theory has been used to estimate elite preferences, where a lawmaker's vote on a bill or a judge's decision on a case can be used to scale their ideological preferences (Clinton, Jackman, and Rivers 2004; Martin and Quinn 2002). In the context of our study, a bill's significance is derived based on whether it was mentioned (coded 1) or not mentioned (coded 0) by the contemporaneous and retrospective raters. Contemporaneous raters—such as the *New York Times* or *American Political Science Review*—publish yearly wrap-ups of the notable legislation passed by Congress that session. Retrospective raters, by contrast, will review a given historical period with the advantages of hindsight. Examples include Faulkner's *Politics, Reform, and Expansion* (1959), which covers 1890–1900, and Goldman's *The Crucial Decade and After* (1960), which covers 1945–60. Simply put, we assume that a mention by a rater is akin to a vote on whether a repeal is notable.

Although these rater mentions are at the heart of our estimates, our statistical approach utilizes additional sources of information—called an "informed prior" in the literature. First, we recorded the number of stories in the *New York Times* and *Washington Post* at the time of the repeal that discuss the repealed statute. Second, we recorded the volume of text (using

TABLE 2.2. Estimates of Repeal Significance

		The Tenure of Office Act	National Maximum Speed Law	Banking Act of 1933 (Glass-Steagall)
Details	Enacted	1867	1974	1933
	Repealed	1887	1995	1999
Significance	Informed Prior	2.3	0.72	2.62
	Uninformed Prior	1.28	−0.22	1.61
	Rank	#7	#68	#2
% of Sources Mentioned	Retrospective Sources	0.43	0.0	0.67
	Contemporaneous Sources	1	0.25	0.5
% of Congress Coverage	WP Mentions	0.005	0.006	0.008
	NYT Mentions	0.009	0.009	0.011
Clinton-Lapinski Estimates	Repealed Law Significance	N/A	0.152	0.13
	Repealing Law Significance	0.769	N/A	N/A
Volume of Text	Words on Repeal	27	80	125

a simple word count) that describes the repeal in each source. A third piece of information is the proportion of sources that mention the repeal. And fourth, we incorporated Clinton and Lapinski's estimates of the enacted and repealing laws' significance on the grounds that when major laws target other major laws, the repeal is notable.[6] As a technical matter, our specific approach uses Bayesian statistics and informative priors to estimate a repeal's significance. Additional details can be found in appendix B.

For illustrative purposes, table 2.2 presents the relevant pieces of data on the three repeals mentioned in the introduction. We show the estimated significance of the repeal using uninformed priors (meaning the significance estimate only comes from the raters) and informed priors (meaning the significance estimate also includes the other bits of information). A few features of table 2.2 are worth mentioning. First, the most important factors in the estimation of significance are the "votes" by the contemporaneous and retrospective raters. Second, we believe these results exhibit face validity: the Tenure of Office Act (ranked no. 7) and Glass-Steagall (ranked no. 2) repeals were clearly generation-defining

TABLE 2.3. The Ten Most Significant Repeals since Reconstruction

Rank	Passed	Enacting Law Title	Repeal	Repealing Law Title	Brief Description
1	1890	Sherman Silver Purchase Act	1893	Repeal of Sherman Silver Purchase Act	Repeal of a law that required the government to purchase silver and issue paper currency. Bimetallism was the defining issue of the late 1800s. Repeal placed US on a de facto gold standard.
2	1933	Banking Act of 1933 (Glass-Steagall)	1999	Financial Services Modernization Act (Gramm-Leach-Bliley)	Repeal of New Deal–era statutes that blocked the cross-ownership of investment firms and commercial banks. Contemporaries debate whether repeal contributed to the Great Recession of 2008.
3	1937	Neutrality Act of 1937	1939	Neutrality Act of 1939	Repealed the arms embargo provision codified in the 1937 act, which blocked weapons sales to warring nations. Repeal was a shift away from America's historic post–World War I neutrality stance.
4	1935	Social Security Act of 1935 (AFDC)	1996	Personal Responsibility and Work Opportunity Reconciliation Act (TANF)	Repealed AFDC, a New Deal–era statute that provided assistance to children of low-income parents, replacing it with TANF, which contained a block grant, workfare requirements, and lifetime limits.

5	1878	Bland-Allison Act	1890	Sherman Silver Purchase Act	Repealed statutes placing the U.S. on a bimetallic standard—following the Coinage Act of 1873—and increased the quantity of silver the federal government was required to purchase in issuing paper currency.
6	1964	Gulf of Tonkin Resolution	1971	Foreign Military Sales Act of 1971	Repeal of the Gulf of Tonkin Resolution, the statutory basis for escalating the war in Vietnam. Along with the War Powers Resolution, repeal represented Congress's effort to reassert its war powers.
7	1867	Tenure of Office Act	1887	Tenure of Office Act Repeal	Repeal of a law that limited the president's ability to remove executive branch officials without the Senate's consent. Notably, the Tenure of Office Act was the basis for impeaching Andrew Johnson in 1868.
8	1882, 1884, 1888, 1892	Chinese Exclusion Acts	1943	Repeal of the Chinese Exclusion Acts (Magnuson Act)	Repeal of a series of laws that blocked Chinese immigration to the United States. Repeal was a response to World War II and a US alliance with China. Repeal allowed Chinese immigration, though at very low levels.
9	1993	National Defense Authorization Act of 1993	2010	Don't Ask, Don't Tell (DADT) Repeal Act	Repealed statutes that banned gays and lesbians from serving openly in the military. While the 1993 law liberalized military policy to an extent, the DADT repeal was a key civil rights victory for gays and lesbians.
10	1988	Medicare Catastrophic Coverage Act	1989	Medicare Catastrophic Coverage Repeal Act	Repeal of one of the most significant expansions in Medicare coverage since the law's creation in 1965. Concerns about rising premiums caused Congress to repeal the law just one year after passage.

actions that had consequential effects on American politics, albeit for very different reasons. By contrast, the National Maximum Speed Law (ranked no. 68), though important in a variety of ways, is less historically consequential by comparison.[7]

We also created a table with the ten most significant repeals in US history, according to the analysis described above. In addition to listing the title of the two laws, as well the dates of enactment and repeal, table 2.3 contains a brief description of each repeal and its historical consequence. We refer to these ten top repeals at various points throughout the book, including in the discussion below.

Lastly, it is important to address how our overall measure of significance is influenced by both the significance of the repealing law and the law it repealed. Consider again the National Maximum Speed Law: a major reform when passed and a minor, though still consequential, repeal when removed from the nation's statutes. When it was passed, the National Maximum Speed Law received front-page attention in the *New York Times* and *Washington Post* and was covered by over one hundred articles overall. By contrast, the repealing law was specifically mentioned twice in the *New York Times*: once in June of 1995 (when the Senate voted), and again in November of 1995 (when the House followed suit and President Clinton promised to sign it into law). At the time of the law's repeal, Americans were no longer waiting in long lines at gas stations and, despite Ralph Nader's warnings about highway safety, the fact is that many Americans ignored the speed limit anyway. Further, the central elements of the GOP's "Contract with America" dominated press headlines in the 104th Congress. In all, the key point is that our estimates thus allow for a repealing law and a repealed law to influence independently the joint measure of overall repeal significance.[8]

SIGNIFICANT REPEALS: A TALE OF TWO CONGRESSES

In this section, we employ our estimates to help us understand the dynamics of repeal. Since repeals are a tale of two Congresses—an enacting Congress that passes a law and a subsequent Congress that repeals it—we present the results in two parts. In the first part, we examine "doomed statutes," or the volume of an enacting Congress's statutes that fell victim to a significant repeal. In the second part, we examine "killer Congresses," or Congresses that repeal a large volume of significant statutes. Because this is the first book on repeals, we believe it is worthwhile to take a step back and examine their basic historical patterns.

Which Congresses Enact Repealed Laws? A Brief Examination of Doomed Statutes

Figure 2.1 presents the volume of each Congress's doomed statutes. On the y axis we report the summed significance of repeal, which is the total significance of that Congress's subsequently repealed statutes. Spikes are an indication that a Congress enacted a large volume of statutes that were "doomed" to be repealed in the future. As a conceptual matter, a higher summed significance score can result from two very significant future repeals, a handful of moderately significant repeals, or something in between. For reasons noted below, we shade periods of unified government in black, while gray bars indicate periods of divided government.

According to our data, the 75th Congress (1937–39) enacted the greatest share of significant doomed statutes. In this Congress, Democrats were in control of both chambers and the presidency, as they continued to grapple with the Great Depression while dealing with the escalating threat of war in Europe. In our database, two repeals of the Neutrality Act of 1937 represent the most significant doomed statutes enacted by the 75th Congress.[9] One repeal, in 1939, repealed the Neutrality Act's arms embargo statute. A second repeal, in 1941, struck down the remainder of the 1937 law. Other

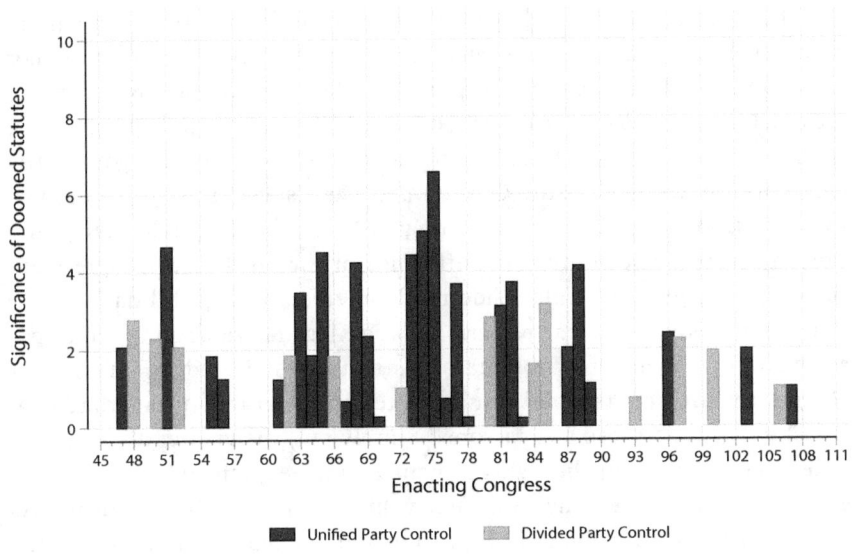

Fig. 2.1. Significance of Doomed Enactments

statutes passed by the 75th Congress that were doomed for repeal include the Agricultural Adjustment Act of 1938, which gave price supports to farmers, and the Miller-Tydings Act, which was a "fair trade" price maintenance law.

Along with the 75th Congress, figure 2.1 shows that the 50th (1887–89), 65th (1917–19), 74th (1935–37), and 88th (1963–65) Congresses had an outsized number of significant statutes repealed by subsequent Congresses. With the expectation of the 50th, these Congresses have one thing in common: single-party control of both chambers and the presidency. Although this provides tentative clues about the importance of parties in explaining when and why repeals occur, we caution that these are only bivariate relationships and do not control for other important partisan factors. Further, we note that the literature on the effects of party control for statutory revision is mixed (see Maltzman and Shipan 2008; Ragusa 2010).

Nevertheless, we see two possible explanations for this pattern. On the one hand, with little input from the minority, unified governments may have a tendency to pass legislation that is a target for repeal because it is ideologically extreme, partisan, or both. On the other hand, legislation enacted with only one party's input may cause policy problems that require subsequent Congresses to revisit those laws. We address these two points in detail in the subsequent chapters. At a minimum, these results emphasize the importance of accounting for party politics in seeking to understand when and why repeals occur.

Of course, a simpler explanation is that unified governments are more productive on average and, because they pass a greater volume of major laws, we should expect them to produce a larger share of repeals in the future. Notably, this alternative gets at one of the central questions of the book: Are repeals a function of the same processes that govern the creation of new laws? Using Clinton and Lapinski's "Top 3500" statutes as our baseline of an enacting Congress's legislative productivity, figure 2.2 presents the summed significance of the laws each Congress enacted (dashed gray line) alongside its doomed statutes (solid dark line).[10] The figure shows no clear pattern between legislative activity in an enacting Congress and the volume of its statutes repealed by subsequent Congresses. In fact, a formal test indicates an insignificant bivariate relationship between these two factors.[11] Simply put, the greater activity that takes place during unified government *cannot* explain why these Congresses' statutes experience a greater volume of repeals in the future. As we have argued throughout, law creation and law repeal seem to be different processes.

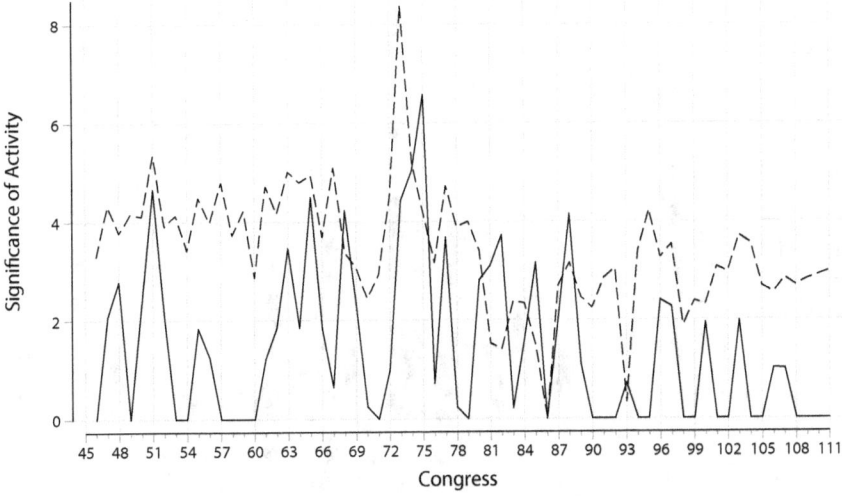

Fig. 2.2. Significance of Doomed and Major Enactmets

Which Congresses Repeal Laws? A Brief Examination of Killer Congresses

Figure 2.3 has the same layout as figure 2.1; however the y axis is the summed significance of each subsequent Congress's enacted repeals. Spikes indicate Congresses that were "killers" in the sense that they were quite active at nullifying significant laws. Once again, a higher summed significance can result from two very significant repeals by a subsequent Congress, a handful of moderately significant repeals, or something in between.

In figure 2.3, the greatest volume of significant repealing activity occurred in the 53rd Congress (1893–95). Not only did the 53rd Congress repeal the Sherman Silver Purchase Act, one we cover in detail in chapter 3; it is also notable for repealing the Reconstruction-era Federal Election Laws.[12] Better known as the "Force Acts," these were a series of laws enacted after the Civil War to combat the Ku Klux Klan and protect African Americans' right to vote by increasing federal oversight of elections and by empowering the president to use military force to uphold the Fifteenth Amendment. Notably, the Force Acts were enacted from 1870 to 1871, at a time when Republicans had large majorities in both chambers. Because the 53rd Congress was the first time after the Civil War when the Democrats had unified control of both chambers and the White House,

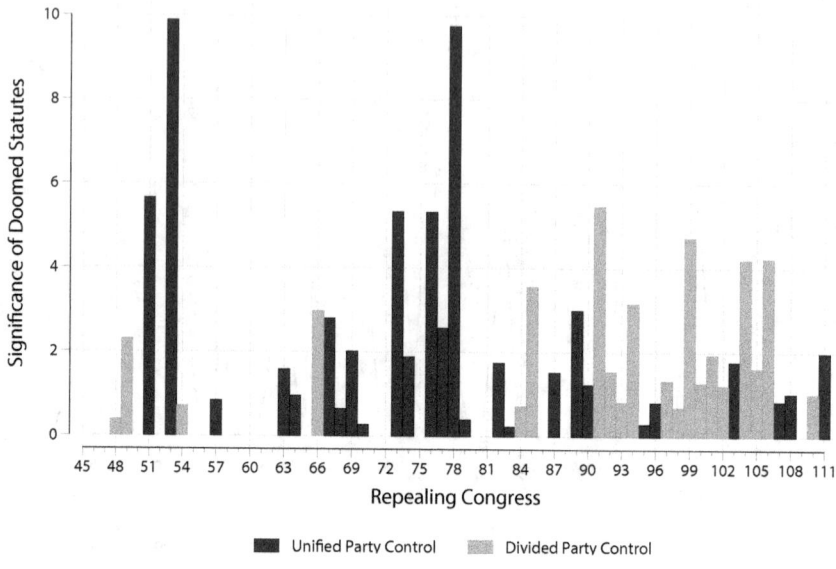

Fig. 2.3. Significance of Repeals Enacted

and the Force Acts were deeply unpopular in the Democratic-controlled South, it is no surprise that they were targets for repeal.

Because our book is mainly focused on the occurrence of repeals rather than the Congresses that enact them, we supplement figure 2.3 with table 2.4, which presents the top ten killer Congresses since Reconstruction. This table helps puts the 53rd Congress into broader context among other repeal-active Congresses. When we focus on the most repeal-active Congresses, we begin by noting that they may be killers for a variety of reasons. Nonetheless, a few broad themes emerge.

First, with only one exception—the 99th Congress—each of these killer Congresses was under unified control of both chambers. That is, the same party that controlled the House of Representatives was also the majority party in the Senate. Interestingly, there is no strong relationship between the party controlling both chambers and White House: just as many of the killer Congresses took place when a unified Congress confronted an opposition president. As with the examination of doomed statutes, although these results are tentative, they once again suggest that party politics is key to explaining when and why repeals occur. Here, however, these results suggest that party dynamics *within* Congress are key to the dynamics of repeal.

On the last point, a second theme that emerges in table 2.4 is that

TABLE 2.4. Top Ten Killer Congresses in US History

	Summed Repeal Significance	Years	Major Statutes Repealed	Party Control		
Congress				House	Senate	President
53	9.89	1893–1895	Sherman Silver Purchase Act; Federal Election Laws Repeal Act; Tariff Bill	D	D	Cleveland (D)
78	9.76	1943–1945	Chinese Exclusion Act; Revenue Act of 1943; Women's Army Corps Act	D	D	Roosevelt (D)
51	5.65	1889–1891	McKinley Tariff Act; Sherman Silver Purchase Act; Sundry Appropriations Act; General Land Revision Act	R	R	Hayes (R)
91	5.46	1969–1971	Tax Reform Act; Drug Abuse Prevention and Control Act; Foreign Military Sales Act Amendments; Gulf of Tonkin Resolution	D	D	Nixon (R)
73	5.34	1933–1935	Economy Act; Emergency Railroad Transportation Act; Gold Repeal; Communications Act; Navy Promotions Act	D	D	Roosevelt (D)
76	5.33	1939–1941	Neutrality Act; Railroad Unemployment Insurance Act; Revenue Act; Army Promotion System Act; Wheeler-Lea Transportation Act; Barbour Fight Film Act	D	D	Roosevelt (D)
99	4.72	1985–1987	Repeal of Clark Amendment; Tax Reform Act of 1986	D	R	Reagan (R)
106	4.23	1999–2001	Gramm-Leach-Bliley Act; Commodity Futures Modernization Act	R	R	Clinton (D)
104	4.21	1995–1997	National Highway Designation Act; Food Quality Protection Act; Personal Responsibility and Work Opportunity Reconciliation Act	R	R	Clinton (D)
85	3.56	1957–1959	Federal Aviation Act; Tax Rate Extension Act; Anti-Secrecy Law	D	D	Eisenhower (R)
94	3.16	1975–1977	Consumer Goods Pricing Act; Tax Reduction Act	D	D	Ford (R)

many of these killers had homogeneous parties in Congress that centralized power in the leadership. As Brady and Stewart (1982) put it, the 51st Congress was marked by a "cohesive Republican party outvoting a cohesive and opposed Democratic party" (351). To do this successfully, the 51st Congress implemented the famous "Reed Rules" that gave Speaker Reed the procedural tools to implement his agenda and stop the minority party's dilatory motions (Binder 1997; Koger 2010). While the Democrats in the 52nd Congress temporarily rescinded the Reed Rules, they restored them in the 53rd Congress and thus maintained this consolidation of powers in the Speaker. Similarly, the 73rd Congress passed most of its repeals under "closed rules"—rules that prevented amendments to the introduced legislation—during a special session called by Franklin Roosevelt. Lastly, Gingrich's tenure as Speaker of the House in the 104th Congress was notable for his willingness to appoint ideological allies to positions of influence, buck the trend of seniority, and utilize various procedural tactics to outflank his opponents (Sinclair 2012).

A third theme is that there are three Congresses in the table—the 53rd, 73rd, and 104th—that saw an ascendant majority take control of both chambers for the first time in decades. As we discussed above, the 53rd Congress saw the southern Democrats wrest control of Congress away from northern Republicans for the first time since before the Civil War. Likewise, the 73rd Congress saw the ascendant "New Deal" Democrats take control of Congress after being in the minority through much of the 1920s. And the 104th Congress was the first time in nearly fifty years that the Republicans held unified control of Congress, pushed into office by Newt Gingrich and his "Contract with America." Despite opposition from a Democratic president, Gingrich and his GOP brethren were able to pass a number of notable repeals.

Fourth, and finally, despite the pivotal role of Congress in explaining when and why repeals occur, presidents still played an important role, at times using the executive powers to compel congressional action, at other times drawing attention to specific issues for repeal. Grover Cleveland called a special session of Congress for the express purpose of repealing the Sherman Silver Purchase Act in 1893 (Brodsky 2000). Similarly, Franklin Roosevelt—riding the electoral wave of New Deal Democrats—called the 73rd Congress into session early (Davis 1986) to bring up a series of repeals, including to establish a statutory basis for his executive actions of taking the United States off the gold standard and to enact a repeal of a 1920 statute that required railroads to relinquish a portion of their profits. Ronald Reagan helped push the 99th Congress to pass the 1986

Tax Reform Act—which repealed a number of previous tax laws—in part through his messaging (Mann 1990). Lastly, though the outcome was considerably more conservative than Democrat Bill Clinton would have preferred, the Gingrich-led Republicans in the 104th Congress successfully used Clinton's campaign promise to "end welfare as we know it" to force his hand in the repeal of Aid to Families with Dependent Children.

A few Congresses buck these patterns, however. First, the 94th Congress is unique, occurring during a long stretch of Democratic control of Congress but also being one of the first Congresses in the postreform House (Rohde 1991). The growing liberal wing of the Democratic Party had become frustrated with the more senior, conservative counterparts who had many positions of power. Two prominent members of the younger liberal wing of the Democratic Party ushered in the Consumer Pricing Act, which lowered the price of many consumer goods. Civil rights hero Barbara Jordan sponsored the bill, and it was cosponsored by Peter Rodino, the new chair of the House Judiciary Committee. The 76th and 78th Congresses also stand out from the others, in that they did not reflect prominent transitions in party power, either, nor were they notable for major institutional reforms. Rather, the killer nature of the 76th and 78th Congresses was largely driven by World War II. The Neutrality Act of 1937 was repealed in 1939 following Hitler's invasion of Poland. Similarly, the 78th Congress's repeal of the Chinese Exclusion Act was a strategic attempt to shore up support from China in an alliance against Japan, whose propaganda had "made repeated references to Chinese exclusion from the United States to weaken the ties between the US and its ally."[13]

It is important to once again assess the relationship between a Congress's baseline productivity and its volume of significant repealing activity. As with our examination of doomed statutes, the uniqueness of the repeals of these killer Congresses is undercut if they are simply a function heightened law creation. Such a conclusion would suggest that the story of when and why repeals occur is the same as when and why Congress enacts new laws. Figure 2.4, like figure 2.2, uses Clinton and Lapinski's Top 3500 statutes as our baseline legislative productivity and compares that baseline (dashed gray line) with repealing activity (solid dark line).[14] As we saw previously, there is no clear correlation between the volume of legislative activity in a subsequent Congress and the volume of repealing activity. Once again, the two correlate weakly, at only 0.15 to be precise, and neither is a significant predictor of the other in a bivariate analysis. For example, the 53rd Congress, which repealed the most significant statutes, was only the nineteenth-most productive Congress. What this tells

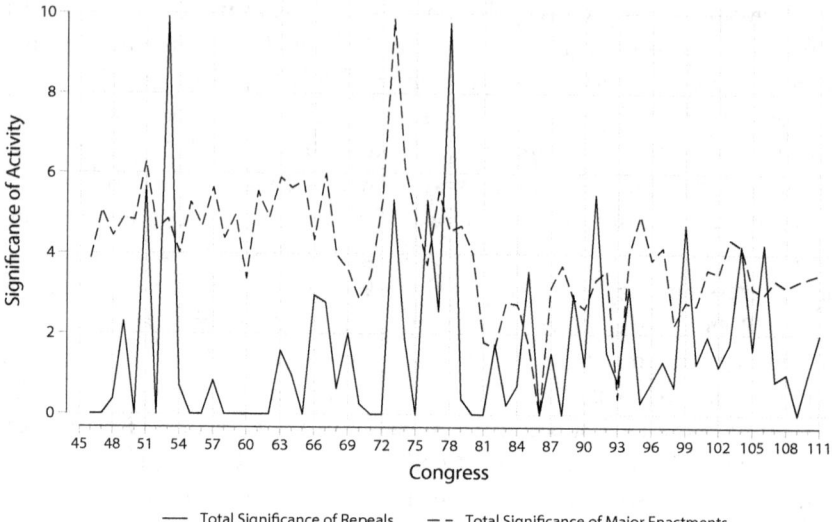

Fig. 2.4. Significance of Repeals and Major Enactments

us is that highly active Congresses do *not* automatically repeal a large volume of laws, lending further support to our claim that the processes of law creation and law repeal are different. Further, it suggests that there are opportunity costs for earnestly pursuing repeals—and that doing so comes at the expense of pushing forward a more "positive" legislative agenda.

THE TIMING OF REPEAL

A final matter concerns when repeals occur in the life cycle of a law.[15] While we have discussed the incidence of doomed statutes and killer Congresses, we have not yet explored how time influences this process. After all, every law is, by the nature of its existence, at a non-zero risk of repeal in any given Congress, irrespective of lawmakers' motivations or the contextual features of the era. Knowing how time affects a bill's risk of repeal is theoretically important as far as why repeals occur, but the effect of time also has important implications for our estimation strategy in later empirical chapters. In this section, we want to answer the following questions: Does repeal become more likely as laws age, less likely as they age, or can no regular pattern be observed in the timing of repeals? Alternatively, does the risk of repeal change directions over time, either rising in magnitude before declining, or vice versa?

Panel A in figure 2.5 provides a graphical depiction of the first three possibilities. First, in the monotonically declining scenario, perhaps lawmakers will work quickly to rectify mistakes made in a previous session.[16] Failing that, the likelihood of repeal falls over time as path dependency and norms of legal stability take root. Second, in the monotonically increasing scenario, the likelihood of repeal increases over time as the enacting coalition is replaced by a coalition that it less committed to protecting legislation from repeal—often referred to as coalitional or legislative

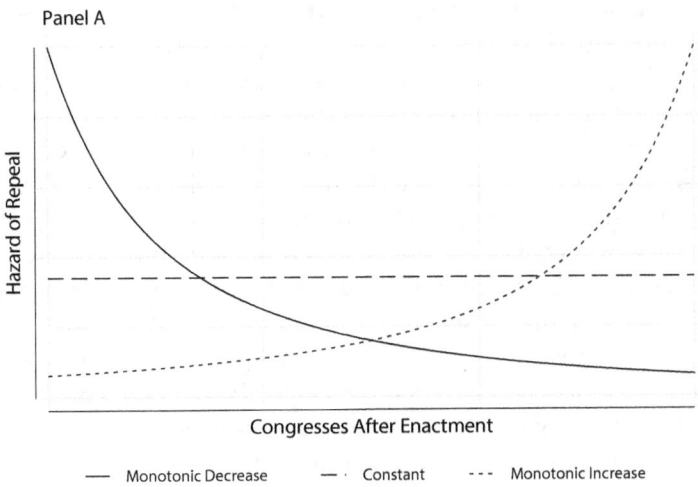

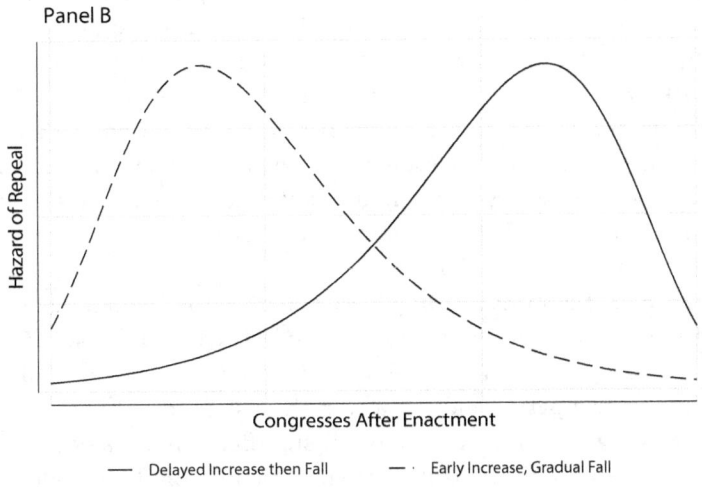

Fig. 2.5. Hypothetical Relationship of Time and Repeal

"drift." In the third scenario, labeled constant risk, the likelihood of repeal is not a function of time at all but rather of the legislation's own features or the characteristics of the postpassage legislative environment. As such, a bill's repeal may not be systematically related to time at all and may depend on other factors.

It is possible, however, that some combination of the three scenarios may present itself and thus the likelihood of repeal is curvilinear. Panel B presents two such hypothetical scenarios. In the dashed line, labeled early increase and gradual fall, perhaps the flaws in a law are not immediately apparent and only present themselves after a few years have elapsed. Perhaps a law is initially popular but is of dubious constitutionality and may be struck down by the courts. In that scenario, the initial likelihood of repeal is low and then increases over time before the countervailing pressures of path dependency or problem salience reduce the likelihood of repeal. Alternatively, depicted by the solid line, labeled delayed increase then fall, the likelihood of repeal is low initially, and although problems in the legislation begin to be apparent, the countervailing pressures of the enacting coalition continue to tamp down repeal efforts. In that respect, the likelihood of repeal is small for quite some time. When the enacting coalition finally gives way, the likelihood of repeal begins to rise. At some point, however, the repeal begins to be less likely as the norms of legal stability and treating legislation as "settled law" take hold.

Which of these views is accurate is, of course, an empirical question. In figure 2.6 we present the hazard of repeal for all significant laws enacted from 1877 to 2011.[17] A greater hazard, on the y axis, indicates a larger likelihood that law i experiences a repeal at time t after passage. Our specific approach uses survival analysis, a method that helps detect when an event is most likely to occur in a given period. Because there are approximately 3,500 significant laws that we observe over this time period, with an average of roughly twenty-five subsequent Congresses per law, the probability a *specific* law experiences repeal in a *specific* Congress is extraordinarily low. Nonetheless, the shape of the hazard tells us something important about when and why repeals occur.[18]

In figure 2.6 the most striking feature is that the likelihood of repeal is curvilinear: a significant law's likelihood of repeal increases from the moment it is signed by the president until about ten years after passage. After that ten-year period ends, however, the risk of repeal drops dramatically. According to our data, 46% of all significant repeals occur within five Congresses, or ten years, of their enactment. From that evidence, we can conclude that there is a general ten-year window that exists wherein

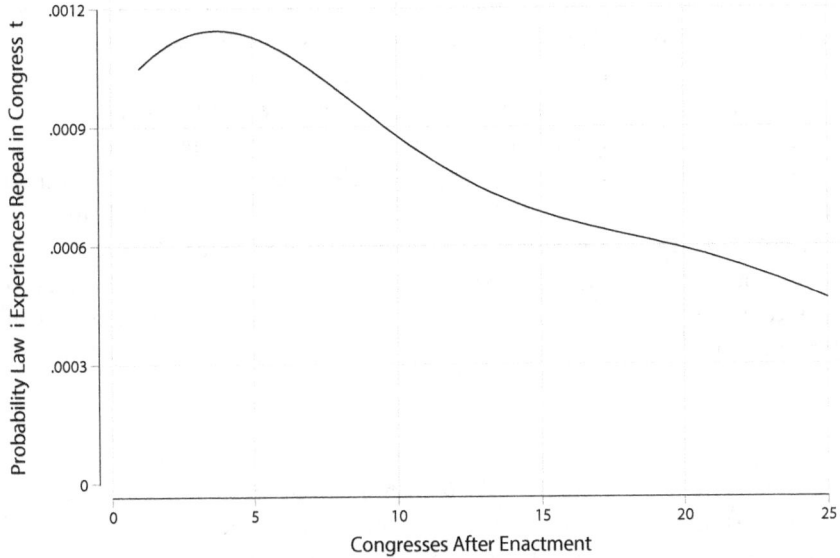

Fig. 2.6. Timing of Repeal

laws are most vulnerable. We do caution, however, that some repeals take decades to take effect: the repeals of Glass-Steagall (1933–99) and Aid to Families with Dependent Children (1935–96) are two notable examples. Nevertheless, these repeals are outliers, despite their notoriety. For the most part, significant repeals occur relatively *quickly* in a law's lifetime. In fact, in our data set there are a number of repeals that happen in the very next Congress after passage. A notable example is the Medicare Catastrophic Coverage Act, which was enacted in 1988 and repealed in 1989 (see Bianco 1994).

How can we explain this pattern as a theoretical matter? We suggest that in the first decade after they come into being, laws exist in a state of uncertainty and are relatively vulnerable to revision. On the one hand, policy problems in the law's domain may arise once the law has been implemented (Adler and Wilkerson 2012). It is only after five to ten years have elapsed that politicians, pundits, the courts, and the public are able to see the true effects of a law and identify its weaknesses. Consider the Gulf of Tonkin Resolution, which was repealed in 1971 after the Johnson administration used it as the statutory basis for escalating the war in Vietnam.

On the other hand, the minority at passage may run in subsequent elections campaigning on a repeal platform, as a way of magnifying their differences with the majority (Lee 2016) and be swept into power in part on the basis of that promise. Indeed, research has shown that Congress's popularity declines when it passes major legislation (Durr, Gilmour, and Wolbrecht 1997). A recent example is the Affordable Care Act: as Nyhan et al. (2012) show, Democrats lost roughly twenty-five seats in the 2010 midterm election because they supported the ACA. If laws can survive an initial period of instability, however, they have a greater likelihood of becoming institutionalized, as path dependency takes hold and the costs of reversing them becomes increasingly significant. As the Republicans found following their attempts to repeal the ACA in 2017, even laws that are initially unpopular can develop strong constituencies given enough time.

CONCLUSIONS

We began this chapter with a discussion of three repeals in our database: the repeals of Glass-Steagall (1999), the Tenure of Office Act (1887), and the National Maximum Speed Law (1995). We selected these laws to illustrate that repeals—even notable ones—come in varying degrees of significance. As with research on legislative productivity, a natural starting point in our examination of when and why repeals occur is to measure the significance of these legislative acts. Doing so provides an important descriptive look at the history of significant repeals and, more importantly, yields some initial answers to the competing theories outlined in the introduction. We believe three broad findings stand out.

First, our examination of enacting Congresses revealed that doomed statutes were more likely to be passed when one party controls both chambers and the presidency. Of the five clear spikes in an enacting Congress's doomed statutes, four were under unified control. An additional analysis showed that this effect is not due to unified governments simply passing more laws, as the passage of new laws and subsequent repeal are not correlated with one another and are thus distinct processes. Forthcoming chapters dive deeper into the precise cause of this effect, but in general terms this confirms that party dynamics—broadly defined—are at work when it comes to repeals.

Second, our examination of killer Congresses indicated that while they vary in their nature and scope, there are a number of important themes. First, all but one of the killer Congresses were under unified control of both chambers and typically under an ascendant—rather than entrenched—majority. Second, many of the killer Congresses occur in close proximity to important procedural changes in Congress's history:

the advent of the Reed Rules in 1890, the "Post-Reform House" in 1974, and the "Republican Revolution" in 1994. Lastly, the killer Congresses had complicated relationships with the executive. In a few cases—the repeal of the Sherman Silver Purchase Act in 1894 or the New Deal package of repeals in 1933—the repeals were forced onto the congressional agenda by the president. At other times, in particular the repeals of AFDC and the Glass-Steagall Act, an active and unified Congress was able to force the president to accept a suboptimal outcome. We also showed that these killer Congresses are not necessarily productive as far as the creation of new laws. Once again, lawmaking and law repealing seem to be distinct processes, a key theoretical claim of ours in this book.

Our third major finding is that repeals tend to occur shortly after a bill is enacted. More specifically, our data indicate that repeals increase in likelihood from the first Congress after passage, becoming most likely at the ten-year point after enactment. After that, the likelihood of repeal drops dramatically. We suggested two explanations for this pattern. Either problems in the new law's policy domain emerge in the first decade after enactment, compelling lawmakers to act, or the opposition party makes a concerted effort in the subsequent years to win back control of Congress and undo their rival's signature accomplishments.

We believe the evidence thus far supports the notion that parties are a key factor that explains when and why repeals occur and that parties use repeals to serve political rather than pragmatic and wholly ideological ends. Throughout this chapter we have stressed that these results are tentative, however. The full examination of partisan dynamics occurs in chapter 4. Beforehand, chapter 3 explores whether the problem-solving motivations that are central to most lawmaking is also evident in repeals.

CHAPTER THREE

Problem-Solving Efforts

> Our current welfare system has failed miserably over the last 30 years. It is time to get under the hood and fix the problem.
> Rep. Joe Knollenberg (R-MI) on the Personal Responsibility and Work Opportunity Reconciliation Act of 1996
> July 17, 1996

> Mr. Speaker, I do not have to get hit full in the face by a 2 × 4 to understand what the people in my district, the senior citizens, are saying about the catastrophic insurance bill. They want it repealed.
> Rep. James Rowland (R-GA) on the Medicare Catastrophic Coverage Act
> November 21, 1989

An intuitive answer to the question of when and why repeals occur is that they serve a problem-solving purpose. One possibility is that repeals target statutes that are defective, outdated, or obsolete. From this perspective repeals can be thought of as a vital statutory tool to improve the nation's laws. Similarly, repeals may occur when historic events—economic recessions, technological advancements, wars, etc.—focus lawmakers' attention on various policies and force them to reconsider statutes in the corresponding area. In other words, repeals may be a legislative response to exogenous problems that require Congress's attention.

As an example of these dynamics, consider the 1971 repeal of the Gulf of Tonkin Resolution. Enacted in 1964, the Gulf of Tonkin Resolution was the statutory basis for the Johnson administration's expansion of the war in Vietnam, in lieu of a formal declaration of war. Despite its tremendous foreign policy implications, the Gulf of Tonkin Resolution was enacted in haste. Senator J. William Fulbright (D-AR), chair of the Senate's Foreign Relations Committee, said of the bill's passage: "We held perfunctory hearings, had a hurried floor debate, and adopted the Gulf of Tonkin Resolution two days after [President Johnson] asked for it" (Glennon 1990, xxii). By 1971, the Vietnam War was deeply unpopular, trust in government was at a record low, and roughly fifty thousand soldiers had been killed since the start of the war. Senator Jacob Javits (R-NY), a member of Nixon's own party, commented that the Gulf of Tonkin repeal was an "end-the-war resolution" that put the president "under a mandate to bring the war to an end and withdraw the troops."[1] In addition to these immediate goals, the repeal of the Gulf of Tonkin Resolution—along with the War Powers Resolution—represented Congress's effort to reassert its constitutional war powers. Simply put, the repeal of the Gulf of Tonkin resolution can be viewed as a case where Congress corrected an error it had made some seven years before and respond to a clear and unambiguous policy problem.

It may go without saying, but problem solving is how *lawmakers* explain just about any action. After all, research suggests this kind of language helps legislators shape how constituents evaluate their efforts and motivations (Sigelman, Sigelman, and Walkosz 1992; McGraw, Best, and Timpone 1995). We suspect this kind of rhetoric is especially common in repeal efforts. Anyone observing American politics from 2011 to 2017 will recognize that the GOP's six-year effort to repeal the Affordable Care Act was steeped in problem-solving explanations. Speaker Paul Ryan repeatedly claimed the law was in a "death spiral" and repeal would improve Americans' lives. Naturally, these claims are not limited to the ACA, or the Republican Party, but are endemic to repeal efforts.

Yet while lawmakers may cite policy concerns as the justification for their repeal efforts, an alternative is that this rhetoric is what political scientists often call "cheap talk" (Austen-Smith 1990; Sides 2006; Sulkin 2009). In other words, the claims about fixing defective statutes or solving policy problems may be cover for partisan and/or ideological motivations. For example, a PolitiFact article[2] rated Ryan's claim that the ACA was in a death spiral as "false," while a Congressional Budget Office analysis[3] concluded that the law was "stable in most areas." Likewise, the simple fact is that Republicans began their repeal efforts *before* the ACA was even enacted (and long before objective problems with the law had a chance to emerge).

At the same time, there are numerous repeals in our data set that seem unrelated to the pressing issues of the day and targeted statutes that were hardly defective. In a few extreme cases, the repeals seem to have *caused* policy problems rather than responded to them. One example is the repeal of the Reconstruction-era Force Acts in 1894, a series of laws enacted in the early 1870s intended to enforce the provision of the Fifteenth Amendment and prevent the intimidation of black voters by groups like the Ku Klux Klan. It is unsurprising that these repeals occurred in the 53rd Congress—the first after Reconstruction where Democrats won majorities in both chambers—and that Jim Crow laws emerged shortly thereafter. Similarly, the repeal of Glass-Steagall occurred at a time of relative calm in the banking industry yet coincides with the electoral ascension of a homogenously conservative Republican majority that was well positioned to realize the deregulatory effort dating back to the Reagan years. While few economists believe the repeal of Glass-Steagall caused the Great Recession, many, including Nobel Prize–winning economist Joseph Stiglitz, believe the recession was worsened by it.[4] With both the Force Acts and Glass-Steagall, it is hard to explain repeal as a clear consequence of an objective "problem" that required Congress's attention.

In this chapter, the first of our three main empirical chapters, we examine the conflicting characterizations described above and ask, "Are repeals the result of problem-solving motivations?" To answer that question, we proceed as follows. First, we discuss the role of legislative issue attention on lawmakers' problem-solving efforts and, consequently, the effect that it may have on repeals. Second, we develop empirical measures associated with the problem-solving theory: issue attention and bill subject area. And third, we evaluate how these measures of problem solving predict repeals by drawing on our database of all major laws enacted by Congress from 1877 to 2011. If we find evidence that repeals are more likely in periods of high issue attention or that repeals target laws in issue domains experiencing upheaval, it offers support for lawmakers' problem-solving rhetoric. On the other hand, if these factors are unrelated to when and why repeals occur, it would suggest that other factors—in particular, partisan and ideological forces—may be at play.

PROBLEM SOLVING

THEORY

Problem solving is vital to our understanding of American politics. In fact, it concerns one of the most important questions in any democratic nation:

Are legislators responsive to the needs of the people, and do they make sincere efforts to enact good laws? From a normative standpoint, the hope is that elected officials monitor the social, political, and economic environment; attend to policy problems when they arise; and make a good faith effort to pass high-quality legislation that addresses citizens' needs.

Although the problem-solving theory rests on a simple theoretical proposition, one of the thorny issues is that the lawmaking environment is riddled with a host of problems and a litany of solutions to consider (Kingdon 1995), raising the question of *which* issues and solutions to prioritize. Given this challenge, many authors propose that legislative action occurs when a "focusing event" brings various policies and solutions together (Cohen, March, and Olsen 1972; Kingdon 1994; Zahariadis 1999). According to this view, a lawmaker's actions are determined less by party affiliation or personal preferences, as many expect, but rather by timing. From this perspective legislative action can be explained by a shock from outside the political system—such as a war, a natural disaster, a recession, etc.—that makes political action urgent (Baumgartner and Jones 1993).

Building on these claims, Adler and Wilkerson (2012) argue that problem-solving motivations are a central component in the behavior of lawmakers. Citing the work of David Mayhew (2005, 211), they define problem solving as "a widespread shared perception that some state of affairs poses a problem and that policymaking should entail a search for a largely agreed upon solution" (5). Adler and Wilkerson base their problem-solving theory on the notion that members of Congress have collective incentives to respond to the country's problems, finding that Congress often acts on such motivations, with the bulk of legislation passed by bipartisan majorities. Two sorts of legislation typically rise to the top of the legislative agenda and are an underpredicted problem-solving action: the reauthorization of expiring programs and responses to crises (Adler and Wilkerson 2012). Simply put, while partisan acrimony may dominate press headlines, most congressional action transcends partisan or ideological infighting and instead constitutes collective decisions to respond to general problems.

Hypotheses

From a problem-solving lens, three empirical concepts are key: issue attention, issue areas, and law quality. In the pages below, we focus on the former two and derive hypotheses concerning when and why repeals should occur. For reasons discussed in more detail in appendix D, we view efforts to measure law quality as inherently problematic given the scope of our research.

Does Greater Issue Attention Lead to More Repeals?

According to the problem-solving perspective legislative action should follow changes in citizens' needs or the emergence of policy problems. A substantial body of research supports these basic claims. On the topic of representation, studies find evidence of a correspondence between a lawmaker's roll-call behavior and the concerns of his or her constituents (Ansolabehere, Snyder, and Stewart 2001; Erikson and Wright 2009; Birkhead 2015; Rogers 2017). With respect to legislative responsiveness, there is also evidence of a correspondence between Americans' preferences for liberal and conservative policy and actual changes in the government outputs at the national (Erikson, MacKuen, and Stimson 2002) and state levels (Erikson, Wright, and McIver 1993). Furthermore, this relationship is well understood to be "thermostatic," with voters shaping a legislature's policy outcomes and those outcomes in turn shaping voters' preferences (Wlezien 1995). Finally, a long-held axiom in research on Congress is that lawmakers genuinely care about good policy (Fenno 1973) and the problem-solving perspective comports with how lawmakers present themselves to their constituents (Harden 2015).

Despite this evidence, the strength of the relationship between policy problems, citizen input, and legislative action depends on the volume of attention the issue receives. Issue attention is generally defined as the range of policy topics at the top of the legislative agenda. For example, Page and Shapiro (1983) show that the relationship between public opinion shifts and policy changes is strongest in issue domains that are "salient." Similar evidence exists at the subnational level: Lax and Phillips (2012) find that across domains, state policy is most responsive to policy-specific opinion on issues that generate more press coverage (see also Caughey and Warshaw 2016). Baumgartner and Jones (1993; Jones and Baumgartner 2005) find "punctuations" in the congressional spending are marked by a large volume of incremental change followed by major disruptions in a few pressing areas (see also Wildavsky 1964). In subsequent work, Baumgartner and Jones (2015) show that the information search led by Congress can explain policy output in a way that transcends common explanations such as party control or ideological polarization (see also Patashnik 2008). Finally, Kingdon's (1995) famous "windows of opportunity" reaches similar conclusions, positing that major policy change is likely when three conditions intersect: a public issue requires attention (the problem stream), lawmakers develop policy solutions (the policy stream), and the institutional environment is favorable (politics stream). In sum, the volume of issue attention in a given policy area is widely accepted as an indicator of the problems lawmakers attend to in a given period.

Finally, Adler and Wilkerson (2012) show that Congress works particularly effectively when a policy domain requires legislative action. In studying amendments to significant laws, they find expiring provisions, salient events, and the volume of issue attention are central to understanding when and why policy change occurs. As they put it, "Issues become the subject of new legislation [because of] events in society and established lawmaking routines that encourage policy updating" (Adler and Wilkerson 2012, xi). Similarly, Patashnik (2008) shows that the survivability of general interest reforms is explained by a mix of factors ranging from the reconfiguration of coalitional patterns to market forces.

As a whole, the foregoing body of work suggests that lawmakers will repeal legislation in response to exogenous shocks to the system in an effort to address salient public issues. Notably, this conjecture contrasts with alternative claims, reviewed in subsequent chapters, that repeals are attempts to kill a rival party's signature accomplishment or are efforts to achieve an ideologically motivated policy outcome. Rather, the implication here is that repeals are best understood as attempts to address a commonly understood problem from the standpoint of good governance.

Are Policies in Some Issue Areas More Durable than Others?

A related matter concerns not just issue attention but the actual policy content of legislation. On this topic, a number of authors have concluded that laws in some issue domains are exceptionally durable. Earlier we noted that social programs are believed to be uniquely resistant to change. Despite the efforts of conservative reformers in the 1970s and '80s seeking cuts in expenditures on social programs, the welfare state wound up being an "immovable object" (Pierson 1994). Echoing one of our central claims, the welfare state's durability owes to the fact that law creation and law change are not governed by the same forces. As Pierson (1994) put it, his "central thesis is that retrenchment is a distinctive and difficult political enterprise. It is in no sense a simple mirror image of welfare state expansion" (1).

Less attention has been paid to the opposite question: Are some laws *more* susceptible to change? Despite the lack of attention, we suggest there are two issue domains that should be particularly vulnerable: issues that face perennial challenge and those enacted around wartime. On the former, we believe laws related to taxes, unemployment, and monetary policy face a greater risk of repeal, given that much of the conflict in American politics concerns macroeconomics (McCarty, Poole, and Rosenthal 2006). While some laws are considered "settled" and certain issue domains remain dormant for long periods of time, the back-and-forth over macroeconomic policy is a constant in American politics. For example, we have multiple repeals in our data set concerning the gold standard, monetary policy, and taxes. Second, laws enacted during wartime for purposes related to the war are also more susceptible to subsequent revision. Unlike macroeconomics, however, these laws are typically bipartisan, enacted in an uncertain political environment, and often temporary by design. For example, the Emergency War Tax Act was enacted at the outset of World War I and was expressly temporary, while the Neutrality Acts of the 1930s were adopted in an uncertain environment. Congress should be more likely to repeal legislation that was intended either as a temporary act or statutes that were passed in eras of international instability and uncertainty.

ANALYSIS OF SUCCESSFUL REPEALS

Data and Method

Our main analysis in this book is an examination of the passage of landmark repeals in a database consisting of all major laws—defined as the most notable 10% of laws—enacted by Congress from 1877 to 2011. As we will do in chapters 4 and 5, laws are arranged longitudinally, spanning the period from the first Congress after a bill's passage to its eventual repeal (or the law is right censored at the 112th Congress). Our survival model—which predicts whether law i experienced a repeal in Congress t after passage—contains variables for preferences and parties in addition to the problem-solving variables, though we focus on the role of problem solving in this chapter. Complete results are available in appendix D.

Regarding our measure of issue attention—testing the key hypothesis in this chapter—we caution that there are no "ideal" measures of this complex phenomenon. Adler and Wilkerson (2012) noted that there are "many potential indicators of changing attention to legislative issues" (148), while Quinn et al. (2010) pointed out that each approach "has particular advantages and weaknesses" (210). Among the various approaches,

Adler and Wilkerson (2012) use the number of bills introduced per issue area, Jones and Baumgartner (2004) utilize data on the proportion of congressional hearings in a given domain, and Quinn et al. (2010) examine the content of floor speeches.

Given the breadth of our research, we do not have the luxury of choosing from a suite of possible measures. Compared to the above studies, the historic scope of our project comes at the expense of data availability, as no database of bill introductions, congressional hearings, or public opinion exists in the late 1800s or early 1900s. Instead, we measure issue attention utilizing data on the description of legislation enacted in a given Congress, a keyword analysis from the Policy Agendas Project codebook, and a supervised machine learning algorithm. In the course of doing so, we classify every law that appears in our analysis according to its policy content.[5] Following other authors (Jones and Baumgartner 2004; Adler and Wilkerson 2012), our measure is simply the number of bills enacted in a given domain divided by the total number of bills enacted in that two-year Congress. Higher values indicate greater attention in a policy domain, with spikes serving as a possible indicator of exogenous focusing events. For complete details, see appendix D.

Figure 3.1 presents our measure of issue attention from 1877 to 2011, the 45th to 111th Congresses, in two issue areas: macroeconomics and energy. Beyond being illustrative, these two domains serve as examples in the results section. In macroeconomics, a few patterns stand out. First, there is increasing issue attention over the entire period, reflecting the federal government's ever-expanding role in economic affairs (for a broader discussion of these trends, see Jones, Theriault, and Whyman 2019). Second, we see three key spikes corresponding to economic crises: a spike in the 111th Congress in the aftermath of the Great Recession of 2007–9, a spike in the 94th–98th Congresses at a time of stagflation in the mid-1970s, and a spike from the 72nd to the 75th Congresses corresponding to the Great Depression. At the other end, the 60th Congress (1907–9) is the low point of issue attention, as just 2.5% of enacted bills concerned macroeconomics. In energy policy, we also see a pattern of increasing attention over time. Unlike macroeconomics, however, there is only one large sustained spike from the 93rd to the 97th Congresses (1973–83), beginning with OPEC's oil embargo in 1973 and coinciding with the energy crisis of those years. According to our data, from 1973 to 1983, an average of 5% of all enacted bills were in the energy domain, a significant increase from the 2% average over the entire time series.

In addition to the absolute measure of issue attention, we calculate a

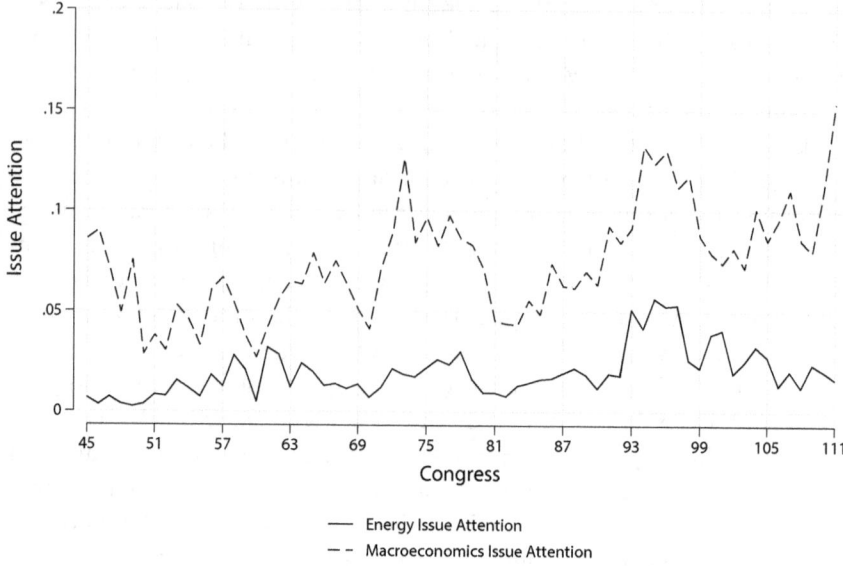

Fig. 3.1. Congressional Issue Attention in Macroeconomics and Energy (1877–2011)

relative measure of issue attention on the grounds that lawmakers may be apt to pay more attention to some policy areas (e.g., macroeconomics) than others (e.g., energy) due to their baseline importance. In other words, it is possible that lawmakers *always* pay more attention to macroeconomics than energy, irrespective of problems in the energy policy environment. In this way, perhaps a spike to 5% in energy (a major increase in a relatively dormant domain) may be equally indicative of an exogenous problem that requires Congress's attention as a spike to 15% in macroeconomics.[6]

We took a number of steps to validate our main measure of issue attention. We detail two key points here, though a full discussion can be found in appendix D. First, our measures of attention in defense, macroeconomics, and banking and commerce are highly correlated with objective problems that should attract Congress's attention (deaths in war, the debt-to-GDP ratio, and bank failures, respectively). While no single variable can capture all the variation in lawmakers' attentiveness, the significance in the relationship certainly suggests our measure is related to objective policy problems. Second, our variable overlaps with Jones and Baumgartner's (2004) preferred measure: congressional hearings. Using the Policy Agendas Project hearings data set, we calculated the percentage of congressional hearings in each domain per Congress and correlated it with our measure since 1947 when the hearings data are available. Again, we would not expect exceptionally high correlations in every domain, yet they should be positive and modestly sized (Jones and Baumgartner 2004; Adler and Wilkerson 2012). Across all eighteen domains in our analysis, the average correlation is a rather robust 0.40.

RESULTS

In our examination of issue attention—the main focus of this chapter—the question is whether repeals are most likely when exogenous problems arise and lawmakers focus their attention on a specific policy area. In the main model, model 1 in table D1 of appendix D, the key finding is that the coefficient on the issue attention variable is *insignificant*. In other words, our analysis finds no meaningful relationship between Congress's emphasis on a specific issue domain and repeals in that area.[7]

Conceptually, this null result indicates that when lawmakers are highly active in a policy area—passing new laws in response to problems that require attention—repeals are no more likely to occur. Likewise, this result suggests that repeals are just as likely even when there are no policy problems and issue attention is calm. Model 2 (a supplementary model in table D3 of appendix D) uses the measure of relative issue attention, testing whether a modest spike in a historically inactive domain indicates a policy problem just like a major spike in a highly active domain, and yields the same insignificant coefficient. Needless to say, these null findings raise serious doubts about the problem-solving nature of repeals.

In an attempt to contextualize these insignificant results, figure 3.2 presents the raw data for macroeconomics and energy, the two examples described earlier. In the figure, we use the relative measure of issue attention to place both series on a similar scale and add a box plot with the number of major repeals per Congress. What this figure shows is the inconsistent nature of the timing of repeals during spikes in issue attention. On the one hand, we certainly see spikes in the number of macroeconomic repeals during the Great Depression and in the mid-1970s / early 1980s, during the period of stagflation and rising unemployment. Some of these repeals were indeed a response to the economic problems of the day. On the other hand, there were no repeals in macroeconomics during the Great Recession of 2007–9, yet there were three major repeals in the post–World War II boom during a period of economic prosperity. Looking at energy, the null results are even starker, as none of the three major energy repeals in our data set occurred during the one sustained spike in energy issue attention in the 1970s. One repeal in energy occurred in the

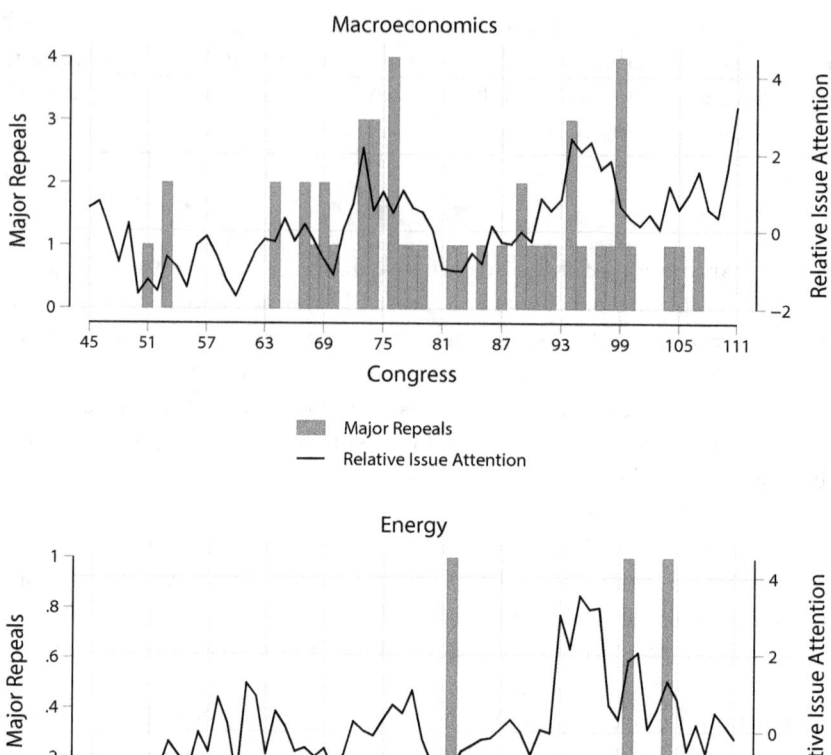

Fig. 3.2. Congressional Issue Attention and Major Repeals in Macroeconomics and Energy

82nd Congress, a low point in the entire series, while the second and third repeals occurred in the 100th and 104th Congresses, which were periods of only moderate energy issue attention.

We believe there are important lessons that can be drawn from one of the energy cases—the repeal of the National Maximum Speed Law in the 104th Congress. During the 1974 energy crisis there was a spike in energy attention, as one would expect if lawmakers are indeed attentive to policy problems, and one of the results was the creation of the National Maximum Speed Law—which imposed a national speed limit of a fuel-efficient fifty-five miles per hour—thereby reducing fuel consumption. Simply put, problem-solving motivations are readily apparent as far as when and why laws are enacted. However, the repeal of the National Maximum Speed Law was heralded by Republicans for "returning power to the states" and occurred after they won unified control of Congress for the first time in forty years. Perhaps most notably, repeal occurred at a time when there were few objective problems in this domain. In at least one way, problems emerged *after* the law's repeal: lifting the law increased traffic fatalities by 3.2%, costing more than $12 billion over ten years, while also increasing gas consumption and emissions (Friedman, Hedeker, and Richter 2009). Overall, while the *enactment* of the National Maximum Speed Law was a clear response to an exogenous problem, the partisan and ideological roots of its *repeal* are unmistakable.

We conducted a series of subsequent analyses to take a more nuanced look at repeals with possible problem-solving intent. In the most important of these additional analyses, we use the objective indicators described earlier—the number of deaths in war, the debt-to-GDP ratio, and the number of bank failures—to directly measure external changes in the policy environment. As the policy environment changes in response to historic social, economic, and political developments, laws from earlier eras may require revision. Returning to a familiar example, the repeal of the Gulf of Tonkin Resolution in 1971—the "end-the-war resolution," in the words of Senator Javits—occurred at a time of great dissatisfaction with the Vietnam War and roughly fifty thousand fatalities to that point. Ultimately, the question is whether this is a systematic relationship or the Gulf of Tonkin Resolution repeal is an outlier.

We present these supplementary analyses in models 3–5 in table D4 of appendix D. In each of these models, we interact the objective indicators above with their corresponding issue domain.[8] Looking at the new interaction terms in these models, all three are insignificant, confirming the null results and casting further doubt on the problem-solving nature of repeals. In substantive terms, these analyses uncover no evidence that objective policy problems (deaths in war, recessions, and bank failures) explain repeals in the corresponding policy domain (defense, macroeconomics, and banking and commerce). In this respect the Gulf of Tonkin repeal in 1971 seems to be an exception rather than a rule, as plainly evident policy problems do not reliably predict the occurrence of repeal.

A related possibility is that technology will become outmoded due to technological advancements, thus increasing their risk of repeal. In this scenario the connection to the previous analyses is the same from a causality standpoint, though here the operative concept does not measure policy *problems* per se: quite the contrary. Nonetheless, technological advancements are another shock to the policy environment that may compel lawmakers to revisit statutes in a given issue domain.

An illustrative example in our data set is a less well-known repeal: the ban on the transportation of boxing films in 1940. Enacted in 1912, two years after the "fight of the century" between Jack Johnson and James Jeffries, the Sims Act outlawed the interstate transportation of fight films. As a multipronged effort to regulate the motion picture industry, prevent race riots like those following Johnson's defeat of Jeffries, and a racist effort to reduce Johnson's popularity, the Sims Act succeeded in causing the demise of the fight film genre (Streible 2008). In the decades after the law's passage, however, the policy environment changed considerably: namely, the law faced serious compliance challenges, and boxing grew in popularity due to a combination of live radio broadcasts and the emergence of televised prize fights (Streible 2008; Thrasher 2015). In many ways, the 1940 Sims Act repeal was a problem-solving action, and in particular, the key dynamic may be that technological advancements made the law anachronistic.

In an effort to measure technological advancements, we draw on the work of economist Robert Gordon (2016) who calls labor productivity the "best available measure of innovation and technological change" (546). Labor productivity spikes in response to technological advancements, including the development of new machinery and materials, transportation improvements, and production advancements. Over the period of this book, there are two major eras of technological advancement. The first was at the turn of the twentieth century: the numerous advancements—from the electrical grid and spread of lighting to improvements in transportation to the creation of the assembly line—helped spawn the industrial revolution (Hounshell 1985). The second era was during and immediately after World War II. In this period, economic boom was the product of doubling the use of machine tools in American factories and improvement in production techniques, which had been necessitated by the war effort (Gordon 2016).

In the analysis evaluating whether technological advancement helps explain repeals, reported as model 6 in table D5 in appendix D, we use Gordon's (2016) measure of "total factor productivity," which serves as our key independent variable, and interact it with laws with a technological component. Using the Policy Agendas Project topics, we use three domains to identify laws with technological content: science and technology, transportation, and energy. In this analysis, we once again find an insignificant coefficient on the interaction term, indicating that technological advancements cannot explain when and why repeals occur in these three domains.[9]

We conducted two final analyses to further examine the problem-solving perspective and assess the robustness of our null results. We list these as models 7 and 8, respectively, in appendix D. Perhaps most notably, we used congressional hearings data as an alternative measure of issue attention. Although this measure has been used in a number of studies (e.g., Jones and Baumgartner 2004) and would therefore be a leading candidate here, the data are only available beginning with the 80th Congress (1947–49). In this restricted analysis, we find no evidence of greater repealing activity when hearings spike in a law's policy domain. We also tested a model that omits "miscellaneous" laws that could not be classified into a policy domain in our main analysis—a function of limited bill descriptions. We found no evidence in this model either. Once again, additional details and complete results of each of these supplementary analyses are included in table D6 of appendix D.

Although issue attention and the related analyses offer little predictive power, we do find that repeals vary systematically as a function of a law's policy content. In the lower portion of the main model, model 1 of table D1 in appendix D, we order the policy domains by their risk of repeal, from the greatest likelihood to the lowest likelihood. While there is not a meaningful relationship between deaths in war and repeals in defense, we find that laws enacted during periods of war with explicit war-related functions are uniquely vulnerable to repeal.[10] In our data set, the bulk of these repeals are related to war financing. After all, for significant portions of United States history, taxes were levied to pay for war efforts. Such was the case during the Civil War, with the adoption of the first income tax, as it was during World War I and World War II, with the enactment of large tax increases. Once the war is over and the need and support for high taxation dissipates, these laws become obsolete. These unique repeals therefore fit one of the tenets of the problem-solving perspective—that external changes in the policy environment cause lawmakers to revisit statutes that become outmoded. Although this certainly represents *some* evidence in support of the problem-solving theory, the reality is that war laws are a small subset in the broader universe of enacted legislation.[11]

After war laws, we find that macroeconomic statutes are the next most likely to be repealed, all else being equal. As fights over inflationary or

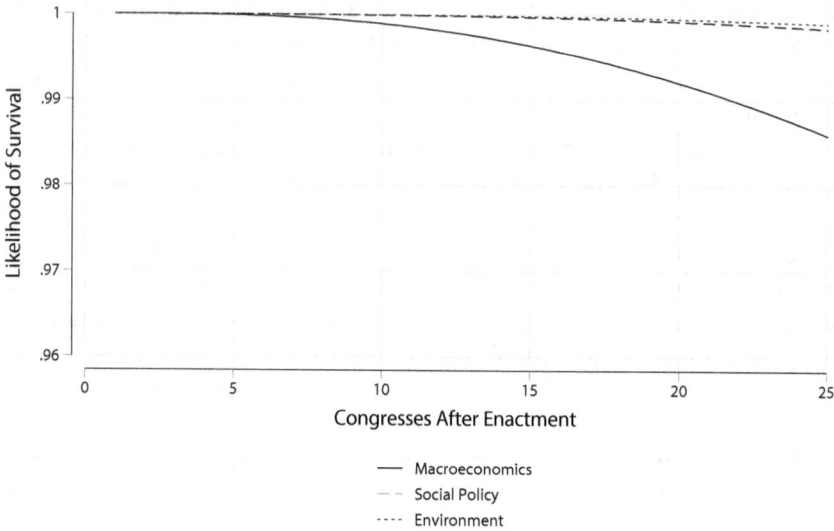

Fig. 3.3. Effect of Issue Domain on Repeal Probability

restrictive economic policies are a near constant in American politics, it is unsurprising to find that there are more repeals in this domain than others. At the other end, social policy is found to be among the most durable subset of laws with the lowest probability of repeal. Needless to say, this result is consistent with a lengthy body of work on the remarkable survivability of the welfare state. Finally, and in something of a surprise, we also find that environmental legislation is considerably less likely to be repealed than legislation in other topic areas.

All in all, we believe these are important findings for understanding the specific topic of repeal, while also characterizing the politics of retrenchment and path dependency. Although scholars have focused on the amazing durability of the welfare state, less work has focused on vulnerability of other law types. Figure 3.3 presents the survivability of laws in the three significant substantive areas—social welfare, environment, and macroeconomics—over twenty-five Congresses after enactment. We can see that while social and environmental policy are quite stable over time, macroeconomic policy is considerably more vulnerable to repeal. In particular, the figure indicates that fifty years after a bill's passage, any given macroeconomic law is about a full percentage point (1.0%) more likely to be repealed than any given social welfare law. Keeping in mind that these are rare events overall, we can see that the issue area can exhibit an important effect on a law's future risk of repeal.

PROBLEM SOLVING AND THE REPEAL OF
THE SHERMAN SILVER PURCHASE ACT

We briefly mentioned a number of cases throughout this chapter, including some that fit the problem-solving perspective, such as the repeal of the Gulf of Tonkin Resolution, and those that did not fit the theory, such as the National Maximum Speed Law. Even though our analysis calls into question the notion that repeals are commonly borne of problem-solving motivations, some are indeed efforts to address a clear policy problem in the spirit of good governance. In this final section, we discuss one historic problem-solving repeal in detail. In fact, the case we selected, the repeal of the Sherman Silver Purchase Act in 1893, is, by the estimates presented in the second chapter, the most significant repeal in our entire data set.

To briefly set the stage, for much of the nineteenth century, the United States adopted a policy of bimetallism, where the nation's currency was backed by a fixed amount of both silver or gold. In 1873, the US moved away from bimetallism and onto the gold standard, effectively demonetizing silver. Although the 1873 law was notable for many reasons, this shift in monetary policy disproportionately hurt those who had debts, in particular farmers, and those from western silver mining states.

In 1890, amid growing public pressure in favor of an inflationary monetary policy and the reestablishment of bimetallism, Congress passed the Sherman Silver Purchase Act. Named for Ohio senator John Sherman, the law required the federal government to purchase a set quantity of silver each month (double the maximum allowed under prior legislation) and increase the amount of paper currency in circulation. Although far less than what proponents of the "free silver" movement sought, passage of the Sherman Act was a key turning point in the battle over the nation's monetary policy (Kemmerer 1944).

In the years after 1890, concerns about the price of gold and silver led to a financial panic (Friedman and Schwartz 1963; Kemmerer 1944). Ultimately the Panic of 1893—the beginning of a severe economic depression—was caused in part by a distrust of the gold standard and a rapid decline in the nation's stockpile of gold reserves, both of which were exacerbated by the Sherman Act (Bensel 2000; Friedman and Schwartz 1963; Kemmerer 1944). President Cleveland called a special session of Congress for the explicit purpose of repealing the Sherman Act. Cleveland, a pro-gold Democrat, along with his "sound money" allies in Congress, blamed the Sherman Act for causing the panic. Economic evidence suggests these claims were justified, at least in part (see Bensel 2000; Friedman and Schwartz

1963). Further, the record is clear that the Sherman Act did little to address the declining price of silver, one of the law's key objectives (Poole and Rosenthal 1997; Hoxie 1893). Lawmakers acquiesced to Cleveland's request, meeting in a special session in 1893 and, after a forty-six-day filibuster by a coalition of Democrats and some prosilver Republicans, passed an act aptly titled "Repeal of the Sherman Silver Purchase Act." Although the United States would not legally adopt the gold standard until 1900, it had a de facto gold standard after the repeal (Kemmerer 1944). Not only can the repeal of the Sherman Act be described as a legislative response to an exogenous policy problem, but the repeal had positive economic effects (Rockoff 1990). Some economists even argue the administration's mere announcement that it would seek the Sherman Act's repeal led to stabilization in the price of gold (Friedman and Schwartz 1963).

Problem-solving evidence can be found not only in the timing of repeal but in the roll-call record as well. By comparing the successful repeal vote in 1893 with a failed repeal vote in the Senate in 1892, we can test whether the depression had a substantial effect on how lawmakers voted, independent of their preferences or party affiliation, which would not change in one short year (Poole 2007). Of the forty senators who opposed repeal in 1892, thirteen, or over 30%, voted *for* repeal the very next year. Although we cannot rule out constituent demands or patronage (Bensel 2000), it is reasonable to infer that the depression was a major cause of this sudden shift in the voting behavior of this key bloc of lawmakers.[12] Moreover, these thirteen "switchers" did not come from one party or region: five were Democrats and eight were Republicans; five were from the Midwest, four from the West, three from the South, and one was from the East. Simply put, while regional dynamics are plainly evident in the repeal vote, as was common with monetary policy in this era, the success of the Sherman Act repeal in 1983—where similar efforts had failed—is explained by a key group of senators that switched positions at the beginning of the 1893 depression.

In addition to the problem-solving motivations that best explain this case, it is worth underscoring the ideological and partisan factors operating in the background.[13] For starters, despite the fact that the Sherman Act increased silver purchases and the amount of currency in circulation, it was an effort by conservatives to *limit* silver's expansion. Indeed, by 1890 the battle over monetary policy was very much one between conservatives who favored sound money (mostly in the Republican Party) and liberals who favored an inflationary monetary policy (mostly in the Democratic Party). Sherman himself makes this clear in explaining why he voted for the law that bore his name: "A large majority of the Senate favored free silver, and it was feared that the small majority against it in the other House might yield and agree to it. . . . Some action had to be taken to prevent a return to free silver coinage, and the measure evolved was the best obtainable. I voted for it, but the day it became a law I was ready to repeal it."[14] It is also worth noting that this repeal occurred during the ideologically motivated presidency of Grover Cleveland. Cleveland's presidency was notable for its record uses of the veto, including his famous veto of the Texas Seed Bill because he argued federal support in disasters was "paternalistic" (Dupont 2014). On the issue of monetary policy, Cleveland fostered an ideological alignment with "gold Republicans" and against the western and populist factions of his own party (Frieden 1997). He eventually won support for the repeal of the Sherman Silver Purchase Act from Democrats in his own party, though he had to rely on patronage pressure to do so (Bensel 2000, 435).[15]

With respect to partisan battles over monetary policy in this era, it is important to keep in mind that the Sherman Act's repeal is an outlier in monetary conflicts of the late 1800s. Bensel (2000) notes that, across the range of votes on monetary policy in this period, the vote on the repeal of the Sherman Silver Purchase Act is a "difficult case." He writes: "Democratic majorities in both the House and Senate were publicly committed to (and, privately, also favored) continued silver purchases by the Treasury but, bowing to Cleveland's blunt use of patronage and other presidential blandishments, voted to repeal the Sherman Silver Purchase Act. At the time, left to its own devices, the [Democratic-controlled] Senate would even have enacted a free silver policy" (371). Ultimately, the cross-partisan coalition that supported the repeal of the Sherman Act was symptomatic of the fraying third-party system and the coming partisan realignment in 1896 that saw the birth of the fourth-party system lasting from 1896 to 1932 (Sundquist 1983; Noel 2013). Within a few years of the Sherman Act's repeal, ideologically conservative northeastern Democrats joined with Republicans, and Democrats aligned themselves with populists to prioritize workers' issues. In the end, the silver issue died in 1896 when Democrats absorbed the tenets of the Populist Party (purifying the party of the "gold Democrats") and Republican William McKinley defeated William Jennings Bryan in the presidential election.

All in all, while the successful repeal of the Sherman Silver Purchase Act is best explained by the problem-solving perspective, we note that it is inexorably linked to one of the most consequential partisan and ideological developments in American history. As we have maintained throughout, no single theory explains *all* repeals, nor is any repeal caused by a *single* process.

CONCLUSIONS

In this chapter we explored whether successful repeal efforts can be characterized as problem-solving actions. At the outset we noted that there are good reasons to believe that this is the case. First, the problem-solving theory is consistent with research on law creation, and, second, it comports with how lawmakers justify their actions. Despite this, we found no evidence that issue attention—the most commonly used measure of problem-solving efforts—has a systematic relationship with repeals, despite the use of multiple measures of legislative attention, including a few that extend from the end of Reconstruction to the present, nor do we find any evidence that repeals are more likely in domains with objective policy problems (deaths in war, recessions, bank failures) or in periods when technological advancement renders some laws obsolete.

Although we find little support for the problem-solving nature of repeals, our data do corroborate the effect of issue attention on law creation—consistent with other work on problem solving. It is important to be clear that our findings do not challenge the link between policy problems and legislative action: quite the contrary. Rather, one of our central claims is that repeals are different from other legislative actions, including both law creation and amendments.

In contrast to the problem-solving perspective, in chapter 1 we offered a series of reasons why repeals are best characterized as partisan contests over the status quo. Relevant to the National Maximum Speed Law repeal, one such reason is the partisan and ideological overtones to the *identification* of problems. Baumgartner and Jones (2015) point out that the search for information can lead to discovering new problems that the government could solve. After the election of Ronald Reagan, Republicans began restricting the quality their information search in attempt to cut down on the number of problems they would discover and solve, and as they did so, the party dramatically reduced Congress's capacity to engage in problem solving (Baumgartner and Jones 2015). Other researchers cite this shift as exacerbating asymmetries in how parties approach their legislative roles. As Grossmann and Hopkins (2016) write, "In contemporary Washington, however, only one major party—the Democrats—conforms to this baseline view of policymaking as an effort to solve social problems through legislative or administrative action" (255). We take up preference-based explanations of repeals in chapter 5. Before doing so, however, in chapter 4 we explore the role that parties play in the repeals process.

CHAPTER FOUR

Partisan Motivations

> Something that Republicans need to be concerned about is that, if we're just going to replace Obamacare with Obamacare-lite, it begs the question, were we just against Obamacare because it was proposed by the Democrats?
>
> Rep. Raul Labrador of the conservative Freedom Caucus, opposing a moderate ACA repeal
> February 15, 2017

> [Regular order on health care] is the only way we might achieve bipartisan consensus on lasting reform, without which a policy that affects one-fifth of our economy and every single American family will be subject to reversal with every change of administration and congressional majority.
>
> Sen. John McCain, a moderate Republican, on his vote against the GOP's ACA repeal bill
> September 22, 2017

In this chapter, we explore whether a partisan lens can explain the dynamics of repeal. In the last chapter, we found little evidence that repeals are a function of lawmakers' problem-solving motivations. An alternative possibility, the second of our "three Ps," is that repeals are instead a function of partisan motivations. Needless to say, parties are a central component of legislative organization (Aldrich 1995), and as Frances Lee (2009) and others have written, party conflict—not ideological conflict—has been the primary schism in the American Congress (see also Koger and Lebo 2017).

Consider, briefly, how parties and partisan conflict shaped the creation of the Affordable Care Act and the partisan nature of subsequent ACA repeal attempts. In general, the ACA's framework mirrored the Massachusetts health care plan—created by Democratic lawmakers and a Republican governor. While both the ACA and the Massachusetts plan dramatically increased the government's role in the provision health care, a few central aspects of the two plans are worth emphasizing. First, both maintained a privately run health care system rather than a government-run "single payer" system supported by liberals. Second, consistent with the conservative belief in the importance of individual responsibility, both plans required Americans to purchase health insurance to prevent taxpayers from footing the bill for emergency room treatment. Notably, this proposal is often credited to the conservative Heritage Foundation.[1] In this respect, the ACA, like the Massachusetts plan, was crafted by drawing on a range of policy alternatives from both sides of the ideological spectrum.

Despite its mix of liberal and conservative provisions, Republicans and Democrats took opposing positions on the law. All Republicans in Congress voted against the ACA, while Democratic leaders used "unorthodox" procedures to pass the bill on a partisan basis (Sinclair 2012). After enactment, no issue received more Republican attention than repealing the ACA. Over the next eight years, from 2011 to 2019, the GOP held roughly one hundred votes to repeal elements of the law even though many of its policy effects were unknown and despite the fact that most repeal proposals had no chance of passing. Yet after these efforts, and despite single-party control of both chambers and the White House, Republicans failed to repeal the law in the 115th Congress (2017–19). Rather, Republicans' lone success was setting the tax penalty associated with the individual mandate to zero dollars, effectively repealing the mandate when they passed the tax reform package late in 2017.

Simply put, it is undeniable that that party politics were at work in the both the passage and postpassage conflict over the ACA, as Republicans Raul Labrador and John McCain plainly admit in the quotes above. Of course, it would be myopic to argue that parties are the *only* explanation of legislative politics and policy outcomes in Congress: lawmakers' ideological motivations, reconciling differences in preferences, or finding solutions to problems are important as well. Even in a clearly partisan issue like the ACA, other factors are at work beneath the surface (Ragusa 2017). Nonetheless, in this book we argue that repeals are best explained as partisan actions for a few reasons.

First, repeals are uniquely difficult to enact because they run counter to the natural path dependency of legislation, exist in a constrained negotiating environment, and aggravate conflict in a system that aids obstruction. Moreover, party conflict reduces the likelihood of passing a repeal, and as partisan conflict increases, the various roadblocks to repeals become more difficult to overcome. Consequently, we contend that it takes an especially homogenous majority to overcome these barriers (Aldrich 1995; Aldrich and Rohde 2001; Rohde 1991). Second, repeals may be more common when a party's grasp on the majority is uncertain. While an entrenched majority may seek to enact new laws, in a competitive environment both the majority and minority party may seek to repeal legislation, for both policy and electoral reasons (Lee 2016). Likewise, a recently ascendant majority may come to power with enhanced cohesion due to its time in the minority (Dodd 1986a, 1986b) and be willing to empower party leaders to act in a decisive manner (Rohde, Stiglitz, and Weingast 2013). And third, the legislative agenda is set by party leaders. Chamber support is not enough to get a bill passed—leaders must be willing to bring the proposal to the floor and expedite its passage (Koger and Lebo 2017; Rohde 1991; Cox and McCubbins 2005). In this respect, party leaders possess the capacity to utilize various tactics to shepherd a bill around the pitfalls and veto points that are common in the legislative process (Curry 2015; Sinclair 1999, 2002).

This chapter proceeds as follows. First, we discuss the ways a partisan lens can make sense of when and why repeals occur: whether unified government influences repeals, whether the majority party's cohesion matters, and whether repeals are related to a party's electoral past. We also argue it is important to consider the majority's cohesion and electoral past in tandem. Second, we test these party-based arguments on data of repeal *attempts*. In this analysis, and in a parallel analysis in the next chapter, we focus on the sponsorship of bills that were intended to repeal legislation, irrespective of whether the effort succeeded, and the characteristics of the lawmakers who introduced them. And third, and most importantly, we proceed to test these partisan-based arguments on our main database of *successful* repeals. Our analysis on adopted repeals is parallel to the analyses in chapters 3 and 5, where the overarching goal is to assess the role of parties, preferences, and problem solving on when and why repeals occur.

PARTIES

THEORY

On the role of political parties in government, E. E. Schattschneider (1942) famously wrote that "democracy is unthinkable save in terms of the parties" (1). Echoing that sentiment, Sartori (1968) claimed that "citizens in Western democracies are represented *through* and *by* parties. This is inevitable" (13:417; emphasis in original). Claims about the critical organizing role of political parties are echoed by modern party theorists as well (Aldrich 1995; Bawn et al. 2012; Cohen et al. 2008; Koger and Lebo 2017; Lee 2016; Rohde 1991). Whereas a substantial volume of this literature has focused on the normative characteristics of parties (e.g., American Political Science Association 1950) or the electoral role that parties play (e.g., Cohen et al. 2008; Hershey 2005), our focus is on the institutional role of the parties in Congress.

In an examination of why parties formed in the United States despite the Founders' best efforts to restrain them, Aldrich (1995) argues that parties are vital tools of individual lawmakers. In Aldrich's theory, parties were created by lawmakers and office seekers to help solve the famous collective action problem by organizing and coordinating members with similar interests and thereby reducing their incentives to work as free agents. The influence of parties in the legislature is not unique to Congress, as efforts to limit the effect of parties at the state level have failed as well (Masket 2016). Simply put, parties are an inevitable feature of legislatures.

While the focus of this section is on the behavior of parties in the legislature, it is appropriate to briefly consider the role of the president in party politics. First, it is well known that the president can help shape legislative productivity. A number of authors theorize that Congress is more likely to pass landmark legislation under unified party government—when the president and lawmakers are more likely to have congruent policy preferences—than it is under divided government, owing to the president's ability to stop legislation with a veto (Edwards, Barrett, and Peake 1997; Binder 1999, 2003; Jones 2001; Howell et al. 2000). Moreover, as the most prominent member of the party, the president is often seen as the de facto leader of the party, frequently invoking mandate rhetoric in policy messages to Congress (Azari 2014; Conley 2001). Though not always successful, this mandate language has the capacity to reshape the legislative agenda.

In the discussion thus far, we focus on two different but related components of the legislative agenda: what the legislature considers but does not pass and what the legislature considers and does pass. With respect to the former—what the legislature considers but does not pass—parties have a near monopoly on the ability to veto legislation or otherwise *stop* a policy proposal from advancing out of the legislature. In the literature, such power is referred to as "negative agenda control." Cox and McCubbins's (1993, 2005) "cartel theory" posits that parties have an electoral incentive to maintain a specific brand, and so it works to bring forward only legislation that benefits the party caucus as a collective body. If the party leadership believes that legislation would hurt the party's reputation or pit the factions of the party against one another, leadership will do its best to prevent the proposal from moving forward.

With respect to the latter, what the legislature considers and does pass, Cooper and Brady (1981), Dodd (1986a, 1986b), Aldrich and Rohde (2001), Aldrich (1995), and Rohde (1991) focus on the benefits of coordinated party behavior. In the literature, that power is most often referred to as "positive agenda control." According to this view, the electoral process helps select politicians who are good policy matches with their constituents, and the politicians set out to achieve the policy goals articulated in the campaign. To the extent that politicians' copartisans share their policy preferences, they will empower the party leadership to achieve those goals. By contrast, when the parties are divided internally on policy matters, the rank and file will not delegate significant agenda-setting powers to their leaders, instead preferring a decentralized legislative structure. Given those tenets, scholars often refer to the theory as "conditional party government," as it suggests that the majority party leadership's power is contingent on the degree of ideological cohesion among the rank and file (Rohde 1991).

In the most recent theoretical work on parties in Congress, scholars are less focused on testing claims about agenda control and are more focused on integrating those theories. In Koger and Lebo's (2017) theory of "strategic party government," parties are forced to balance two goals—winning elections and delivering policy—such that too little party influence (nothing gets done) can hurt, as can too much party influence (members vote with their party and against their district). Koger and Lebo argue that ideologically cohesive parties are expected to delegate more positive agenda-setting power to party leaders in pursuit of agreed-upon policy outcomes, much like in conditional party government. In order to win election, however, the rank and file will unite behind their leaders even on items that divide the caucus, and party leaders will on occasion block policy items that their members support. In Lee's account, not only is a sizable amount of partisan conflict nonideological (Lee 2009), but nonideological conflict is based on the party's expectation that it might win the next election (Lee 2016). When party control is uncertain and either side could become the next majority, the rank and file will work to burnish their own party's reputation by magnifying differences between the parties, both in ideological and nonideological conflicts. By contrast, when party control is certain—such as during the long period of Democratic control after 1932—fewer incentives for pursuing ideological conflict exist.

Hypotheses

In the sections that follow, we discuss the specific partisan factors that may explain when and why repeals occur. As in the last chapter, and the next, while the partisan perspective is intuitive, the question is *how* parties matter. In the ensuing discussion, each factor dovetails in some form with the theoretical discussion above.

Do Unified Governments Repeal More Legislation?

Unified government is an intuitive explanation of when and why repeals occur. It stands to reason that when one party wins control of both chambers in Congress and the White House, it will feel empowered to target laws enacted by its rival and, due to its institutional position, is more likely to succeed in that effort. As a theoretical matter, the effect of unified government is consistent with the notion that, in a system of checks and balances, parties serve as the "glue" that bonds fragmented institutions (Fiorina 1980; Wilson 1885; Schattschneider 1942). Divided government, by comparison, exacerbates the separation of powers, leading to gridlock and inaction.

In the literature, however, researchers reach mixed conclusions about the efficacy of unified party control. Initial research supported the conventional wisdom: unified government leads to increased legislative activity (Sundquist 1988; Cutler 1988). But in 1991, Mayhew's *Divided We Govern* reached the opposite conclusion. Examining the volume of landmark laws enacted in the post–World War II period, Mayhew found that important legislation passes in roughly the same proportions during single- and split-party control. Mayhew's finding led many to conclude that lawmakers' preferences—not their party—is pivotal in the legislative process. (We explore this competing perspective in the next chapter.) On balance, however, recent work supports many researchers' initial conclusions (Edwards, Barrett, and Peake 1997; Howell et al. 2000; Binder 1999, 2003; Jones 2001). As Edwards, Barrett, and Peake (1997) aptly put it: "The pre-Mayhew conventional wisdom was correct: divided government inhibits the passage of important legislation" (562).

Unlike the body of work on law creation, research on statutory revision reaches mixed conclusions on the effect of unified government. Carpenter and Lewis (2004) conclude that unified government increases the risk of bureaucratic termination; Maltzman and Shipan (2008) find no effect on amendments; and Berry, Burden, and Howell (2010) conclude that federal programs are more likely to survive during unified control. In other words, three studies reach three competing conclusions.[2] Our work reaches mixed conclusions as well: in Ragusa and Birkhead (2015), we find no effect of unified government on the likelihood of repeal, consistent with Maltzman and Shipan, while Ragusa (2010) found a greater risk of repeal when one party controls both chambers and the White House, consistent with the study by Carpenter and Lewis. In chapter 2 of this book, descriptive statistics showed a modest correlation between unified control and the occurrence of significant repeals. Simply put, we lack clear expectations on whether unified governments repeal a greater volume of legislation, though on balance there seems to be a modest relationship.

Do Unified Governments Enact More Repealed Legislation?

A parallel question is whether laws enacted *during* unified party control have a higher likelihood of repeal in subsequent Congresses. A study by Maltzman and Shipan (2008) reaches what they call a "counterintuitive" conclusion (255). According to their analysis, statutes enacted during single-party control are less likely to be amended by future Congresses. Maltzman and Shipan argue that this effect is due to the fact that unified government enables lawmakers to craft laws that are legally consistent and more likely to have self-executing provisions. During divided government, by comparison, lawmakers tend to pass inconsistent and inflexible laws, thus increasing the need for future revisions. Likewise, laws enacted with bipartisan support are unlikely to satisfy both sides of the aisle, increasing the risk of amendment when one party gains unified control in the future.

An alternative view is that divided government is associated with greater deliberation and moderation, therefore producing more durable legislation. On the one hand, because each party has a de facto veto over any bill, divided government may lead to greater minority party input (Weatherford 1994; Austen-Smith and Riker 1987). This deliberation may lead to the creation of laws that more adequately address the problems they were intended to solve, thus reducing the need for revisions in the future (Bendix 2016; Lascher 1996; Page 2007; Sunstein 2005). At the same time, given the body of work concluding that divided government decreases legislative productivity, perhaps the laws that *do* pass during split-party control are more moderate and thus less likely to be a target for repeal when the governing majority switches (Niskanen 2003; Thorson 1998).

In an earlier study (Ragusa 2010), we found mixed evidence on this question. In the immediate aftermath of a landmark law's passage, repeals are more likely to occur if it was enacted during split-party control, consistent with Maltzman and Shipan's study. Over the long term, however, our data indicate that laws enacted during divided government are less likely to be repealed, consistent with the alternative view that emphasizes deliberation and bill moderation. On the question of whether unified governments repeal more laws, we conclude that the literature on statutory revision is mixed on whether laws enacted by unified government are more or less likely to be repealed.

Are Cohesive Majorities Better at Repealing Laws?

Given the inconsistent link between summary measures of party control and statutory revision, we explore a host of partisan factors that are less intuitive but nonetheless have strong backing in the literature. One such factor is the majority party's ideological cohesion. We have argued throughout that the majority's cohesiveness is likely a key factor in explaining when and why repeals occur.

In discussing the partisan nature of repeals earlier, we noted that because repeals are uniquely hard to pass, due to a combination of unique institutional constraints and the contentious nature of statutory revision, it often requires a cohesive majority and strong party leaders to shepherd repeals though the legislative process. Unlike the majority's ability to block the passage of unwanted proposals, which is historically constant (Cox and McCubbins 1993, 2005, 2007), the governing party's capacity to act in a positive manner is thought to be conditional (Rohde 1991; Aldrich and Rohde 1997). In eras when the majority's rank and file exhibit ideological cohesion, not only is there greater policy agreement a priori, but, under such conditions, the party's caucus can be expected to empower their leaders to set the legislative agenda, exploit the chamber's institutional rules and procedures, and compel members to support the party's policy goals. In our earlier work (Ragusa and Birkhead 2015) we found considerable support for these claims.

To illustrate these points, consider two Congresses, the 53rd (1893–95) and 81st (1949–51), which exemplify the contrast between homogenous and heterogeneous parties. Figure 4.1 is a density plot of the distribution

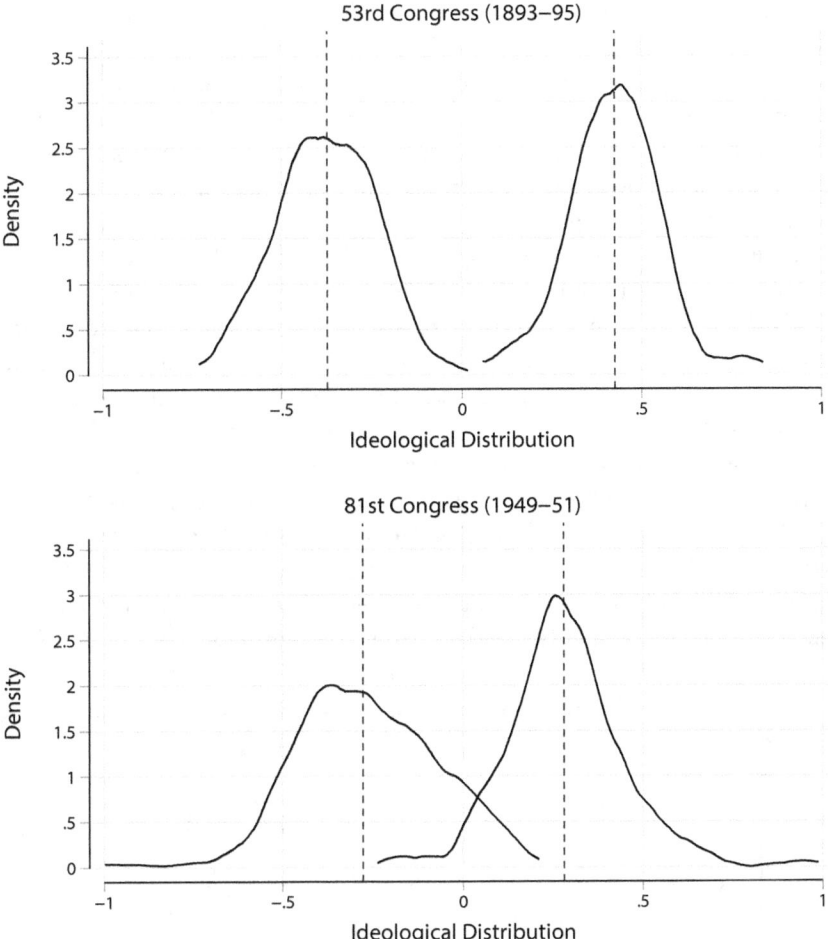

Fig. 4.1. Distribution of Liberal and Conservative Lawmakers

of liberal lawmakers (left) and conservative lawmakers (right) in both parties in these two Congresses.[3] Vertical lines denote each party's median member. We can see that the 53rd Congress had two ideologically homogenous parties, while the 81st Congress had two ideologically heterogeneous parties. Not only are members of the 53rd Congress tightly clustered around their party's median member, but there is literally no overlap in the ideological middle. In other words, the Democratic majority in the 53rd Congress was fairly liberal on economic matters—by the standards of that era—and no Democrat was more conservative than the most liberal Republican. In the 81st Congress, by comparison, there were a number of extreme members in both parties (on the far left and far right) but also an overlap in the middle of the spectrum. In addition to exhibiting greater ideological diversity, each party's median member in the 81st Congress was closer to the middle of the spectrum. Simply put, an ideologically cohesive majority, like Democrats in the 53rd Congress, should be better positioned to repeal legislation owing to their preexisting policy agreement and capacity to unite behind strong party leaders who can expedite repeal bills.

In Figure 4.2 below, we display the majority's ideological cohesion for each Congress in our analysis.[4] We see cycles of polarization that are familiar to most students of Congress (Dodd 2015; Poole and Rosenthal 1997). From 1877 to 1911, the 45th to the 61st Congresses, majorities tended to be very cohesive. Congressional scholars often refer to this as the era of "Reed's Rules," an eponymous term for parliamentary reforms adopted in 1890 by then Speaker Thomas Bracket Reed that allowed the majority to thwart minority obstruction. After the famous revolt against Speaker Joe Cannon weakened the majority's power in 1910, ideological cohesion waned over the subsequent decades. In the middle part of the time series, from 1945 to 1969, the 79th to 90th Congresses, we can see that majorities tended to be ideologically heterogeneous. Congressional scholars often refer to this as the "textbook era" Congress. Finally, after a series of reforms reempowered parties in the 1970s, ideological cohesion trends back upward. From 1993 to 2011, the 103rd to 111th Congresses, majorities were

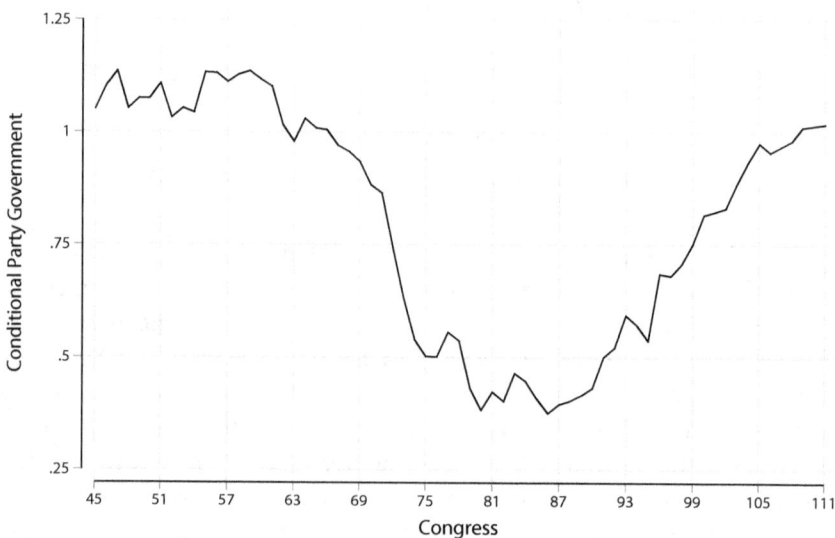

Fig. 4.2. Conditional Party Government Index (1877–2011)

cohesive again, though slightly less so than from 1877 to 1911. Scholars often refer to this as the "postreform era."

Does a Party's Electoral Past Lead to Repeal?

In the discussion thus far, we have focused on a party's institutional position, in particular the governing majority's capacity to overcome constitutional and procedural impediments to legislative action. Such a view would surely be incomplete, however. In particular, based on Lee (2016), Koger and Lebo (2017) as well as many others, it is also important to also consider the party's recent electoral experiences. We consider two specific processes, what we call "party mandates" and "party cycles" for simplicity.

A long line of work has studied party mandates: landslide electoral victories that legitimize one party's legislative agenda. In 1964 V. O. Key Jr. noted: "In a landslide the might of the electorate in a democratic order appears in a most spectacular fashion." (523). Party mandates can affect the legislative process, and statutory revision in particular, in two basic ways. First, landside electoral victories usually coincide with shifts in the public's preferences for liberal or conservative policies (Stimson 1999). Second, large seat swings afford the majority greater institutional power due to their increased numerical size. Although journalists, pundits, and politicians tend to overinterpret the results of any given election, research suggests that dramatic electoral victories do indeed lead to notable shifts in national policy (Bond and Fleisher 1990; Brady 1988; Erikson, MacKuen, and Stimson 2002; Skocpol, Finegold, and Goldfield 1990; Stimson 1999). Such effects may be especially pronounced when they occur alongside national crises or economic downturns (Lewis-Beck 1988). In the literature on statutory revision, however, there are mixed results regarding whether the size of the majority's seat share—a proxy for the size of a party's mandate—leads to a greater risk of revision (Berry, Burden, and Howell 2010) or has no effect (Ragusa and Birkhead 2015).

Party cycles, by comparison, are historic transitions from one governing majority to the next. Unlike mandates, which occur in every election to some degree, party cycles are rare, occurring when a newly ascendant majority replaces a previously entrenched majority. A long line of work explores how to define and classify these critical elections (Key 1955; Campbell et al. 1960; Burnham 1970; Sundquist 1983). For our purposes, however, we are interested in whether party cycles shape legislative politics. We believe the answer is yes, owning to the fact that parties alter their legislative strategies based on their experience in and out of power (Koger and Lebo 2017; Lee 2016). In a competitive environment, when either party could become the majority, parties will eschew compromise (Lee 2016), making it harder to pass new laws and repeal old ones. In an uncompetitive environment, when one party governs for a decade or more, the majority will focus on passing new laws, often with input from the minority (Lee 2016).

We extend this logic, arguing that repeals will not be a priority in an uncompetitive environment with an entrenched majority, as the most recently enacted laws are the majority's own, and the demand for repeal wanes with each passing Congress. In contrast, repeals *will* be a priority in an environment when a newly ascendant majority comes to power. Due to the fact that they were in the minority for a considerable length of time, there will be a backlog of statutes the new majority wants to repeal. Of this dynamic, Dodd (1986a) writes that in their "early days in power," a newly ascendant majority can "offset" their ideological divisions given their time in the minority opposing the majority's legislative accomplishments (94). Furthermore, newly ascendant majorities often campaign on reversing statutes enacted by an entrenched rival and may act decisively by empowering leaders in an effort to keep these promises (Rohde, Stiglitz, and Weingast 2013). For these reasons, we hypothesize that repeals are most likely in the early stages of a party cycle, when a new majority comes to power after a long stint in the minority.

In figure 4.3, we chart party cycles from 1877 to 2011 using a variable that counts the majority's time in the minority based on the number of House and Senate chambers out of power over the past decade. As we note in the analysis below, we call this "historical minority status" since it records the past chambers controlled by the majority's rival in the five previous two-year Congresses. As we explain, our measure utilizes changes in control of Congress, ranging from a minimum of zero, if the majority had control of every chamber over the past decade, to a maximum of ten, if the majority regained control after spending all of the past decade in the minority. Conceptually, higher values indicate a newly ascendant majority, and lower values indicate an entrenched majority. As a reference point, we include a horizontal line at the series average, which is 3.6 chambers in the minority.

We first see a spike in the 46th Congress (1879–81), when Democrats controlled both chambers for the first time since the Civil War. A competitive environment in the 1880s saw split control of the two chambers, before the modest spike of the 53rd Congress (1893–95), when Democrats once again regained both chambers. Following the 53rd Congress, and

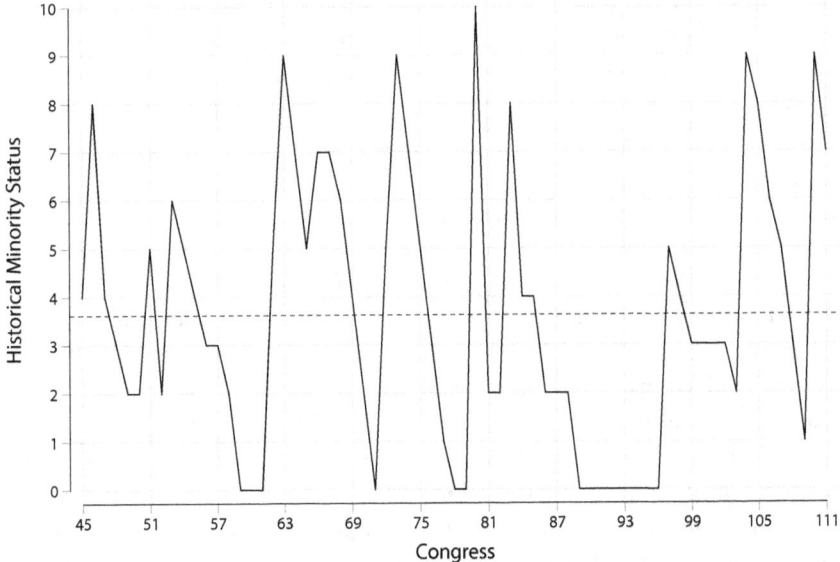

Fig. 4.3. Cycles of Party Control of the House and Senate

after William Jennings Bryan's defeat in the 1896 presidential election, Democrats were relegated to the minority for the next eight Congresses. It wasn't until the 63rd Congress (1913–15), which coincided with Wilson's first election, that Democrats retook unified control of Congress. The plateau in the 66th and 67th Congresses corresponds with the Republicans regaining both chambers in the election of 1918. Another lull occurs as Republicans retained control through the 1920s until the Democrats swept into power along with FDR in 1932. Except for Republican control of both chambers in the 80th and 83rd Congresses (1947–49 and 1953–55), and control of the 97th Senate (1981–83) following the 1980 election, there is a long lull in the post–World War II period due to Democrats' near universal control of Congress. In the series, the last spikes occurred during the famed Republican revolution in 1994, and in the 110th Congress (2007–9), when Democrats won control of Congress for the first time in over a decade in the waning years of George W. Bush's presidency.

What about the Combined Effect of a Party's Institutional Position and Electoral Past?

A final matter concerns the combined effect of a party's cohesion and time in the minority. While these two concepts are distinct, the former reflects institutional dynamics, and the latter reflects electoral dynamics, it is entirely possible they work in tandem. For example, the majority may be in a favorable institutional position, but its electoral ascension may not be conducive for repeals. Likewise, the majority may come to power under favorable electoral conditions but possess an unfordable institutional position. On rare occasions, however, the majority finds itself in a favorable institutional position *and* the characteristics of its electoral ascension are conducive for repeals.

In our earlier work, we found just such an effect (Ragusa and Birkhead 2015). Drawing on the notion that the majority's agenda-setting capacity is a function of its ideological cohesion and the size of the agenda (Rohde, Stiglitz, and Weingast 2013), we hypothesized that repeal is most likely when a newly ascendant majority is cohesive. First, due to limited plenary time and constant pressure on the agenda, the rank and file must prioritize some issues over others (Walker 1977). But this agenda scarcity is not constant; it waxes and wanes from one Congress to the next. In particular, a newly ascendant majority that spent considerable time in the minority will exert greater pressure on the agenda compared to majorities that hold onto control for a decade or more. In such a scenario, Rohde, Stiglitz, and Weingast (2013) maintain that cohesive majorities that have *recently* won control are more likely to centralize agenda control in the leadership due to the fact that the rank and file are likely to agree on what items to prioritize (see also Fenno 1997; Barnes and O'Neill 2006; Dodd 1986a, 1986b). Notably, this hypothesis joins the work of institutionally focused partisan theorists (Aldrich 1995; Cox and McCubbins 1993, 2005; Masket 2016; Rohde 1991) with the more recent wave of party theorists who focus on electorally induced party actions (Bawn et al. 2012; Koger and Lebo 2017; Lee 2009, 2016).

ANALYSIS OF REPEAL INTRODUCTIONS

In the introductory chapter, we conducted a test of our theory that repeals are uniquely difficult to enact using data on repeals introduced in Congress in the post–World War II era. We return to that data set in this section and examine the members who sponsor repeal bills. Rather than exploring whether repeals pass or fail, here we are interested in why a lawmaker introduces a repeal bill in the first place. Although our main analysis of successful repeals is in the next section, an examination of repeals sponsored helps us understand repeal dynamics more broadly.

Data and Method

Our data set contains all bills introduced in the House and Senate from the 83rd to the 114th Congresses (1953–2017).[5] The dependent variable is a count of the number of repeal bills lawmaker i introduced in Congress t. Recall that repeal bills are classified based on whether their bill title includes the word "repeal." As we noted, it is quite common for bills to make their effect on other laws known in this manner. Because the dependent variable is a count, we estimate negative binomial count models, and because of the multilevel nature of the data set, we include member random effects. Complete details are in appendix C.

In the analysis, we have independent variables in three categories: parties, preferences, and electoral factors. We discuss the measurement of these variables, and their expected directions, in this chapter and the next. In the pages below, we focus on the partisan variables in the model. Lastly, because the unit of analysis is a member of Congress and not a law as in our main model of repeal success, we have no way of testing problem-solving variables, which require a bill-level analysis.

We tested four partisan institutional variables in the repeal introduction analysis. *Majority* is a dichotomous measure of whether the lawmaker is a member of the chamber's majority party. On the one hand, members of the majority may sponsor more repeals owing to the greater chance they actually pass. On the other hand, members of the minority may sponsor more repeals as a form of electoral messaging. *Unified government* is a dichotomous measure of whether one party controls both chambers and the White House. We hypothesize that unified government is associated with greater repealing activity owing to increased odds of passing both chambers and being signed into law. *Ideological cohesion* measures the homogeneity of the lawmaker's party.[6] Given the earlier discussion, we expect a positive effect, indicating members of cohesive parties sponsor a greater number of repeals. Finally, *historical minority status* captures whether the member's party is ascendant or entrenched.[7] We expect recently ascendant majorities will sponsor a greater number of repeals.

We also included two partisan electoral variables in the analysis. *District / state partisanship* is the two-party vote for the Democratic presidential candidate in the district/state in the most recent election. (In the next chapter, we test whether the public's ideology—known as the public mood—explains repeal efforts instead.) We suspect that Republican-leaning constituencies, conservative publics, or perhaps both, pressure lawmakers to sponsor a greater volume of repeals. Lastly, *safe seat* uses the same presidential vote data to determine how far a member's district/state leans in their favor. Higher values indicate a Republican (Democratic) lawmaker represents a district with a large pro-Republican (pro-Democratic) constituency, while lower values indicate the extent of the mismatch between the member's party affiliation and his or her constituents. We suspect that members from safe seats will sponsor fewer repeals, all else being equal.

Results

In the analysis of repeal sponsorship—reported as model 1 in table C1 of appendix C—we find support for two of the partisan hypotheses. First, the results indicate that members of recently ascendant parties indeed sponsor a larger number of repeals relative to members of parties that are entrenched. In other words, parties that govern for an extended period in an uncompetitive environment focus on the creation of new laws, not repeals, while parties who ascend to power after a long time in the minority will introduce a greater volume of repeals. We hypothesized that this may stem from a backlog of statutes the newly ascendant majority wants to undo and the propensity of ascendant majorities to rally behind strong party leaders and a unified agenda.

Second, the repeal introduction results reveal that lawmakers from Democratic-leaning districts and states sponsor fewer repeals, while members from Republican-leaning districts and states sponsor more repeals. We noted that this effect likely stems from the Republican Party's ideological commitment to limited government, where a repeal is viewed as a tool to roll back the size and scope of the federal government, and the Democratic Party's commitment to enacting new laws to aid various demographic groups (Grossmann and Hopkins 2016).

An important caveat, however, is that these two effects are small in magnitude. Specifically, the *historical minority status* variable indicates that for every additional year the member spent in the chamber's minority party, there is only a 2% increase in the expected number of repeal bills he or she sponsors. Likewise, a 1% increase in a district or state's Democratic leaning decreases the expected number of repeal bills sponsored by only 0.4%. Compounding these small effect sizes is the fact that, of the six variables in the partisan category, only these two are significant. Variables for unified government, the majority's ideological cohesion, being a member of the majority party, and whether the member represents a safe partisan seat do not predict the number of repeals a member sponsors. As we discuss in the next chapter, the results indicate a greater role of preferences in explaining a member's repeal efforts. We do, however, find a notable interaction between a party variable and a preference variable. We report on that in the next chapter as well.

ANALYSIS OF SUCCESSFUL REPEALS

Data and Method

As in the last chapter, our main analysis is an examination of successfully enacted repeals. Recall that our data set consists of all major laws—defined as the most notable 10% of laws—enacted by Congress from 1877 to 2011. Laws are arranged longitudinally, spanning the period from the first Congress after a bill's passage to its eventual repeal (or are right censored at the 112th Congress). Our survival model—which predicts whether law i experienced a major repeal in Congress t after passage—contains the same variables reported in chapters 3 and 5, though here we focus on the partisan variables described above. As always, complete results are available in appendix D.

Earlier we noted that the partisan causes of repeal can reflect a party's institutional position, its electoral past, or a combination of the two. In the analysis of successful repeals we test three variables for the majority's institutional position. First, we include a variable for party control in the enacting Congress. *Unified at enactment* is coded 1 if one party controls both chambers and the White House and 0 if divided government exists at the time of the law's enactment. Second, we have a variable for party control of each Congress after enactment. *Unified at subsequent* is coded the same as the enactment variable, with 1 representing unified government and 0 indicating divided government. Despite mixed results in the literature, given the preliminary analysis from chapter 3, we expect unified government, both at the time of passage and in subsequent Congresses, is associated with a greater risk of repeal.

Our third measure of the majority's institutional position is a variable for its ideological cohesion. Following Aldrich, Berger, and Rohde (2002), *conditional party government* is a single-factor score derived from four common measures of the majority's ideological heterogeneity and distance from the minority.[8] We utilize this measure over alternatives because it is favored by the theory's main proponents and has been used in a number of studies (Finocchiaro and Rohde 2008; Lebo and O'Green 2011; Miller and

Overby 2014; Ragusa and Birkhead 2015; Birkhead 2016). Figure 4.2, above, charts this measure over the entire time series, where higher values indicate more cohesive majorities and lower values indicate less cohesive majorities. We hypothesize that cohesive majorities have a greater capacity to shepherd repeals though the legislative process due to their agenda-setting powers and greater policy agreement.

On the electoral partisan variables, we use two measures for how the majority ascended to power. Electoral mandates are measured using the size of the majority's seat swing since the Congress that enacted the law. For *seat swing*, higher values indicate the majority gained seats since it enacted the law, while lower values indicate the majority lost seats. Conceptually, when the majority experiences a large positive seat swing, not only is it better able to safeguard its signature laws, but the swing itself is a proxy for popular support of the party's agenda. Large negative seat swings, by comparison, often coincide with changes in party control and declining public support, both of which may embolden a new majority to pursue repeals. Party cycles are measured with a rolling average that counts the number of chambers the majority was in the minority over the past decade. Our variable ranges from a minimum of zero—if the majority had control of every chamber over the past decade, to a maximum of ten—if the majority regained control after spending all of the past decade in the minority. Figure 4.3, above, plotted *historical minority status* for the entire time series. We hypothesize that a newly ascendant majority will seek to reverse the statutes enacted over the past decade by its rival, while an entrenched majority will focus more on law creation.

Lastly, we argued that there will be an interaction between a majority's institutional position and the nature of its electoral ascension. Specifically, we hypothesize that there is an increased risk of repeal when a majority is ideologically cohesive *and* it regained power after a long time in the minority. Given the importance of this combined effect to this chapter's main claims, we present a brief illustration of party cycles, ideological cohesion, and successful repeals. Table 4.1 is a 2 × 2 chart with four Congresses—the 53rd, 57th, 83rd, and 81st—that represent each possible condition: (1) high party cohesion and an ascendant majority, (2) high party cohesion and an entrenched majority, (3) low party cohesion and an ascendant majority, and (4) low party cohesion and an entrenched majority. A key point is that these factors are independently necessary but not sufficient conditions for repeal to occur. In other words, ideologically homogenous majorities and those that seize power after a long time in the minority are not *automatically* successful in adopting repeals.

TABLE 4.1. 2 x 2 Table of Party Cycles and Ideological Cohesion

Ideological Cohesion	Party Cycle	
	Ascendant Majority (high time in the minority)	Entrenched Majority (low time in the minority)
Homogenous Majority (high conditional party government)	53rd Congress 1893–95 Description: Democratic control of both chambers and the White House for the first time since the Civil War. Democrats were ascendant, having controlled just four chambers over the past decade, including no control of the Senate. Democrats were highly cohesive. Outcome: 53rd Congress adopted the largest volume of significant repeals in history, according to the analysis in chapter 2. Landmark repeals include the Sherman Silver Purchase Act, the Reconstruction-era Federal Election Laws, and the McKinley Tariff.	57th Congress 1901–3 Description: Republican control of both chambers and the White House. Republicans were entrenched, having controlled seven of the last ten chambers over the past decade, including both chambers in the prior three Congresses. Republicans were highly cohesive. Outcome: 57th Congress adopted just one repeal of modest significance, a series of war taxes enacted in 1898 to fund the Spanish-American War.
Heterogeneous Majority (low conditional party government)	83rd Congress 1953–55 Description: Republican control of both chambers and White House for the first time in twenty years. Republicans were ascendant, having controlled just two chambers over the past decade. Republicans lacked ideological cohesion. Outcome: 83rd Congress adopted just one repeal of modest significance, a movie theater admissions tax for films costing 50 cents or less.	81st Congress 1949–51 Description: Democratic control of both chambers and the White House. Democrats were entrenched, having controlled eight of the last ten chambers over the past decade. Democrats lacked ideological cohesion. Outcome: 81st Congress adopted no major repeals.

Recall from figure 4.2 that the period from the 45th Congress to the 61st is one of ideologically cohesive and polarized parties. On the surface, we might expect a consistent stream of repeals in this era. But, as figure 2.4 in chapter 2 showed, while the 53rd Congress enacted a large volume of repeals, the following Congresses enacted very few. We believe this disparity can be explained by the fact that the 53rd Congress had an ascendant Democratic majority, while every Congress for the next sixteen years (54th to 61st Congresses) developed into an entrenched Republican majority. Of course, this period also coincides with Bryan's defeat in the realigning election of 1896 and Republican dominance in national elections around the turn of the century. For example, in the 57th Congress, our example of a homogenous majority but entrenched majority, just one repeal was successfully enacted, a unique case in that the repeal targeted a war law from the Spanish-American War that was temporary by design.

Unlike the Congresses around the turn of the century, the post–World War II Congresses were characterized by ideologically heterogeneous parties, with a sizable number of conservative Democrats and liberal Republicans. Figure 4.2 shows that the period from the 79th Congress to the 90th (1945–69) is the low-water mark for cohesion. Consistent with our general expectations, figure 2.4 in chapter 2 shows that this is an era of limited repealing activity. Emblematic of this period is the 81st Congress. Despite control of Congress and the White House and a strong push by labor unions to repeal the Taft-Hartley Act enacted in the previous Congress, Democrats enacted no major repeals. In addition to their low cohesion, Democrats were an entrenched majority, having been in the minority for just two of the last ten chambers. By comparison, the 83rd Congress featured a heterogeneous but ascendant Republican majority during Eisenhower's first two years in the White House. Notably, this was the last time the GOP controlled both chambers over the subsequent forty-two years. In the 83rd Congress, one major repeal—the repeal of an excise tax on movie admissions—was passed, which we estimated to be of only modest significance.

Results

Consistent with the results in table 4.1, above, our main finding in model 1 is the significant interaction between the majority's ideological cohesion and the amount of time it was in the minority in prior Congresses. In the model in appendix D, the negative interaction effect indicates that when the conditional party government indicators are high *and* the majority is recently ascendant, landmark laws are vulnerable to repeal. In other words, a homogenous majority that comes to power after a long stint in the minority is most likely to expedite the passage of repealing legislation and undo an existing law. As noted previously, we see this joint hypothesis as unifying the work of institutionally focused partisan theorists (Aldrich 1995; Cox and McCubbins 1993, 2005; Masket 2016; Rohde 1991) with those who focus on electorally induced party actions (Bawn et al. 2012; Koger and Lebo 2017; Lee 2009, 2016).

Figure 4.4 shows how likely repeal is when the majority is cohesive and ascendant. In the figure, we plot the likelihood of a new law's survival over twenty-five Congresses (fifty years) after enactment. As noted elsewhere, it is important to keep in mind that, because major repeals are rare, even the strongest predictors vary the probability of repeal by only a few percentage points in any given Congress. In the top panel of the figure, we calculate the survival probabilities for three conditions of ideological cohesion and time out of power: a homogenous and ascendant majority, the average of both variables, and a heterogeneous and entrenched majority. We discuss the bottom part of the panel below.

A few things stand out in the top panel of figure 4.4. First, we can see how consequential the majority's ideological cohesion and electoral past are for the occurrence of repeals. Although there is no appreciable difference between the average effect and that for a heterogonous and entrenched majority, a law's survivability drops *precipitously* when the majority is homogenous and ascendant. Second, the size of this effect is quite large in a comparative sense. Recall from the last chapter that policies on macroeconomic policy are about 1% more likely to be repealed than a given social welfare law. By contrast, a bill has a 3.5% greater risk of repeal when the majority is homogenous and ascendant. Clearly, while the issue area of a bill influences its longevity, its longevity is particularly affected by the patterns of party conflict.

In brief, the interaction of a majority's cohesion and electoral ascension matters, and it matters quite a lot relative to other significant factors. These results dovetail with two of the most repeal-active Congresses in history: the 53rd Congress (1893–95), when a cohesive Democratic majority won unified control for the first time since the Civil War, and the Gingrich-led 104th Congress (1995–97), when a homogenous Republican majority seized both chambers for the first time in forty years.

We pause here and address the question, Which factor is more important? Of course, the interaction effect indicates that both matter and the effect of one depends on the level of the other. For this reason we cannot

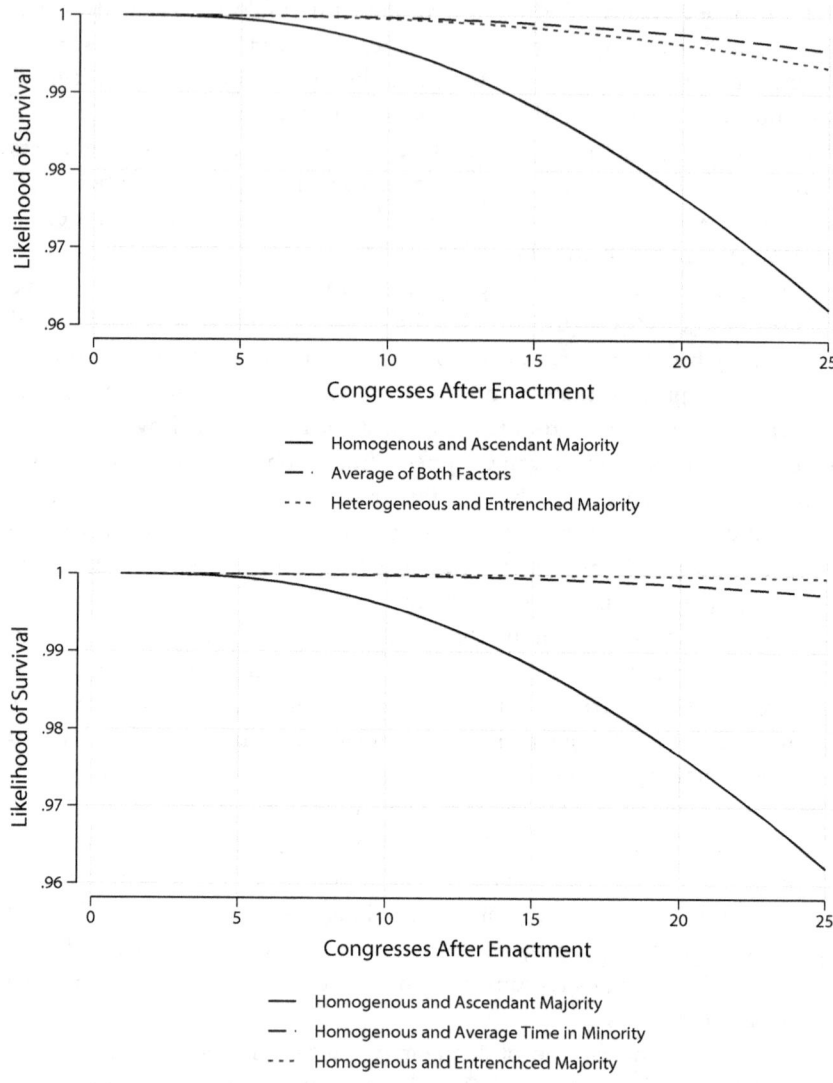

Fig. 4.4. Effects of Majority Cohesion and Electoral Ascension on Repeal Probability

simply "eyeball" the base terms as if they are the unconditional main effects (Brambor, Clark, and Golder 2006). We therefore computed survival curves and marginal effects of each variable when the other variable's condition is met: the majority is homogenous or ascendant.[9] In brief, the results indicate that the two factors matter about equally. Individually, they both have significant and similarly sized effects on a bill's risk of repeal. Although the rival party control variable has the larger effect size, the difference is not significant at conventional levels.[10]

A second interesting result emerges from the joint effect if we consider the alternative: when repeals do *not* succeed. Needless to say, we are focused on when and why landmark repeals occur, which are historically notable events, whereas the nonoccurrence of repeals is a routine outcome. On occasion, however, the factors that explain an event's occurrence are not mirror opposites of why they do not occur and thus yield insights on the causal dynamics at work. In figure 4.4 the bottom panel is the same as the top panel except that we estimate a bill's survival probability for a homogenous majority exclusively while varying the party's experience in the minority from the minimum, mean, and maximum. Note that the third condition—a homogenous and ascendant majority—is recorded in the top panel as well and thus serves as a comparative baseline.

Looking at the top line in the bottom panel of figure 4.4, we see a remarkably low likelihood of repeal when the majority is ideologically cohesive but entrenched. A subsequent analysis confirms that this reduced probability of repeal is significantly different from the average condition.[11] What this reveals is that a homogenous party is actually the *least* likely to repeal legislation if it is *also* an entrenched majority. Specifically, the top line in the bottom panel of figure 4.4 indicates that even twenty-five years after enactment, a given law has a 99.95% of surviving when the majority is homogenous but entrenched.

We believe this additional result dovetails with our theoretical claims on the following grounds. First, we argue that electoral competition incentivizes the parties to burnish their own reputation by magnifying their differences (Lee 2016; Koger and Lebo 2017). A repeal targeting an aspect of the other party's brand is a great way to achieve this, as we have argued. For these electoral reasons, as well as a desire to adopt policy change (Aldrich and Rohde 2001; Aldrich 1995; and Rohde 1991), repeals are especially likely when a majority ascends to power after a long time in the minority and is ideologically cohesive. However, when the majority has governed for an extended period of time, they can be expected to focus their agenda on enacting new laws and even seek compromises with the minority (Lee 2016). Furthermore, because they have governed for an extended period, an entrenched majority will be less likely to prioritize repeals owing to fact that the most recent laws are their own (Dodd 1986a, 1986b; Rohde, Stiglitz, and Weingast 2013). In short, a homogenous but entrenched majority can be expected to avoid repeals, choosing instead to defend their recent enactments from such efforts and pursue the creation of new laws.

We presented the 57th Congress earlier in table 4.1 as an example of a homogenous and entrenched majority. Although it passed one repeal of note, that repeal was a war financing law enacted during the Spanish-American War and was therefore expressly temporary. In a broader timeline, any Congress from the 55th to the 62nd (1897–1913) could be used as an example, as the raw data reported in chapter 2 shows a long lull in significant repealing activity coinciding with an entrenched and homogenous Republican majority. In fact, the repeal of the war law is the *only* one in this long period of Republican dominance.

In the model, two additional partisan factors are found to explain when and why repeals occur. First, there is a marginally significant effect ($p = .06$) of unified government in a subsequent Congress. Because the effect is negative, the model indicates that unified control of both chambers and the White House increases a landmark law's risk of being repealed by that Congress. We again plot a law's survival probability over a fifty-year period to visualize this effect. Looking at figure 4.5, we can see that, at twenty-five Congresses after passage, whether the government is unified or divided varies a law's likelihood of repeal by about a half percentage

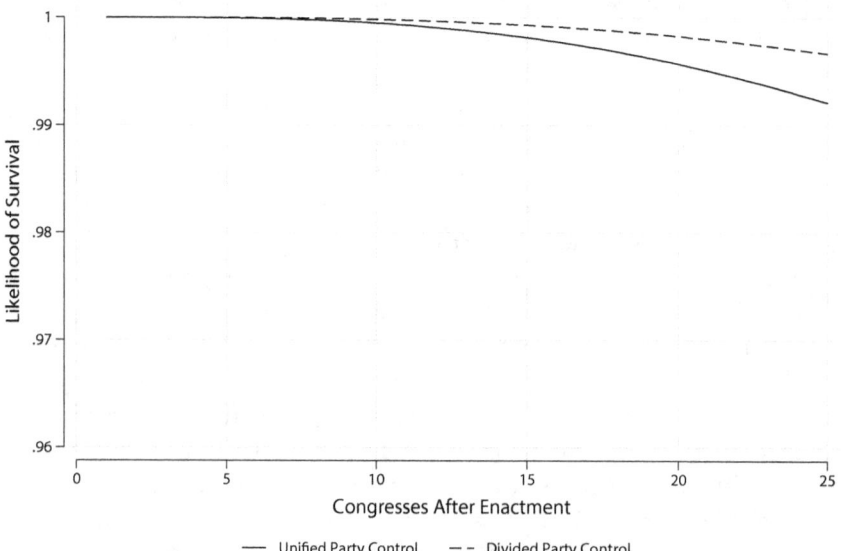

Fig. 4.5. Effect of Unified Government on Probability of Repeal

point (0.5%). Thus the difference unified to divided government, when controlling for all other factors, is about half the effect size of the difference between the most repeal-prone policy area (macroeconomic policy) and the most durable policy area (social welfare).

In a broader context, this result lends support to our claim that law creation and law repeal are not driven by parallel processes. Given that party control is a key factor in most models of law passage (see for example Binder 1999, 2003), the fact that unified government in our model of repeal is only marginally significant and small in magnitude is an indication that that repeal is not governed by the same basic forces as bill passage. As was evident in the GOP's seven-year attempt to repeal the Affordable Care Act, including their control of government during the 115th Congress, our results indicate that unified party control is no guarantee of repeal success. Like with the Democratic effort to repeal Taft-Hartley in the 89th Congress (1965–67), a party with sole control of the government can nonetheless fail to repeal a law it opposes if its caucus is ideologically divided. Again, repeals are hard to adopt, and it takes a homogenous majority to overcome the unique barriers to repeal.

Lastly, we find a significant effect on a control variable that, upon closer inspection, has roots in party politics. In the main model, model 1, the variable that records a bill's margin of passage is positive and significant, indicating that laws enacted with wide support are more likely to survive repeal efforts. As a theoretical matter there are two competing ways to explain this result, each of which has important implications for our understanding of legislative politics. On the one hand, it could be that laws that attract wide support are of higher quality, and high-quality laws, in turn, are less likely to be targets for repeal in the future. Such an effect would fit the problem-solving perspective in the last chapter. On the other hand, it could be that moderate bills attract wide support, and moderate laws are less likely to be targets for repeal. Partisan bills, by comparison, face a greater risk of repeal in the future. Such an effect would fit the partisan perspective in this chapter. Which is right?

In an effort to disentangle these competing processes, we conduct a secondary analysis that disaggregates a bill's final passage vote into two components: the majority's yeas/nays and the minority's yeas/nays.[12] While bills that pass unanimously are bipartisan by their very nature, there is enough variation on non-unanimous votes to discriminate between the two hypotheses. At the extremes, some bills pass with a *bare majority* and are *partisan* (garnering 100% majority support yet 0% minority support), while others pass with a *bare majority* and are *bipartisan* (garnering 50% majority support and 50% minority support). Conceivably, if bill quality is at the root of the passage margin effect, both variables, majority support and minority support, should be significant and positive, indicating that the raw number of lawmakers that approve of the law matters most. If, on the other hand, the passage margin effect is simply picking up how moderate the bill is, the minority party variable should be significant and positive, while the majority variable should be either insignificant or negative.

In this additional analysis, reported as model 9 in table D7 in appendix D, the results indicate that partisanship drives the passage margin effect. In the model, the minority passage margin variable is significant and positive, indicating that the greater the extent of minority support, the more likely a bill is to survive, while the majority party variable is marginally significant but negative,[13] indicating greater support from the majority *reduces* a law's likelihood of survival. Simply put, partisan laws are more likely to be repealed by future Congresses, irrespective of how many lawmakers voted for the bill in the aggregate. In the hypotheticals cited earlier, the results suggest that a bill supported by 100% of the majority but 0% of the minority is more likely to be repealed than a bill supported by 50% of the majority and 50% of the minority, even though both bills would be approved by roughly the same number of lawmakers. Complete details can be found in appendix D.

As a final matter, it should be noted that not all partisan variables are significant in our analysis. First, unified government at enactment does not seem to affect a law's future risk of repeal. In this respect the bivariate relationship we uncovered in chapter 2 is not supported once additional measures are included in the analysis. Past work reaches mixed conclusions about whether unified governments enact laws that have a greater or lower risk of future alteration. Although the evidence continues to be mixed, we believe it is clear that the ideological composition of the parties matters quite a bit more than simple measures of party control. Second, whether the enacting party gained or lost seats after enactment is unrelated to repeal. Although it is intuitive that parties that gain seats after enacting major laws will be better positioned to block repeal attempts, while those that lose seats run the risk of having their major laws repealed, we do not find evidence to support this conclusion. Of course, we do find that a party's electoral fortunes play a key role in when and why repeals occur, just in terms of their ascension to power in historical terms.

PARTISANSHIP AND THE REPEAL OF AFDC

In this chapter we focused on broad explanations for the roles parties play in explaining when and why repeals occur. To provide some additional context for these results, we focus on one of the most significant repeals in our data set—the 1996 welfare reform effort led by Newt Gingrich and congressional Republicans, when Aid to Families with Dependent Children was replaced with the Personal Responsibility and Work Opportunity Act.

Enacted in 1935 as part of the Social Security Act, AFDC provided financial assistance to children born to low-income parents and became a central element of the modern American welfare state. At the time of its enactment, AFDC was a federal program that provided modest financial assistance to families, but it allowed states to retain enormous discretion over the program's administration. Over the subsequent decades, AFDC grew in size and scope, particularly when it stopped providing support to white women exclusively and included black women in its entitlements in the 1960s.[14] Opposition to the program mounted at this time, with critics citing its growing cost and claiming that it incentivized women to have children and avoid seeking employment (Gilens 1996, 1999; Soss 2000).

Efforts to repeal or reform AFDC from 1960 to 1994 showed the unique durability of the welfare state. The failure of Nixon's "Family Assistance Plan" in 1970 offers one example of the challenges of welfare reform. Nixon's proposal would have eliminated AFDC and replaced it with a negative income tax. Like most negative income taxes—championed by libertarian economists like Milton Friedman—Nixon's plan covered individuals who were to be provided a basic cash transfer that was taxed back above a certain income threshold.[15] Proponents believed it would provide poor Americans a minimum income, incentivize recipients to seek employment, and reduce the size of the federal bureaucracy. Ultimately, the plan failed because it lacked a cohesive group of lawmakers in Congress who would help overcome various institutional and policymaking "traps" unique to welfare reform (Weaver 2000). Indeed, a bill with Nixon's proposal passed the House but died in the Senate when liberals and conservatives on the Senate Finance Committee opposed it from opposite ends of the ideological spectrum.

With welfare spending continuing its upward trend in the 1990s, a legitimate policy problem to many, Bill Clinton's 1992 campaign called for an "end to welfare as we know it." Yet despite unified party control in the 103rd Congress, Democrats never got a bill out of committee in either chamber. Observers generally cite two of factors in explaining the Democratic failure on welfare reform in that Congress. First, agenda space was scarce: Democrats passed several other notable bills in that time, including the Family Medical Leave Act, the "Motor Voter Act," the Brady Bill, NAFTA, and the Violent Crime Control and Law Enforcement Act (Weaver 2000). Second, the Democratic Party itself was ideologically divided on the issue of welfare, and party leaders were concerned about their ability to protect a welfare reform proposal on the floor from a coalition of Republicans and conservative Democrats (Weaver 2000). For these reasons—a lack of ideological consensus and lack of plenary time—Democratic leaders failed to win a reform bill's passage in the first two years of Clinton's term.

When Republicans won control of the House and Senate in the 1994 midterm for the first time since 1946, reform was thrust back onto the legislative agenda in a powerful way. After all, welfare reform was a core component of the GOP's "Contract with America." After Clinton twice vetoed GOP proposals, he acquiesced and signed a bill that repealed AFDC, replacing it with Temporary Assistance for Needy Families. Under the TANF program, states were provided with a block grant—allowing states discretion in the program's administration—and the law made assistance conditional on "work effort" while also imposing a sixty-month lifetime limit on benefits. In addition to changing the delivery of aid—from a federal entitlement to a block grant—the repeal of AFDC and replacement with TANF altered the fundamental nature of federal aid to children: from helping single mothers stay home with their children to getting parents back into the workforce.

We believe there are two elements about the Gingrich-led congressional Republicans who repealed the New Deal–era statute that are worth emphasizing: they were an ideologically motivated majority, and they had just won control after a long stint out of power. First, it is unquestionable that the landmark Republican victory in 1994—winning both chambers for the first time after forty years out of power—was the deciding factor in when and why repeal occurred. In his oft-cited book on welfare reform, Weaver (2000) calls the GOP victory the "most obvious answer" (365) to the question of why major reform succeeded in 1996 while earlier efforts failed. Second, and relatedly, once in power Gingrich's recruitment of ideologically driven Republican candidates—who were supportive of restrictive floor procedures that would help assure high levels of party discipline—was quite consequential in the success of various GOP legislative priorities (Theriault 2013; Haskins 2007). As we and others (Cox and McCubbins 2005; Rohde 1991) have argued, cohesive majorities are more likely to use institutional rules and procedures to their advantage.

Supporters of the AFDC repeal at the time cited public concerns about welfare and the program's growing cost as the impetus for their efforts. We believe there are reasons to be skeptical that problem-solving motivations are the only explanation of the repeal effort, though they certainly played some role. First, if public opinion is the most proximate cause, repeal could have occurred any time between 1960 and 1994. Indeed, the percentage of Americans who believe the government spends "too much" on welfare had been consistently above 50% since the late 1960s (MacLeod, Montero, and Speer 1999). At the same time, the role of public opinion is undermined by the fact that most Americans support "helping the poor" in the abstract (MacLeod, Montero, and Speer 1999). Second, claims about the "growing size and scope" of AFDC do not match the broader environment of the program. For example, while it is true that the number of AFDC recipients grew from the mid-1980s to 1989, that growth was slower than normal population growth.[16] Likewise, though federal outlays for AFDC increased in the aggregate, the average per-family AFDC payment declined markedly from 1970 to 1993 in constant 1993 dollars, from $663 to $377 per family.[17] In short, AFDC had certainly grown in size since the 1930s, which can be legitimately cited as a problem motivating the repeal effort, but the program was hardly *broken* or in *need* of repeal.

Rather than originating purely from concerns about the program's solvency or public opposition, welfare reform should be understood as a key element of conservative reformers' fifty-year effort to undo the core elements of the welfare state. Beginning in the 1960s, against the backdrop of the Cold War, conservative insurgents like Barry Goldwater derided welfare as a collectivist program that undermined Americans' spirit of individualism. By the 1980s, the rhetoric about the ills of welfare shifted to the "undeserving" recipients of aid, captured most famously by Reagan's "welfare queen" trope (Gilens 1996, 1999). Naturally, the program's costs and ill incentives were a constant concern cited by conservative opponents. Notably, this effort to scale back the size and scope of the welfare state unified various strands within the conservative movement—and thus the Republican Party—who coalesced in 1994 on economic, moral, and racial grounds (Layman and Carsey 2002).

Yet a puzzle remains: How can we describe the circumstances surrounding AFDC's repeal as "partisan" when a Democratic president signed the repeal law? As Weaver (2000) puts it, with the GOP's sudden victory in 1994 and the party's growing conservatism in the 104th Congress, Republican leaders were able to exercise strict agenda control and could "confront the president with a 'bad choice' between reform on their terms and the status quo" (367). Moreover, Republican leaders were able to use Clinton's campaign promise to "end welfare as we know it" against him in response to his veto threats. Coupled with the failure to get a reform bill out of committee in the 103rd Congress, these factors backed Clinton into a corner while weakening Democratic cohesion in opposition to welfare reform. As Weaver (2000) writes, "That they succeeded in doing so is a tribute to an extraordinarily effective Republican leadership, which centralized authority over political and policy deal-making, thus weakening the impact of fragmented political institutions and multiple veto points" (367). In other words, the ascendant, cohesive Republican majority was able to engineer a dramatic repeal despite the unique difficulty of undoing the welfare state.

CONCLUSIONS

Our central finding in this chapter is that repeals are, to a large degree, a function of the majority's ideological cohesion and its time in the minority in the previous Congresses. In plain English, homogenous majorities that ascend to power after a long period out of power are more likely to succeed in their repeal efforts than are heterogeneous and entrenched majorities. Not only is this effect significant in the analysis, but closer inspection reveals it has a substantively large effect on a law's probability of repeal. Because repeals are exceptionally difficult to enact, it takes a strong majority party—united in common purpose, buoyed by its electoral ascension, and with empowered party leaders—to overcome the various barriers to repeal. Although unified government explains when and why repeals occur repeal and the president is *an* important actor in any repeal effort, its effect size is rather small in comparative terms.

Given our results, we wish to emphasize three broader points. First, while others have found that ascendant majorities differ in their legislative behavior from entrenched majorities in uncompetitive electoral eras (Dodd 1986a, 1986b; Lee 2016; Rohde, Stiglitz, and Weingast 2013), the result that ascendant majorities are significantly more likely to repeal legislation is a new finding. We believe this result further underscores the importance of broadening our focus from a party's ideological characteristics to also include its recent electoral experience. Second, and relatedly, the interaction between a majority's cohesion and its time in the minority joins the work of institutionally focused partisan theorists (Aldrich 1995; Cox and McCubbins 1993, 2005; Masket 2016; Rohde 1991) with the more recent wave of party theorists who focus on electorally induced party actions (Bawn et al. 2012; Koger and Lebo 2017; Lee 2009, 2016). And third, our results underscore that "conventional" explanations of legislative creation are, in some cases, insufficient to explain efforts to undo legislation. In the case of repeals, it is perhaps surprising that single-party control is not the *leading* determinant. Yet this comports with the fact that the GOP failed to repeal the ACA despite the similar institutional conditions that saw Democrats enact the law. As Representative Steve Womack (R-AR) said after the GOP failed to repeal the ACA in July of 2017: "We've been given this opportunity to govern and we are finding every reason in the world not to."[18]

In conclusion, in our examination of the "three Ps" thus far, the evidence indicates that partisan factors play a key role in when and why repeals occur. While we have noted throughout that no one perspective has a monopoly on explaining repeals, as efforts to fix defective statutes matter as well, our results suggest that the problem-solving perspective offers far less explanatory power by comparison. Of course, we have yet to specifically examine the role of lawmakers' preferences, which we do in the next chapter.

CHAPTER FIVE

Preferences of Lawmakers

> I have little interest in streamlining government or making it more efficient, for I mean to reduce its size. I do not undertake to promote welfare, for I propose to extend freedom. My aim is not to pass laws, but to repeal them.
>
> Republican Barry Goldwater in *Conscience of a Conservative* (1960)

In the last two chapters we examined whether repeals are the product of lawmakers' problem-solving and partisan motivations. We found substantial support for the partisan nature of repeals and little support for the problem-solving perspective. In this chapter, we examine the last of the "three Ps" of repeal: whether they reflect the policy preferences of lawmakers. We consider three distinct ways in which preferences—broadly defined—might affect both repeal efforts and repeal successes.

First, we test whether Goldwater's quote above extends to his ideological counterparts: Are conservatives focused on repeals to a greater extent than liberals? A recent book by Grossmann and Hopkins (2016) argues that there are indeed asymmetries in each party's orientation to the legislative process. In particular, Grossmann and Hopkins argue that liberals are committed to helping various constituents overcome structural disadvantages and thus focus on creating new laws to ameliorate the problems these groups face. Conservatives, by comparison, are motivated by an ideological opposition to government involvement in the economy. Although there is considerable evidence documenting that liberals are indeed more active in creating new laws (Baumgartner and Jones 2015; Mayhew 1991; Volden and Wiseman 2014), the proposition that conservatives are more active in pursuing repeals as a means of limiting the government's size and scope has not been tested to this point.

Second, we examine whether shifts in the distribution of preferences within Congress explains when and why repeals occur. We focus on two aspects of shifting preferences: the ideology of key members, or what is commonly called "legislative pivots" (Krehbiel 1998), and ideological differences between the two chambers, or what Binder (2003) calls "bicameral distance." As we describe below, the focus on legislative pivots involves calculating a zone in the ideological spectrum where policy change is impossible for each Congress. By comparison, bicameral distance focuses on the fact that members of the House and Senate often have very different policy goals due to differences in the length of their terms, their method of election, chamber norms, etc. (Baker 2008). Nonetheless, both posit that legislative outcomes can be explained based on the distribution of policy preferences in Congress.

And third, we test the claim that legislative drift—the gradual replacement of the enacting coalition—explains repealing activity (Horn and Shepsle 1989). Over the life cycle of any piece of legislation, the enacting coalition is ephemeral: lawmakers inevitably retire or lose reelection. An intuitive possibility is that as the arrangement of the preferences in a legislature evolves, so too does lawmakers' willingness to retain or repeal an existing statute. Rather than treat preferences as an ideological construct, legislative drift tests lawmakers' unique attachment to the laws they helped create. While the theory of legislative drift is most often applied to the maintenance of federal programs (Carpenter and Lewis 2004; Lewis 2002; Berry et al. 2010), it makes sense that lawmakers may act in a similar manner by repealing old statutes and enacting their own.

As an example of how preferences might explain repeals, consider the 1999 repeal of Glass-Steagall, which had been passed in 1933. Following the Wall Street crash in October of 1929, the United States sank into an economic depression marked by high unemployment, deflation, and low consumer confidence. Ultimately, the economic frustration in this period gave way to political frustration, and Democrats won control of the House in 1930 and the Senate and White House in 1932. Among the various New Deal laws passed in response to the Depression was the Banking Act of 1933, which contained two central components: (1) the establishment of the Federal Deposit Insurance Corporation and (2) the creation of a series of banking regulations. Modern commentators refer to the act's banking regulations as "Glass-Steagall," a name given for its principal sponsors: Senator Carter Glass and Representative Henry Steagall. In brief, Glass-Steagall was an effort to regulate the financial services industry and prevent future depressions by blocking the cross-ownership of investment firms and commercial banks (Critchlow and VanderMeer 2012). FDR referred to it as it the "best banking law since the Federal Reserve System was created."[1]

In chapter 2 we estimated that Glass-Steagall is the second most significant repeal in our data set, for a few reasons. First, it undid one of the most significant laws in history, one that governed our financial system for sixty years (Clinton and Lapinski 2006). Another reason is the ideological controversy over whether the repeal exacerbated the economic turmoil in the Great Recession of 2007–9 (Hacker and Pierson 2011). Robert Kuttner, a prominent economic journalist, testified that "since repeal of Glass-Steagall in 1999 . . . super-banks have been able to re-enact the same kinds of structural conflicts of interest that were endemic in the 1920s."[2] Former Secretary of Labor Robert Reich agrees—arguing that denying the linkage between the repeal and the recession is "baloney."[3] By contrast, the CATO Institute's Oonagh McDonald said, "Glass-Steagall would have been irrelevant [in 2008], since an examination of the causes of the crisis shows that the fault lay entirely elsewhere,"[4] while economist Tyler Cowen calls the link between repeal and the 2008 Great Recession a "myth."[5] Whether the Glass-Steagall repeal caused the Great Recession is not a question we can resolve here. What is indisputable, however, is that the repeal itself was quite consequential and continues to be contentious decades later.

Unlike debates about the effects of the financial law, we believe it is clear that the *effort* to repeal Glass-Steagall was driven by ideological considerations. First, undoing the New Deal–era law was a cornerstone of the deregulatory movement that began in earnest during the 1970s. Furthermore, decades of lobbying by banks and investment firms persuaded lawmakers in *both* parties to support less government regulation of the financial services industry (Hacker and Pierson 2011). In our data there are two eras when repeal efforts spiked, which correspond with ideological periods of change but not objective policy problems in the banking industry. The first wave followed Ronald Reagan's victory in 1980 and Republican control of the Senate, when efforts to undo Glass-Steagall gained momentum with multiple repeal bills passing the upper chamber. A second wave of repeal efforts followed the Republican revolution in 1994, when Republicans won control of both chambers for the first time since 1952. Although the presence of a Democratic president would seem to make those efforts unlikely to succeed, Bill Clinton's record on financial services regulation was hardly liberal and, perhaps, slightly conservative (Hacker and Pierson 2011). In fact, prior to Clinton's signing the Glass-Steagall repeal bill, key actors in his administration—namely Treasury Secretary Richard Rubin and Federal Reserve Chairman Alan Greenspan—allowed banks and investment firms to essentially ignore the New Deal–era law, while Clinton signed a number of other laws loosening up financial services regulation (Sinkey 2001). Indeed, a newsletter from the libertarian Cato Institute wrote that "[Clinton] and his administration deserve credit" for the major banking regulation reforms.[6]

Overall, we believe preferences are quite clearly the key factor that explains the Glass-Steagall repeal effort. But *how* did preferences matter in this case? Was the success of the Glass-Steagall repeal effort in 1999, and not in the 1970s or '80s, due to the fact that the 106th Congress was one of the most conservative since the Eisenhower years? Alternatively, did repeal occur because of the replacement of the pivotal lawmakers who enacted—and subsequently, helped protect—the Great Depression-era law? Or perhaps repeal was a function of the factors outside Congress, such as the American public's greater conservatism in the 1990s?

In this chapter, we explore the power of preferences to explain when and why repeals occur, and in doing so we test each of the above possibilities. First, we discuss three ways lawmakers' preferences can explain when and why repeals occur: whether repeals are conservative actions, whether repeals occur during periods of ideological change, and whether repeals are caused by the replacement of a law's enacting coalition. Second, we test these preference-based arguments on data of repeal *attempts*. In an analysis parallel to that in chapter 4, we focus on the sponsorship of bills that were intended to repeal legislation, irrespective of whether the legislation passed, and the characteristics of the lawmakers who introduced them. And third, we proceed to test these preference-based arguments on our main database of enacted—or successful—repeals. Our analysis of adopted repeals is identical to the main analyses in chapters 3 and 4, where the overarching goal is to assess the role of parties, preferences, and problem solving on when and why repeals occur.

PREFERENCES

Theory

One important element unexplored thus far is that policy problems and their solutions can be subjective: what one lawmaker may see as a failed policy in need of change another lawmaker may see as a successful program. Consequently, we also need to take into consideration lawmakers' personal preferences to understand when and why repeals occur. As a normative matter, this view can be tracked back to Burke's (1996) model of policymaking premised on the notion that lawmakers ought to act with a degree of autonomy from the general public's desires and adopt policies *they* believe are best.

In his 1991 book *Divided We Govern*, David Mayhew challenged the conventional wisdom that parties serve as a bridge between separated institutions and thus help the government operate more efficiently under unified control. Rather, in his analysis of landmark legislation after World War II, Mayhew found that major legislation was equally likely to pass under unified government as it was under divided government. Consequently, Mayhew suggested that researchers would be better served by considering parties as factions of policy demanders with common policy preferences rather than unified teams.

Mayhew's theory of lawmaking was elaborated further by Keith Krehbiel (1993). In his article "Where's the Party?" Krehbiel put the issue this way: "Do individual legislators vote with fellow party members *in spite of their disagreement* about the policy in question, or do they vote with fellow party members *because of their agreement* about the policy in question?" (238; italics in original). Stated another way, because we cannot discern whether parties truly exert an independent influence over lawmakers, as the two go hand in hand, it's appropriate to focus at least as much on the preferences of lawmakers as on their party affiliation. Krehbiel extended that argument in his 1998 book *Pivotal Politics*, wherein he argued that the arrangement of ideological preferences in a legislative body was decisive in explaining legislative output. Krehbiel found that once the preferences of super-majoritarian actors like the cloture pivot—which could stop a filibuster—and the veto-override pivot were accounted for, preference-based explanations of lawmaking predict gridlock best.

Further empirical evidence in support of the role of preferences stems from the fact that lawmakers' voting patterns are very stable (McCarty, Poole, and Rosenthal 2001). Poole (2007) famously concluded that members "die in their ideological boots" (435), the implication being that lawmakers have relatively fixed preferences. Related work has reported evidence of consistent voting patterns even under conditions that would seem to change legislative behavior: when members move from the House to the Senate (Grofman, Griffin, and Berry 1995), in lame-duck sessions after an election (Jenkins and Nokken 2008), following the passage or failure of statewide ballot measures (Huder, Ragusa, and Smith 2011), and even when members retire (Lott and Bronars 1993). At best, the evidence suggests that changes in voting behavior occur gradually over time (Asher and Weisberg 1978).

Although the preferences of individual lawmakers may explain variation in the collective behavior of Democrats and Republicans, it is also possible that the effects of those preferences on legislative behavior are asymmetric. In a recent book, Grossmann and Hopkins (2016) theorize that the two parties are not mirror images of one another: quite the contrary. Rather, they contend that while Republicans are motivated by an ideological commitment to restraining the size and scope of the federal government, Democrats are best understood as a group of coalitions interested in helping various constituencies. As they put it: "While the Democratic Party is fundamentally a group coalition, the Republican Party can be most accurately characterized as the vehicle of an ideological movement" (3). Notably, Grossmann and Hopkins contend that this asymmetry explains why the two parties adopt fundamentally different legislative strategies.

For our purposes, the implications of the theories articulated by Mayhew, Krehbiel, Grossmann and Hopkins, and others are clear. If we want to create a full account of the dynamics of repeals, we must not simply focus on which party is in power or whether objective problems are in need of fixing. Rather, a complete account of repeals requires that we consider the arrangement of preferences in Congress and ideologically driven asymmetries in the parties' orientation to the legislative process.

Hypotheses

In the sections that follow, we discuss the various ways that preferences may influences when and why repeals occur. As in the previous two chapters, our emphasis is on *how* preferences influence repeals while trying to hold constant lawmakers' problem-solving or partisan motivations.

Do Repeals Occur during Periods of Ideological Change?

Instead of viewing lawmaking through a partisan or ideological lens, pivotal politics focuses on the preferences of key actors in Congress.[7] Designed to explain gridlock in Congress and reconcile why divided and unified party control differ only slightly in their legislative output, Krehbiel's (1998) model argues that the decision to proceed with a bill, or allow the status quo to remain, depends on the preferences of the filibuster pivot and the veto pivot (see also Brady and Volden 2005). In a spatial sense—where lawmakers are aligned from left to right—the filibuster pivot is the fortieth senator, whose support on a bill is necessary to invoke cloture and prevent a filibuster from occurring. Similarly, the veto pivot is the sixty-seventh senator, whose support for a bill is necessary to override a president's veto on a bill. According to the theory, any policies passed by Congress will be located somewhere within the gridlock interval. For example, when it was passed in the 73rd Congress, the Glass-Steagall Act was liberal enough to satisfy Franklin Roosevelt but was conservative enough that it was not filibustered in the Senate.

According to this theory, if an existing law is located between the filibuster and veto pivots, Congress will not change the law and gridlock will ensue. In such a scenario, a liberal filibuster pivot may block any conservative policy endorsed by a conservative president, while a conservative president would veto any effort to shift the law further to the left. Under a conservative president, the ideological space from the fortieth-most liberal senator (the filibuster pivot) and the sixty-seventh-most liberal senator (the veto pivot) is what Krehbiel calls the "gridlock interval." Overall, the prospect of policy change depends on where the status quo is relative to the gridlock interval, as policy change only occurs when the status quo policy is located somewhere *outside* the interval.

In figure 5.1, below, we estimate gridlock intervals for each Congress from the 65th to the 112th to illustrate how pivotal politics can be extended to form a hypothesis about repeals.[8] In figure 5.1 there are three aspects worth noting. First, some Congresses have much smaller gridlock intervals than others. In the figure, the 75th Congress (1937–39), when Roosevelt's New Deal coalition fully asserted itself in the Senate, had the smallest interval.[9] By contrast, many of the Congresses in the late 1990s and 2000s had large gridlock intervals, making legislative change difficult. Second, while some Congress-to-Congress shifts in the size of the interval were dramatic—such as the shift from the 110th to the 111th Congress—most often the shifts are quite modest. For example, the shift from the 108th to the 109th Congress is barely noticeable.

Finally, and most important, it is necessary to account for the gridlock interval exposed by a shift from one session to the next. In particular, the likelihood of a Congress's enactments being repealed should be positively associated with the amount of the *exposed space* in these shifts. Consider the shift from the 96th Congress (which met during the last two years of the Carter administration) to the 97th Congress (which met during the first two years of the Reagan administration). In this case the gridlock

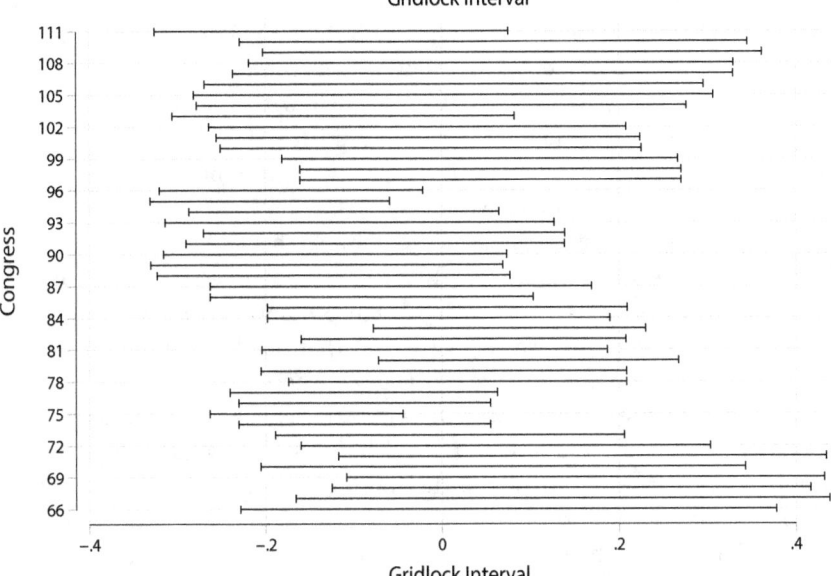

Fig. 5.1. Gridlock Intervals from the 66th to the 111th Congress

interval shifted dramatically to the right, meaning that more liberal bills were vulnerable to repeal. By contrast, there is very little space exposed from the 107th to the 108th Congress (from 2001 to 2003 and 2003 to 2005). Any policy enacted in the 107th was quite likely to endure in the 108th due to the pivotal blocking power of key lawmakers, meaning that repeals of the 107th Congress's policies were unlikely.

It is important to note that we tend to see these dramatic shifts in gridlock intervals—and thus large amounts of exposed space—during wave elections, when a new majority is swept into power. The first years of the Reagan administration marked a dramatic shift to the right in the country's policies, whereas the first years of the George H. W. Bush administration largely marked a continuation of what came before. And while we, and the congressional literature more broadly, treat preferences as distinct from partisanship, it is appropriate to acknowledge that big changes in partisanship tend to covary with changes in preferences.

A related approach is to focus on preferences in Congress with a keen eye to the fact that Congress is an institution with two distinct chambers. After all, there are important differences in the membership, procedures, and norms of the House and Senate (Baker 2008). As Binder (1999, 2003) notes, much of the policy gridlock in the post–World War II Congress can be explained by House-Senate differences rather than the usual suspects such as divided government or party polarization. For example, Binder finds that "quasi" divided government—when the House and Senate are controlled by rival parties—is not associated with greater policy stalemate. In this respect, Binder's work finds a critical effect of preferences in the functioning of bicameralism in the US Congress but no explicit role for partisanship and bicameralism.[10]

Existing research suggests that the distance between House and Senate not only affects Congress's ability to pass new legislation, as Binder an others find, but also influences Congress's ability to revise existing legislation. In our earlier work, we found that as the distance between House and Senate grows, it decreases the likelihood that Congress will be able to reverse existing policies (Ragusa 2010; Ragusa and Birkhead 2015). Similarly, Maltzman and Shipan (2008) show that the greater the level of disagreement between chambers, the more difficult it is for Congress to amend existing legislation. In this way, irrespective of partisan control of the legislative chambers, ideological differences between the chambers can have an independent and meaningful effect on Congress's ability to act—either in the creation of new legislation or the revision and repeal of existing legislation.

Are Repeals Conservative?

In the last chapter, we explored whether repeals are partisan efforts to undo a rival party's enactments and shift the status quo in a direction consistent with that party's brand. In that chapter, our main focus was on the majority's ideological cohesion and its position in a party cycle. By focusing on these aspects, we largely considered the parties as mirror opposites who battle on similar terms but from opposing positions on both policy and electoral grounds. What we left unexplored, however, is how the parties' ideological goals, and thus approaches to government, may differ in fundamental ways.

As noted in the theory section, Grossmann and Hopkins (2016) challenge the common perception that the parties operate in parallel, arguing that one key feature of the asymmetric nature of party conflict is variation in each party's governing style. Specifically, Grossmann and Hopkins argue that Democrats are more likely to focus on passing legislation to benefit various constituencies, while Republicans emphasize the philosophical goal of limiting the federal government's reach. For this reason, Democrats are more active in the legislative arena than their Republican counterparts.

Numerous studies support this contention: Grossmann and Hopkins (2016) find that Democrats introduce more bills, pass more bills, and meet in committee more often; Baumgartner and Jones (2015) show that Democrats hold more hearings, conduct more investigations, and pass more laws; Mayhew (1991) found that Democratic presidents propose more landmark laws; and Volden and Wiseman (2014) show that Democrats are more effective in passing substantive and significant legislation. Simply put, the consensus view is that liberals, in the Democratic Party, prioritize the passage of new laws to a greater extent than conservatives, in the Republican Party.

What remains unexplored is whether the asymmetric orientation is also manifest in repealing behavior. Grossmann and Hopkins do hypothesize that that repeals are a conservative action, noting that Republicans express greater support for repeals in their communication with colleagues (300–301). Critically, however, they do not examine actual repeal behavior—through either bill introductions or legislation. A logical extension, based on the numerous studies documenting that liberals are more active in law creation, it is likely that liberals will be *less* active when it comes to repeals. In this respect, although both parties are interested in changing the status quo, perhaps liberals want to layer additional polices onto the existing arrangements while conservatives want to remove those existing layers.[11]

An additional dynamic concerns asymmetries in party polarization, and not just asymmetries in the parties' legislative strategies. While the word "polarization" implies that the parties have moved to the extremes in tandem, the academic literature suggests the Republican Party has shifted rightward to a much greater degree than Democrats have shifted left (Hacker and Pierson 2005; Mann and Ornstein 2012; Theriault and Rhode 2011). Research has shown that this pattern is largely a function of the replacement of moderate members with more extreme members (Theriault 2006) and the disincentives for moderates to run in the modern era (Thomsen 2017). For these reasons, we explore whether the conservative commitment to the repeal of existing law has increased over time while the liberal commitment to law creation has pushed their volume of repeals in the opposite direction.

Are Repeals Caused by the Exodus of the Enacting Coalition?

A final way the preferences of lawmakers may matter for repeals is in the longevity of the enacting coalition. A distinct possibility is that the group of lawmakers that worked to create and pass a particular law may have a unique stake in its continuation. Having invested critical resources into the law's passage, the enacting lawmakers may be particularly averse to reversing their own policies. As the enacting coalition's membership turns over and, in particular, as oppositional coalitions replace the enacting coalition, policies may be more vulnerable to reversal (Horn and Shepsle 1989; Shepsle 1992).

In the relevant literature, this "coalitional" or "ideological" drift has a mixed relationship with policy reversal. On the one hand, drift is associated with the mutation or death of federal programs: programs are more vulnerable to alteration when the enacting party loses seats (Carpenter and Lewis 2004; Lewis 2002; Berry et al. 2010). Similarly, Thrower (2017) finds that executive orders—particularly those based on weak statutory authority—are more likely to be revoked when there is ideological drift between the enacting and current presidents. On the other hand, Corder (2004) finds that drift is not an explanation for program termination and that the hazard of an agency's termination *decreases*—rather than increases—over time. As a whole, although there are ample theoretical reasons to expect that coalitional drift will have a positive relationship with repeals, the empirical evidence is mixed.

ANALYSIS OF REPEAL INTRODUCTIONS

Data and Method

As in chapter 4, we conducted an initial analysis to see who sponsors repeals, irrespective of whether they succeed. Our data set of repeal efforts contains all bills introduced in the House and Senate from the 83rd to the 114th Congresses (1953–2017) with the dependent variable being a count of the number of repeal bills lawmaker *i* introduced in Congress *t*. Complete details on this analysis are in appendix C.

In this portion of the analysis, we use two measures of a lawmaker's personal preferences. Our primary variable of interest—*conservatism*—is a legislator's first-dimension DW-NOMINATE score, which ranges from -1 (liberal) to 1 (conservative). *Extreme* is a measure of a lawmaker's ideological extremism, which is the absolute value of *conservatism* subtracted from zero. Lower values indicate moderates, with 0 being a perfect moderate, while higher values indicate extremely liberal or conservative members.

We also include two other measures that address the effect of ideology, albeit in different ways. *Polarization* is a measure of partisan-ideological conflict and is the distance between the median Democrat and median

Republican averaged for both chambers, with higher values indicating a more ideologically polarized Congresses. Finally, we include a variable for the public's policy preferences. *Public mood* is a measure of the public's liberalism or conservatism, where higher values indicate a more liberal public and lower values a more conservative public (Stimson 1999).

Results

Our main hypothesis in this section is that conservative lawmakers will seek to repeal legislation at a higher rate than their liberal counterparts. We address this descriptively before presenting a multivariate analysis. Based on the total number of repeal bills introduced, we find that conservative lawmakers are indeed more active in their repeal efforts.[12] From 1953 to 2017, liberal lawmakers sponsored an average of 0.31 repeal bills per Congress, and conservative lawmakers sponsored an average of 0.44 repeal bills. While this may seem like a small difference, it represents 42% greater repealing activity on the part of conservatives, a disparity that accounts for nineteen additional repeal bills introduced per Congress on average.[13] Notably, the difference in repeal activity between liberals and *moderates* is nearly indistinguishable, indicating that conservatives are uniquely driving this disparity in the sponsorship of repeal bills.[14]

Figure 5.2 presents the rate of repeal bill introductions over time, as the parties have polarized, which depicts the impact of ideology in an important way. The *y* axis is the percentage of repeal bills (repeal bills sponsored / all bills sponsored) per party per Congress, with Democrats depicted in gray and Republicans depicted in black.

The trends shown in figure 5.2 support the hypotheses outlined earlier. From the 83rd to 92nd Congresses (1953–73), an era marked by ideologically heterogonous parties, the volume of repeal efforts by Democrats and Republicans is nearly identical. Not only is the rate the roughly same, but the volume of repealing activity goes up and down in tandem. By the end of the time series, however, a large gap emerges in each party's repeal efforts. Roughly speaking, the number of Republican repeal bills doubled from the 1950s to today, while the percentage of Democratic repeal bills declined by about 30%. Overall, the fact that Republicans increased their repeal efforts as they became more conservative while Democrats decreased their efforts as they became more liberal dovetails with the asymmetric nature of each party's legislative goals (Grossmann and Hopkins 2016) and the greater rate of polarization on the Republican side of the aisle (Hacker and Pierson 2005; Mann and Ornstein 2012; Theriault and Rhode 2011).

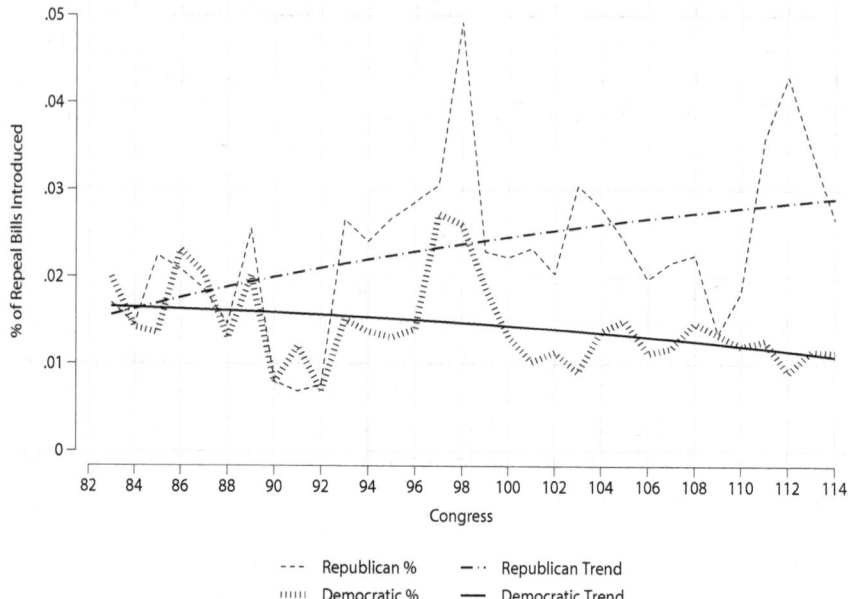

Fig. 5.2. All Repeal Efforts (1953–2016) by Party and Congress

Although these trends support the claim that repeal efforts have an ideological basis, additional evidence can be leveraged by looking at variation in repeal bills *within* the Democratic Party. For most of the post–World War II period, the Democratic Party had a racially conservative white southern bloc and a more liberal bloc, allowing us to effectively control for the effect of party affiliation and explore whether these two ideological factions behaved differently in their repeal efforts. We believe this is an especially stringent test of the proposition that ideology is at the root of repeal sponsorship.

Using the same data as above, figure 5.3 presents the average number of repeal bills introduced by white southern Democrats, all other Democrats, and Republicans from 1957 to 1994 in the area of civil rights.[15] We can see that 5.0% of all civil rights bills introduced by white southern Democrats were repeals, compared to just 1.7% for nonsouthern Democrats. A one-way analysis of variance indicates that this is a significant difference ($p < 0.01$). Based on the findings, the descriptive results once again point to a strong effect of conservative ideology in lawmakers' repeal efforts, even when we restrict the analysis to a single party.

In the comprehensive multivariate analysis of repeal sponsorship, we confirm the conclusion from these trends. Not only is the ideology variable statistically significant, but the model indicates that legislator ideology is one of the *strongest* predictors of repeal efforts overall.[16] For example, the model indicates that the effect of ideology is eleven times greater than the effect of unified party control, a key partisan effect discussed in the preceding chapter. According to the model, a strong conservative is expected to sponsor 67% more repeal bills in Congress than a strong liberal.[17] As noted earlier, the substantive effect of this difference is dozens of additional repeal bills introduced per Congress by conservative members, an effect that has increased in recent Congresses due to the Republican Party's outsized shift to the right.

We find that preferences matter in other ways as well. First, extreme lawmakers on both sides of the ideological spectrum sponsor a greater number of repeals than moderates. According to the analysis, lawmakers on the far left or far right sponsor 17% more repeal bills than ideologically moderate lawmakers.[18] It is important to contextualize this result by noting that the size of this effect is much smaller in magnitude than a lawmaker's raw ideology—thus indicating that conservatism is a stronger predictor of repeal introductions than ideological extremism. In addition, lawmakers introduce fewer repeal bills in ideologically polarized Congresses, a result that likely reflects the reduced likelihood of bill passage in polarized eras. Finally, we find that the public's preference affect the

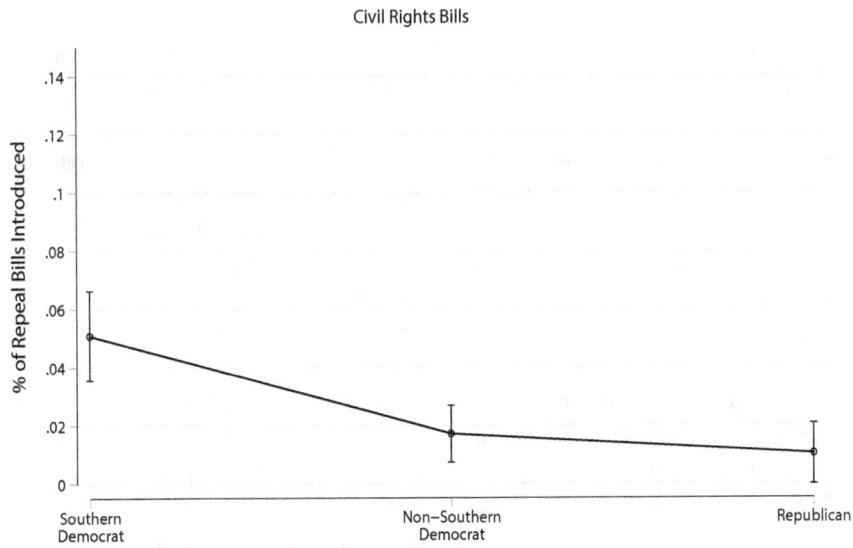

Fig. 5.3. Repeal Efforts (1957–1994) by Democratic Party Faction on Civil Rights

number of repeal bills a lawmaker sponsors, all else being equal. In liberal eras, fewer repeal bills are introduced, while in conservative eras, more repeal bills are introduced. We note that these last two effects are small in magnitude as well when compared to the effect of a lawmaker's personal ideology.

Across the board, there is overwhelming evidence that the decision to sponsor a repeal is shaped by a lawmaker's personal preferences. From their own ideology (*conservatism*) and ideological extremism (*ideological extremism*) to the distribution of preferences in Congress (*polarization*) and even the preferences of the public (*public mood*), the evidence for the preference-based explanations of repeal sponsorship is clear and consistent.

We also find an interaction effect between preferences and partisanship. Recall that in the last chapter there was scant evidence in favor partisan explanations of repeal sponsorship. For example, we hypothesized that members of the majority would sponsor more repeals, while members of the minority would sponsor fewer repeals, yet we did not find evidence of this effect. In a supplementary model, reported as model 2 in appendix C, we tested an interaction between majority status and ideology (*majority * conservatism*). Consistent with the notion of ideological asymmetries between the parties, perhaps liberals and conservatives behave differently depending on whether they are in the majority or minority. In this supplementary model the interaction term is significant, confirming this intuition.

We depict this interaction effect in figure 5.4. Lawmakers in the chamber's majority are represented by the solid dark line, and those in the minority by the gray dashed line. On the x axis we vary a member's ideology, where -1 indicates the most extreme liberal and 1 indicates the most extreme conservative. On the y axis is the number of repeal bills that member is predicted to sponsor (holding all other variables at their mean). In figure 5.4 we can see that there is little difference in the number of repeals that liberals sponsor whether they are in the majority or the minority. By comparison, conservatives introduce the greatest volume of repeals when they are in the *minority*.

An example of this effect was on display after the Affordable Care Act's passage in 2010: Republican members sponsored fewer ACA repeal bills and held fewer repeal votes once they were in the majority.[19] Although counterintuitive, this effect underscores differences in liberal and conservative legislative and electoral strategies. When they are in the minority, conservatives are more likely to unite in opposition to recently

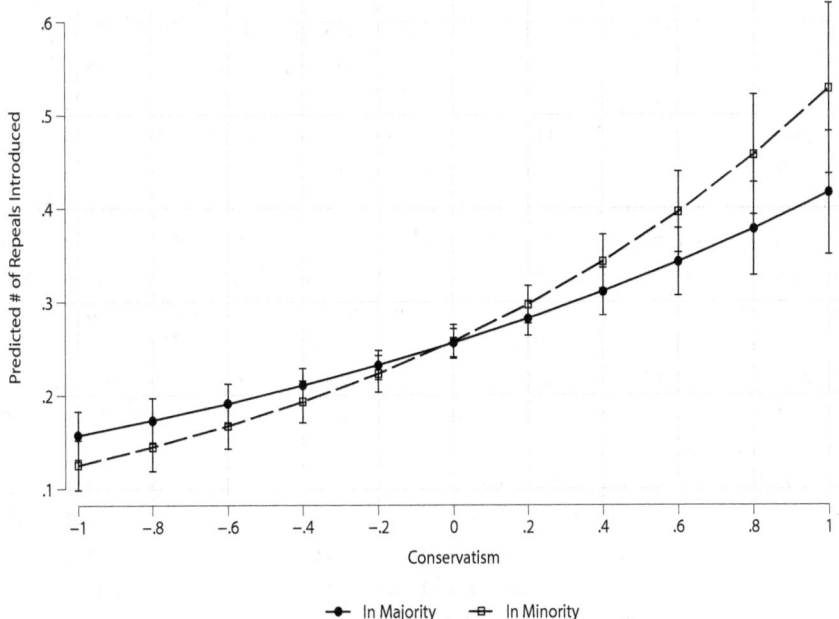

Fig. 5.4. Interaction of Ideology and Majority Status

enacted laws, enhancing the GOP's conservative image and helping the party win back control of Congress, particularly in a competitive electoral environment (Koger and Lebo 2017; Lee 2016). When they are in the majority, however, the compromises needed to enact repeal legislation is anathema to conservative ideology (Grossmann and Hopkins 2016). Overall, while the idea of limited government is appealing in general terms, rolling back specific policies may be widely panned by the public and politically damaging.

ANALYSIS OF SUCCESSFUL REPEALS

Data and Method

In the analysis of bill sponsorship above we showed that conservative lawmakers are more active in their repeal efforts. In the main analysis of successful repeals below we conceptualize the relationship between conservatives and repeals in three ways. First, we account for the *conservatism of Congress*, a variable that is the two-chamber ideological median of each subsequent Congress. Using Poole and Rosenthal's common space

DW-NOMINATE scores, we average the ideological medians of the House and Senate, where higher values indicate a more conservative Congress. We expect conservative Congresses to pass more repeals than liberal ones. Second, *conservative shift* is a variable for the Congress-to-Congress change in conservatism. For each bill, we measure the ideological shift in each subsequent congressional median relative to the enacting Congress. Higher values indicate the subsequent Congress is more conservative than the enacting one. We expect bills enacted by liberal Congresses will have a higher risk of repeal when the subsequent Congress is conservative. Lastly, the variable *sponsor ideology* is the DW-NOMINATE score of the member who introduced the bill, where higher values indicate conservative sponsors and lower values indicate liberal sponsors.[20] If conservatives target the work of liberals, the more liberal the sponsor, the greater the bill's risk of repeal.

In the hypothesis section we introduced the concept of coalition drift, a term used in the literature to refer to the enacting coalition's survivability and their inability to permanently shield their enactments from future revision. We account for coalitional drift by measuring whether members of the enacting Congress are still members of the subsequent Congresses. An ideal measure would be the survivability of the lawmakers who *voted* for the law, but this is impossible given the historic scope of our data set. Our variable *coalition degradation* is therefore the percentage of the enacting Congress that remains in each subsequent Congress. Consistent with the theory, we expect to find a positive effect in the model, indicating that coalition degradation is associated with the greater the risk of repeal in a subsequent Congress.

We measure shifting pivots by accounting for the exposed space of the enacting Congress's gridlock interval in each subsequent Congress after a bill is passed. Given that we can reliably predict that the enacted bill will be somewhere inside the gridlock interval (Krehbiel 1998; Richman 2011), we hypothesize that a bill's probability of repeal is positively associated with the amount of the enacting Congress's gridlock interval exposed by subsequent shifts. For illustrative purposes, consider the 88th Congress, which saw the passage of the Equal Pay Act, Civil Rights Act, the Gulf of Tonkin Resolution, and the Food Stamp Act, among other major pieces of legislation. On the left *y* axis of figure 5.5, we depict the gridlock interval for each Congress after the 88th. On the right *y* axis we compute the *exposed space*, the variable used in the analysis, which is the amount of the 88th Congress's interval that was uncovered by the shifts in

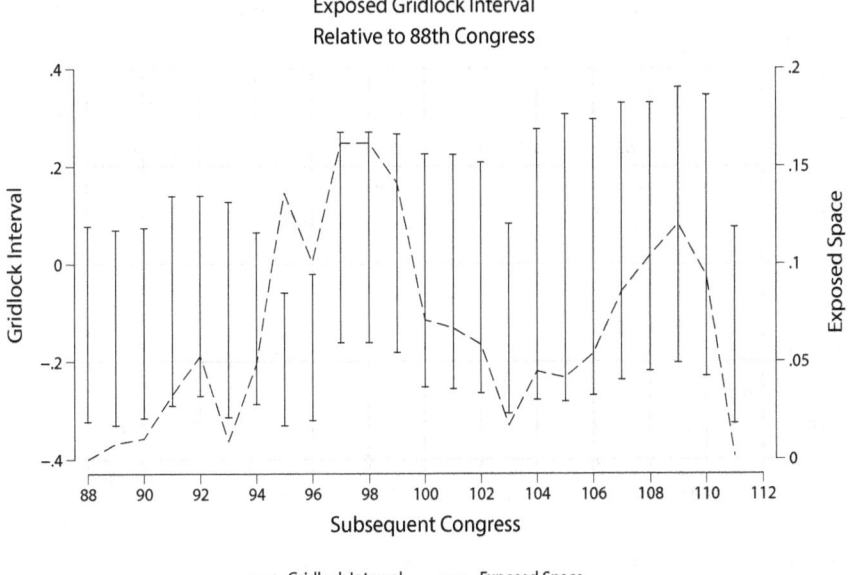

Fig. 5.5. Exposed Space Relative to the 88th Congress

each subsequent Congress's gridlock intervals.[21] According to the theory, repeals should be more likely when the exposed space is higher.

In figure 5.5, the gray dashed line on the right y axis shows that from the 88th to the 89th Congress, only the tiniest sliver of the 88th Congress's interval was exposed, and thus the 88th Congress's policies were not particularly vulnerable to repeal. By contrast, based on the gridlock interval, the 88th Congress's enactments were most vulnerable to repeal in the 97th–99th Congresses, when nearly half of the 88th Congress's gridlock interval was exposed by a large conservative shift in congressional preferences. Notably, this period coincided with Ronald Reagan's presidency, and the Republicans regaining control of the Senate for the first time in thirty years.

Lastly, to account for the ideological gap between the House and Senate, we use the absolute difference between the median legislator in the House and the median legislator in the Senate using Poole's (1998) common space scores (Chiou and Rothenberg 2008; Hughes and Carlson 2015).[22] Because research shows that the variable *bicameral distance* is one of the strongest predictors of gridlock (Binder 1999, 2003), when the House and Senate are separated ideologically, perhaps repeals will be less likely to occur as well. While the gridlock interval and bicameral distance are based on the same logic, the measures produce different predictions in a few key cases. For example, in figure 5.5 the gridlock interval predicts a high probability of repeal in the 97th–99th Congresses for laws enacted by the 88th Congress. By contrast, we might see a *lower* risk of repeal in these Congresses given that the House and Senate were divided by party, with a large ideological gap between the chambers.

Results

As in chapters 3 and 4, our main analysis is an examination of major repeals in a data set of the most significant laws in history—once again, the most notable 10% of laws enacted by Congress from 1877 to 2011. Laws span from the first Congress after a bill's passage to its eventual repeal (or are right censored at the 112th Congress). Our survival model contains the same variables reported in the prior two chapters, though here we focus on the preferences variables described above. Complete results are available in appendix D, with the main results reported in model 1.

One of the more surprising findings in this chapter is the null effect of ideology on the likelihood of a successful repeal. Across three variables that test this hypothesis, we find that the asymmetric effects that reliably explain repeal *efforts* are not predictive of repeal *successes*. First, conservative Congresses are no more likely to repeal legislation than liberal Congresses, all else being equal. Second, conservative shifts from the enacting Congress to the subsequent Congress are unrelated to repeals as well. And third, there is no evidence that the ideology of the bill sponsor is a factor in the likelihood of repeal—bills introduced by liberals are not more likely to be repealed.[23] In a broader sense, these results indicate that repeal efforts and the success of repeals are governed by different processes.

In a set of secondary models, reported as models 10 and 11 in table D8 of appendix D, we explored two alternative hypotheses. First, we tested a variation of the repeals-are-conservative hypothesis by examining whether conservative Congresses are more likely to repeal bills introduced by liberal sponsors. In other words, maybe conservative Congresses do not target *all* bills equally, just liberal ones. However, the interaction effect is insignificant in this additional model. Second, we tested a model restricted to the post–New Deal era. Because the asymmetric nature of the modern party system only dates back to the New Deal (Grossmann and Hopkins 2016), perhaps the long time span in our analysis may be obscuring the effect of conservatism in the contemporary party system. Yet here, too, we do not find evidence to support the role of conservative ideology in successful repeals.

Although these results are perhaps surprising, they are in keeping with our earlier finding that Republicans, as the conservative party in the modern period, introduce more repeal bills when they are in the minority. In this respect, we believe the results are entirely consistent with the notion of partisan asymmetries, particularly the inherent challenges facing a conservative party. Whereas conservative *minorities* are aided electorally by pushing ideological efforts to "roll back" federal laws (Koger and Lebo 2017; Lee 2016), conservative *majorities* must confront the reality that undoing government programs is unpopular and often requires the forging of compromises that are anathema to their governing philosophy (Grossmann and Hopkins 2016). Both analyses—repeal efforts and successful repeals—point toward this general conclusion.

We find null effects of the coalition drift variable as well. Simply put, the degradation of the enacting Congress is unrelated to the likelihood of its bills being repealed. In the main analysis, however, the variable *coalition degradation* is negative and significant, which seems to suggest that repeals are more common when a large number of the enacting Congress's membership remains in the legislature. Stepping back, it is worth remembering that repeals are most likely to occur in the first decade after enactment, an effect documented in chapter 2. A secondary analysis in appendix D—one that accounts for these temporal dynamics, presented as model 12 in table D9—reveals a null result on the coalition drift variable. Overall, we find that the retention of the enacting coalition does not exert an impact on repeals one way or the other, and with the notable exception of the Medicare Catastrophic Coverage Act notwithstanding, Congress does not routinely suffer buyer's remorse on the policies it just enacted.

In contrast to the null effects of conservatism and coalition drift, we find a significant and negative effect on the interaction between the exposed space variable and the cloture-era variable (which marks the passage of Rule 22 in 1917, permitting senators to defeat a filibuster with a super majority vote). What this interaction effect indicates is that as an enacting Congress's gridlock interval is uncovered by subsequent shifts in the pivotal actors, there is an increased risk that Congress's major enactments will be repealed. Notably, this result fits the expectations from the pivotal politics theory articulated by Brady and Volden (2005), Krehbiel (1998), and others: the status quo is quite resistant to change and thus is difficult to reverse, especially a decade or more after enactment. Even with an energetic group that desires to repeal a statute, the ability to do so is affected

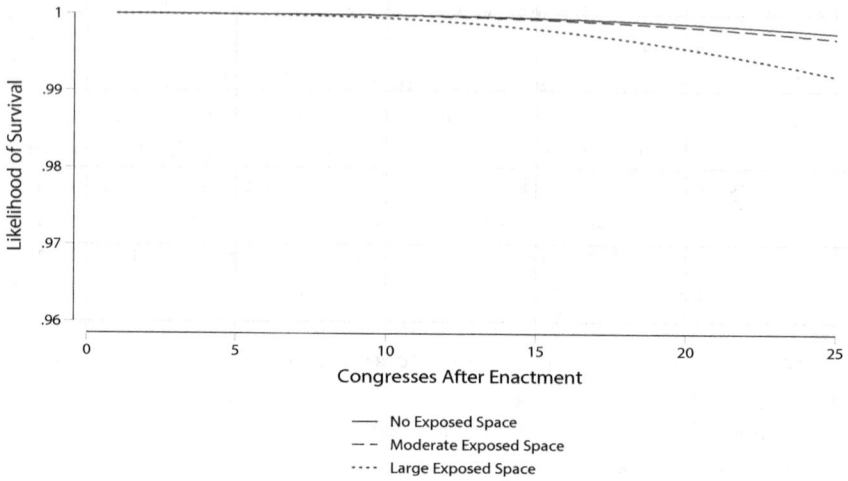

Fig. 5.6. Effect of Gridlock Shift on a Law's Survivability

by the requirement to make a bill palatable to the filibuster pivot on one end of the spectrum and the veto override pivot on the other end. Repeal is possible, however, provided the gridlock interval shifts in a decisive way.

In an effort to contextualize this result, figure 5.6 plots the likelihood of repeal for no shift (black line), a moderate shift (dark gray line) and a large shift (light gray line) in the gridlock interval over twenty-five Congresses (fifty years). Higher values on the y axis indicates a greater likelihood the law will survive over its postenactment life, while lower values indicate a greater probability of repeal. Figure 5.6 reveals two findings of note. First, the effect of gridlock interval shifts is generally small in magnitude. At fifteen Congresses after passage, or thirty years, there is only a miniscule decrease in the likelihood of survival for large gridlock shifts relative to small gridlock shifts. Although we see a sizable gap in the likelihood of survival at twenty-five Congresses after enactment, the difference is just one-half of one percent. Second, and perhaps most important, only a large gridlock shift exerts a substantively meaningful effect on the likelihood of repeal. Even at twenty-five Congress after enactment, there is little difference between the "no shift" and the "moderate shift" lines. Rather, the big gap is evident for a "large shift" in the gridlock interval. All in all, while the gridlock interval is indeed a significant predictor of repeal in the Rule 22 cloture era, a closer look at the data reveals that it does not have a substantively large effect.

Lastly, the model indicates that bicameral distance is not a significant predictor of repeals when controlling for the effect of the gridlock interval and other elements in the model. We believe this null result is partially a function of the interrelated nature of bicameral distance and gridlock interval, as the Senate median is always within the interval, and the House median is nearly always located somewhere within the gridlock interval. In other words, the result does not undermine the logic of the effect of bicameral distance on productivity in general, but the gridlock interval often subsumes the impact of bicameral distance on when and why repeals occur.

PREFERENCES, TAFT-HARTLEY, AND THE TAX REFORM ACT OF 1986

At the end of each chapter we discuss an example of a successful repeal to illustrate key findings from the statistical analysis. In this chapter, we present two cases. First, the failed effort by Democrats to repeal Taft-Hartley and, second, the successful Tax Reform Act of 1986. Given the mixed role of preferences uncovered in this chapter, we felt it appropriate to discuss one example that did not succeed in addition to one that did.

Enacted by a Republican-led Congress in 1947 over Truman's veto, Taft-Hartley is best known for prohibiting compulsory union membership, therefore allowing states to enact "right-to-work" laws. Specifically, Taft-Hartley's famous section 14(b) amended the National Labor Relations Act of 1935 and banned so-called closed shops. In practical terms, this statutory change meant that employees could not be required to pay union dues, thus reducing the size and bargaining capacity of the union, putting them at a disadvantage in states that enacted right-to-work laws.

In the subsequent decades, most repeals aimed at Taft-Hartley targeted this one section of the law. From the 81st to 95th Congresses (1949–79), roughly a dozen attempts to repeal Taft-Hartley were introduced by Democrats in each Congress. One repeal effort, which would have blocked state right-to-work laws, passed the House in 1965 but failed to overcome a filibuster waged by an ideological coalition of southern Democrats and Republicans. In this respect, Democrats were unable to repeal Taft-Hartley (despite large majorities in both chambers) due to the party's lack of ideological cohesion on labor relations (Greenstone 1969; Roof 2013). As Roof (2013) aptly put it: "All the arm-twisting in the world was unlikely to produce another 14 votes for cloture, which would have required the support of numerous Southerners and senators from right to work states" (106). From the 1980s to the present, Democrats shifted strategies: rather than continuing to introduce Taft-Hartley repeals bills, they attempted to pass new laws to expand the welfare state, increase the minimum wage, improve working conditions, increase federal aid to education, and so on (Roof 2013). In this way the case of Taft-Hartley underscores our claim in this chapter that liberals and conservatives approach legislating differently, with conservatives much more committed to undoing previously enacted legislation and liberals more apt to pass new laws to achieve their policy objectives (see also Grossmann and Hopkins 2016).

Another reason for the failure to repeal Taft-Hartley is the countervailing effects on shifting pivot points and the Democratic Party's ideological diversity. In our data set, the "exposed space" from the 80th Congress's gridlock interval suggests that this Congress's enactments should have been most vulnerable to repeal in the 95th Congress, when there was quite a bit of exposed space to the liberal side of the spectrum. However, when that window was open, the Democratic Party's lack of ideological cohesion on the issue, coupled with agreement on other policies, including the Civil Service Reform Act, the Clean Water Act, and the Community Reinvestment Act (all passed in the 95th Congress), led to Taft-Hartley remaining the law of the land.

On the other side of the coin, the Tax Reform Act of 1986 shows how ideological cohesion can—on occasion—transcend party lines to facilitate a repeal. To properly motivate the repeal, we offer a very brief primer on the history of tax reform. America's first income tax was enacted during the Civil War but was repealed after the war in 1872, and a second income tax was declared unconstitutional by the Supreme Court in 1895. In response, reformers advanced a constitutional amendment—eventually becoming the Sixteenth Amendment—that empowered the federal government to levy income taxes. Notably, the Sixteenth Amendment was not borne of partisan conflict but was, rather, an ideological effort by progressive reformers in both parties. Indeed, the constitutional amendment passed with large, bipartisan majorities in each chamber in the 1909 vote.[24] After the amendment was ratified, the 1913 law creating the first permanent income tax was enacted by a coalition of Democrats (who had recently won control of both chambers) and members of the new Progressive Party populated by ideologically moderate former Republicans (Howard 1999).

After losing these initial battles, conservatives pursued a strategy of tax reform—piecemeal efforts at first—with the goal of cutting taxes and curtailing the power of the federal government (Huret 2014). In the decades after World War II, calls for reducing the progressivity of the tax code moved from the super rich and business elites to a mass-based conservative movement among white, suburban, middle-class Americans (Huret

2014). Despite winning the passage of various tax *cuts* in these decades, it was not until the Tax Reform Act of 1986 that conservatives successfully enacted a sweeping reform of the tax *code*.

For our purposes, we are interested in a few major repeals contained in the Reagan-era tax reform law. First, the repeal of both a capital gains exclusion and the state and local sales tax deduction undid many of the structures in the Revenue Act of 1942.[25] FDR called the Revenue Act of 1942 "the greatest tax bill in American history."[26] Second, a major repeal in the 1986 tax reform targeted the investment tax credit, which had been enacted in the Revenue Act of 1962.[27] Although the investment tax credit was a probusiness tax break, the repeal of the Kennedy-era statute fit the goal of conservatives to simplify the tax code by repealing deductions and credits while simultaneously lowering the corporate rate. In the end, the 1986 tax reform package was passed with bipartisan support in both chambers in an era when a conservative reformer—President Ronald Reagan—confronted a Democratic-controlled House led by liberal Tip O'Neill. As a *New York Times* article at the time noted, the bill achieved the conservative values of flattening tax rates, while also reflecting the preferences of various groups of lawmakers.[28]

How did preferences influence these repeals? We see two answers. First, the 99th Congress, which passed the 1986 Tax Reform Bill, represented a substantial rightward shift in the gridlock interval relative to the 77th and 87th Congresses gridlock intervals, exposing their enactments to conservative policy shifts. Second, Reagan was successful at pushing for tax reform while the policy window was open, the public's policy mood was more conservative, and the multifaceted nature of tax policy meant that more liberal members could vote in favor of expanding the earned income tax credit, while more conservative members could vote in favor of reducing the top tax rate. Thus, through a confluence of factors, the Tax Reform Act of 1986 was a preference-driven repeal that matched the goals of tax reformers.

CONCLUSIONS

In this chapter, we explored whether repeals are the product of the preferences of lawmakers. We have two key findings, the first of which reveals something of a paradox. On the one hand, preferences best explain a lawmaker's behavior vis-à-vis repeal efforts. Our analysis of repeal sponsorship reveals that the single greatest determinant of a lawmaker's introduction of a repeal bill is his or her personal ideology, with conservative lawmakers introducing a greater volume of repeals, all else being equal. Additional results suggest that this effect is in large part electorally motivated, as conservatives sponsor more repeals when in the minority and fewer repeals when they are in the majority. Liberals, by comparison, sponsor a consistently low volume of repeals, no matter the electoral circumstances. Yet at the same time, our analysis reveals that ideology is wholly unrelated to repeal success. Consistent with the finding that conservatives sponsor more repeals when in the minority, and thus fewer in the majority, the results show that conservative Congresses are no more likely to succeed in repealing significant statutes than liberal Congresses.

We believe the paradoxical relationship between ideology, party, repeal efforts, and repeal outcomes dovetails with the notion of party asymmetries and electoral competition. While conservative lawmakers support repeals on philosophical grounds, these attempts are more likely to be driven by symbolic position-taking motivations rather than genuine attempts to shift the contours of national policy. As the effort to repeal the Affordable Care Act in 2017 demonstrates, conservatives faced contrasting incentives when they transitioned from the minority to the majority. Put simply, repeals are hard. In the case of the ACA, the shift from campaigning to governing forced conservative legislators not only to emphasize the unpopular elements of the legislation but also to acknowledge the various elements that were in fact popular. This transition yielded a failed effort to repeal the ACA with little success in passing a new health care law or amending the existing statutes. In contrast, our results suggest that liberal efforts to repeal legislation are largely the product of policy concerns, in particular a commitment to bettering the lives of its various constituencies. As the failed effort to undo Taft-Hartley in the 1950s and '60s illustrates, the repeal was not a goal in and of itself but an attempt to improve the condition of workers. Once the repeal effort died, liberals adjusted strategies, focusing instead on passing new laws to aid the working class.

Our second key finding in this chapter is that repeals are more common when the enacting Congress's gridlock interval is exposed by subsequent shifts in the ideological location of pivotal lawmakers. Although repeal outcomes are unrelated to the ideological location of Congress, this is not to say that preferences have no impact at all on policy reversals. In particular, the results show that since the establishment of cloture in 1917, the ability of lawmakers to repeal an existing statute is determined by the ideological location of the statute and the shifts in the filibuster and veto override pivots in each subsequent Congress. We find that this effect is small in magnitude, however, as it takes an especially large shift in the gridlock interval to exert a meaningful effect on the risk of repeal.

It is worth considering these results alongside the results from the preceding chapter on parties. In that chapter we found that while partisan factors are key determinants of repeal outcomes, the most consequential effect is conditional: with repeals most likely when the majority is ideologically homogenous and recently ascendant. In other words, repeals are especially likely when the majority's members have similar policy goals, come to power after a long stint in the minority, and are willing to target the statutes enacted by their rivals. We believe that chapter's conclusion, when paired with this chapter's findings—that repeals are more common when the enacting Congress' gridlock interval is exposed by preferences shift over time—point to an overarching conclusion: repeals are exceptionally difficult to enact due to the ability of pivotal lawmakers, particularly those in the minority party, to block any repeal effort. For this reason, it takes an ideologically homogenous majority, and one willing to allocate scarce agenda space to a repeal effort, to overcome these institutional impediments. Simply put, parties and preferences are intertwined when it comes to explaining when and why repeals occur.

CHAPTER SIX

Conclusions and Discussion

REPEALS ARE DIFFERENT . . . AND IT MATTERS

We have argued that repeals are different from other types of legislation, on both normative and empirical grounds. As a normative matter, we note that repeals challenge the tradition of treating enactments as "settled law." Although it is certainly in the public's interest to repeal defective or outdated statutes, too much repealing activity, especially when unrelated to objective policy problems, weakens the rule of law and undermines democracy itself. A number of prominent thinkers, including James Madison and Alexis de Tocqueville, warned of the dangers of too much repealing activity and the "capricious tendencies" of the American political system. As an empirical matter, we have argued that one of the defining characteristics of repeal bills is that they are harder to pass than any other types of legislation. In this respect, law creation and law repeal are not mirror opposites of one another, even though they face the same institutional and constitutional constraints, and scholars have erred in treating all types of enactments as though they have the same empirical dynamics.

On the former point, there are several reasons why repeals are different and can be more difficult to pass than alternative forms of legislation. First, repeals typically present lawmakers with a more constrained policy environment. Unlike other types of legislation, where lawmakers have greater flexibility to choose any policy location from a series of potential policy solutions, repeals can shrink the menu of possibilities to a familiar reversion point or the status quo. Second, repeals are uniquely difficult because they disrupt the path-dependent nature of legislation in ways that amendments or changes in funding levels do not. As we have argued, a new law creates constituencies and activates interest groups that benefit from the new policy area and have a stake in the law's continuation. Repealing legislation—particularly legislation dealing with social policy—often means overcoming considerable interest-group or citizen-based opposition. And third, from an institutional perspective, the major structural and procedural powers in the American political system are negative rather than positive, which gives the repeal's opponents many opportunities to block it from going forward. Consistent with research on the importance of "party brands," we argue that there are electoral incentives for the opposition to seek to undo its rival's signature accomplishments and, likewise, for the enacting party to resist future repeal efforts.

A number of findings throughout the book confirm our basic proposition that repeals are more difficult to pass than other forms of legislation. In chapter 1 we tested the likelihood of passage for various kinds of bills and showed that repeals indeed have the lowest probability of passage, all else being equal. And in chapter 2 we showed that Congress's productivity does not have a clear relationship with the volume of its repealing activity: some of the most productive Congresses repealed no landmark legislation, while some of the least productive Congresses repealed several major laws.

In an effort to explain when and why repeals occur, chapters 3–5 set out to test three leading theories of the legislative process and assess their suitability in the context of this study. To impose some intellectual order on the various dynamics of repeal, we referred to these as the "three Ps," as they emphasize the role of lawmakers' problem-solving efforts, partisan motivations, and preferences. Although legislative scholars have focused their attention on the factors that lead to the creation of new laws, we thought perhaps one or more of these theoretical perspectives explain repeals as well. And while *each* helps us understand when and why repeals occur, our theory suggests, and our results confirm, that the partisan lens offers the greatest explanatory power on balance.

In chapter 3 we examined the extent to which problem-solving efforts explain Congress's repealing behavior. As noted in that chapter, most of the rhetoric by politicians suggests that repeals are driven by their sincere problem-solving motivations. Moreover, there are salient examples that support this explanation: the Neutrality Acts, the Sherman Silver Purchase Act, the Medicare Catastrophic Coverage Act, and the Gulf of Tonkin Resolution. In analyzing the broad corpus of legislative repeals, however, we reach a different conclusion. While there is no objective indicator of a law's "problems," we find that a commonly used proxy—legislative issue attention—is unrelated to repeals. In other words, when issue attention spikes in response to some exogenous problem, repeals are not more likely to occur in that policy domain. Likewise, repeals are just as likely when there are *no* exogenous problems in an issue domain. As we note, these results are actually consistent with Adler and Wilkerson's (2012) work, for they show that problem-solving motivations are more common for routine legislation—expiring provisions and reauthorizations—and less common on major items. In our view this distinction only reinforces our claim that repeals do not have the same dynamics as other types of legislation.

We then explored the role parties play in successful repeal efforts in chapter 4. In that chapter, we found that multiple partisan factors explain when and why repeals occur. However, our key finding is that repeals depend largely on the ideological characteristics of the majority as well as that party's position in recent electoral cycles. Unified control of government—a leading predictor of law creation—has only a weak effect on the probability of repeal, according to our analysis. We reach a similar conclusion regarding the partisan environment at the time of a law's passage: although laws passed on a partisan basis are more likely to be repealed in the future, the effect is small in magnitude compared to other factors. Instead, the main finding in chapter 4 is that repeals are most common when an ideologically cohesive party is willing to allocate scarce agenda space to reversing the legislative achievements of the opposing party *and* the majority gained power after having supplanted a previously entrenched rival. As we have noted, the importance of these Congress-level factors helps explain why repeals occur in bursts in some periods. In a broader sense, these results blend the work of institutionally minded party theorists and more recent work on electorally motivated party efforts.

We then focused on the role of ideology in chapter 5, exploring the relationship between lawmakers' preferences and their repealing behavior. Our results reveal something paradoxical: while most ideological measures are unrelated to *successful* repeals, we find a clear and consistent relationship between ideology and repeal *efforts*. Specifically, conservative lawmakers are far more likely to sponsor repeals than their liberal counterparts, and this gap has grown since the 1970s, but repeal attempts by conservatives are not more likely to succeed. In this respect, while it is easy to propose a repeal, and indeed a repeal may be politically popular, successfully repealing a piece of legislation is quite difficult. Furthermore, we found that conservatives sponsor the most repeals when they are in the minority, suggesting that a nontrivial volume of their repeal attempts are messaging bills rather than sincere attempts at changing the nation's laws.

However, we do find that repeals tend to succeed when the preferences of lawmakers shift dramatically relative to the enacting Congress. Namely, we find that when an enacting Congress's gridlock interval is exposed by subsequent shifts in the ideological location of pivotal lawmakers, repeals are more likely to occur. Yet like the effect of unified government, shifts in the gridlock interval have a substantively small effect on a law's likelihood of repeal compared to the majority's ideological cohesion and the timing of partisan electoral cycles. Rather, ideology's effects are realized through parties: ideologically homogeneous and ascendant majorities are most likely to repeal legislation.

AN APPLICATION TO THE AFFORDABLE CARE ACT

It is worth applying the themes of this book to the Republican efforts to repeal the Affordable Care Act, as it is one of the most dramatic legislative events in decades and is certainly germane to our research. Moreover, the fight over the ACA took place almost exclusively outside our period of study and thus constitutes an "out of sample" test, which we can use to assess our central claims. Although an entire book can be written on this one case, we think an extended discussion is in order now that we have our full range of findings.

As a starting point, it is important to characterize the political and policy context of the bill's passage and the subsequent repeal attempts. First, the ACA was passed in 2010 when the Democratic Party had unified control of government and a first-term president who took office promising to enact sweeping health care form. The final bill had four main parts: an expansion of Medicaid coverage, a set of regulations on what insurers are obligated to cover (known as "essential health benefits"), subsidies to help low-income Americans afford health insurance, and a tax provision that penalized citizens for not carrying health insurance (the "individual mandate"). Republicans regained the House later that year in part because of the unpopularity of the ACA (Nyhan et al. 2012). Subsequently, the GOP took the Senate in 2014 midway through Obama's second term. With Democrats able to block any repeal bill from 2011 to 2016, it wasn't until Donald Trump's victory that many expected that the ACA to be repealed. Nonetheless, the only major ACA repeal that passed in the 115th Congress (2017–19) was a lone tax provision—the individual mandate—leaving the bulk of the law intact. Although the individual mandate is a notable repeal, and no doubt a key victory for the GOP, it surprised many that Republicans failed to repeal much of the ACA despite the same institutional conditions that saw Democrats enact the law. In order to explain these events, we begin by examining the repeal attempts through the lenses of our three theoretical perspectives: problem solving, parties, and preferences.

Starting with the problem-solving theory, we doubt the rhetoric of Republican lawmakers that their actions can be explained as sincere efforts to fix a defective law. First, we note that the GOP's repeal effort began quite literally *before* the law was even enacted, with three repeals introduced in the House and one in the Senate the day before the White House signing ceremony. Although it is difficult to say at what point lawmakers can "observe" a new law's flaws, it is certainly impossible before enactment. Second, while bad policy is subjective, one of the main justifications for repealing the ACA—that the law was in a "death spiral" and doomed to force its own repeal—has been repeatedly proven inaccurate. In a prior chapter we cited a PolitiFact article that rated Speaker Paul Ryan's death spiral claim as "false" as well as a Congressional Budget Office analysis that concluded the law was "stable in most areas." And third, numerous Republicans criticized their party's repeal effort on both procedural and policy grounds, with some *admitting* that the effort was partisan from the start. In a speech on the Senate floor in July, where he called for a return to "regular order," John McCain (R-AZ) criticized the bill in blunt terms: "It's a shell of a bill right now. We all know that." Likewise, Raul Labrador (R-ID) asked, rhetorically, whether his party was "against Obamacare because it was proposed by Democrats?"

A few caveats are in order at this point. First, our argument against Republican lawmakers' problem-solving rhetoric is not unique to the GOP or contemporary American politics: quite the contrary. In our data set of landmark repeals dating back to the 1800s, it is easy to find Democratic examples of non-problem-solving repeal efforts or similar cases in earlier time periods. Second, even though we believe the ACA is a poor fit for the problem-solving theory, there are obvious problem-solving repeals in our data set. In this respect our argument is simply that problem solving is not the *main* driver of repeals.

Another caveat is that there is nothing inherently wrong with ideologically motivated legislative behavior. While the ACA repeal effort may not reflect sincere problem-solving motivations, it may simply represent a conservative party opposing a law on principled grounds. We believe the evidence is mixed on this point, however. For starters, the full scope of the repeal effort—spanning 2011–17—was characterized by journalists, politicians, and pundits as a conservative revolt against the expansion of federal government's role in health care.[1] In aggregate, we believe this is a reasonable characterization and is consistent with our findings in chapter 5, where we showed that conservatives tend to introduce a greater number of repeal bills. Applying this to the ACA repeal effort, conservative Republicans—particularly those affiliated with the Tea Party and Freedom Caucus wings of the party—were indeed more likely to introduce an ACA repeal bill (Ragusa 2017).

Yet the main critique of a preference-based explanation of the ACA repeal effort lies in the challenges of disentangling lawmakers' sincere preferences from their strategic partisan behavior. Although we find a key role for both in this book, our results suggest that partisan motivations supersede policy preferences. Namely, although conservatives introduce more repeals, we also showed that the effect of ideology is mediated by electoral considerations, with conservatives sponsoring more repeals when they are the minority party. We see this as consistent with Grossmann and Hopkins's (2016) notion of ideological asymmetry: when out of power conservatives benefit by trying to "roll back" federal laws, while conservative majorities confront the fact that the compromises needed to actually govern is anathema to their underlying philosophy. Likewise, guided by Lee's (2016) recent work, we argued that repeal attempts are an excellent way to magnify party differences in a competitive electoral environment (see also Koger and Lebo 2017).

A handful of pieces of evidence support our skepticism about conservative ideology being the primary determinant of the GOP's ACA repeal attempts. First, it is important to note that the conservative Heritage Foundation advocated a similar health care plan, including the controversial health insurance mandate, as far back as 1989.[2] A number of commentators have argued that the ACA is in fact an ideologically moderate law—containing a mix of liberal and conservative ideas—and that the Republican opposition was based on more than just ideology.[3] Second, the fact is that Republicans sponsored fewer ACA repeal bills in the 115th Congress with unified party control than in prior Congresses when a repeal bill had little chance of passing, a pattern clearly consistent with the mediating effect described above. And third, of the three Republican senators who voted *against* the "skinny" repeal in 2017, when it had a high chance of passing, two voted *for* an even *bigger* repeal just two years earlier when it was clear Obama would veto it.[4] We doubt the ideology of these two members—John McCain and Lisa Murkowski—changed in two short years.

Although it is hard to see clear and consistent evidence of problem solving or preferences in the ACA repeal effort, we believe a partisan lens offers considerable explanatory power. First, there is no doubt that the overall effort was quite good for the Republican Party from an electoral standpoint. After all, research suggests the ACA vote alone cost Democrats control of the House in the 2010 midterm (Nyhan et al. 2012). Likewise, the partisan lens can help explain the most important question: why the ACA repeal effort failed despite an intense multiyear effort. Simply put, failure was driven by the disjuncture between the Republican Party's electoral goals and its governing goals. As we argued at the outset, repeals are uniquely difficult to enact, and to overcome the unique barriers to repeal, the majority benefits from ideological cohesion. In this respect one of the key conditions for repeal did not exist, as the GOP had deep divisions among its competing factions (Ragusa and Gaspar 2016).

We are certainly not the first to note that in the ACA repeal effort Republicans in Congress were split into three factions: an extreme conservative wing, represented by the Freedom Caucus; a bloc of mainstream Republicans, represented by many party leaders and committee chairs; and a group of moderates, represented by lawmakers like Senators Susan Collins and Lisa Murkowski. In an analysis of the failed ACA repeal, Sarah Binder (2017) wrote that while "ideological disagreement among Senate Republicans has been on the rise for over a decade" the gap is "particularly wide on health care." Indeed, the defining issue in the ACA repeal effort in the 115th Congress was how to placate conservatives, who favored something approximating "full repeal," on one end, and moderates, who supported less dramatic changes that kept some ACA provisions in place while replacing others. On the defeat of a scaled-down "skinny" repeal bill in July of 2017, Senate majority leader Mitch McConnell put it bluntly: "It's pretty obvious that we don't have 50 members who can agree on a replacement."[5] While it is easy to diagnose why the repeal effort failed with the advantage of hindsight, we noted the importance ideological cohesion in repeal efforts two years earlier (Ragusa and Birkhead 2015).

Magnifying the GOP's ideological divisions on health care is our finding in chapter 3 that social policies are among the most difficult to repeal. In particular, the ACA repeal was an example of what we referred to as "concentrated costs and diffuse benefits," the opposite of Olson's (1965) oft-cited claim. In simple terms, the GOP repeal effort energized a diverse group of actors that had a stake in the law's continuation—ranging from the health care industry to millions of Americans who faced the prospect of losing their health care coverage—while doing little to galvanize those who would receive modest tax savings from repeal.

In stark contrast to the party's divisions on health care, the GOP is more ideologically cohesive on taxes, which the analysis in chapter 3 indicates is the policy area where statutes are among the most vulnerable. When House leaders unveiled their tax reform plan, Mark Walker (R-NC), chair of the moderate Republican Study Committee, said of the various GOP factions, "Guys from different caucuses, from different groups, were all speaking in favor of it. . . . I was actually a little taken aback at how much unity there was in the room at the overall package."[6] As a whole, variation in the GOP's ideological cohesion *across* issue domains helps explain why the broader ACA repeal effort failed while the individual mandate repeal succeeded in the tax reform effort.

Switching the focus to the Democratic side of the aisle, another reason why the ACA repeal was so difficult is that it would have reversed a signature element of the Democratic Party's brand. For this reason, Republican leaders knew in advance that they could not count on votes from the minority. Unlike when the ACA was enacted, where thirty-four Democrats voted against the bill at passage, not a single Democrat voted for any of the GOP repeal proposals in the 115th Congress, including three members who opposed the ACA in 2010. Moreover, Democratic opposition in the Senate stymied attempts at passing the repeal legislation through conventional measures and forced the Republican leadership to attempt the repeal via budgetary reconciliation bill. The reconciliation process allowed Republican leaders to circumvent Democratic opposition in the Senate and pass the bill with a simple majority vote, but it came at the cost of preventing leadership from including nonbudgetary items (such as restrictions on abortion) in the repeal.

All in all, Republican attempts to repeal the ACA support our claim that repeals are (a) uniquely difficult and (b) mostly partisan. Yet even when the majority is willing to allocate agenda space to its repeal and allows party leadership to use a variety of unconventional tactics (Curry 2015), all under unified government, repeals are by no means a sure thing—particularly on matters of social policy. Given how difficult it is to repeal a landmark law, it takes an especially homogenous majority, particularly one that has seized power after a long period out of power, to overcome the extra legislative barriers. Ultimately, the durability of the ACA—as well as the repeal of the individual mandate—can be attributed to universal Democratic opposition and the ideological divisions within in the Republican Party, which had little agreement on health care but ample agreement on taxation.

IMPLICATIONS FOR OTHER SCHOLARSHIP

Repeals, Responsible Parties, and the Legislative Agenda

At various points in history, the American two-party system has suffered criticism for failing to offer voters clear alternatives on important policy issues and producing too much gridlock. In 1950, the American Political Science Association (APSA) issued a widely cited report calling for the creation of a "more responsible" two-party system. In particular, the report noted two deficiencies among the parties: first, they did not articulate clear policy alternatives to constituents, and second, when in power, the parties lacked the capacity to enact their agenda. The APSA's report also had requirements for the party out of power, calling for the opposition to be responsible for "the development of alternative policies and programs." Simply put, the "responsible parties" model has shaped how academics and nonacademics alike think about the virtues of political parties in the American system of government. Where do repeals fit in this normative "ideal?

A natural argument is that repeals play a key role in the responsible party thesis insofar as a party's preoccupation with repealing legislation helps present voters with clear policy alternatives. A repeal is, after all, a natural a vehicle for a party to oppose their rival on a policy matter and provide an unambiguous alternative. At the same time, however, our reading of the responsible parties thesis is that a party placing too much emphasis on repeals is a violation of the theory's tenets. While the primary focus of Schattschneider (1942) and his contemporaries is on the normative benefits of policy differentiation, an implicit tenet of the theory concerns the virtues of a *positive* policy agenda. As the report states, "The parties [in power] are able to bring forth programs to which they commit themselves," while the role of the party in opposition is similarly clear, to "develop, define, and present the policy alternatives which are necessary for a true choice" (quoted in Ranney 1962, 9). To be sure, a party that reflexively opposes the enactments of its counterparts is *an* alternative: we simply argue it may be a poor alternative from a responsible parties standpoint. Stated differently, if the responsible parties approach only required mere "options," it would not incorporate the additional requirement that the opposition "develop, define and present" clear alternatives. In this way, campaigning to repeal the other party's policies, without articulating alternatives, is, in our view, inconsistent with the central thrust of the

APSA's report and falls short of the electoral benefits of affording voters clear *positive* alternatives.

Switching the focus from the parties in the electorate to the parties in Congress, a similar argument can be made that, while repeals are a vital legislative tool, too much emphasis on undoing a rival's prior legislation can have negative implications for a party's capacity to enact its agenda. If we return to the lessons from Aldrich (1995), Döring (1995), Adler and Wilkerson (2012), Rohde, Stiglitz, and Weingast (2013), and others, a party comes into power with far more legislative proposals than members actually have time to work on. If we also include the number of reauthorizations that Congress must consistently enact, there is little time for party leaders to allocate for "chosen problems." This, in turn, makes party leadership's decisions to focus on a particular policy all the more consequential, and the decision to allocate resources to *undoing* their opponent's legislative achievements rather than promoting a positive policy platform erodes Congress's capacity to respond to emerging issues and solve policy problems. It is natural for parties to devote attention to salient policy issues—particularly those that are particularly salient among the party's base—and repeal is a viable alternative worthy of the party's attention. In our view, the problem is not whether a repeal is part of the governing majority's platform. Rather, the problem is when repeal functionally becomes the party's raison d'être.

A colloquial way of expressing this is that repeals are part of a "balanced diet" in a healthy two-party system: with too much emphasis on repeals, parties do not offer voters positive policy alternatives and damage their governing capacity, while with too little emphasis on repeal parties fail to differentiate themselves in a meaningful way and become complacent toward laws their coalition opposes. And like any diet, there are disagreements about the proper balance between law creation versus law repeal and what constitutes "too much" or "too little" emphasis on undoing existing law. In what follows, we draw on reports from journalists, pundits, and politicians to discuss various critiques of both parties' approach to repeals.

On one side of the aisle, the Republicans in Congress have been criticized for focusing too much on repealing the Affordable Care Act over the seven-year period from 2011 to 2017. First, by concentrating so intently on repealing the ACA, some argue that the GOP failed to develop and articulate a conservative alternative for health care and was forced to fight on Democrats' terrain. In this way, the party was unable or unwilling to present the various conservative health care policies to voters and establish genuine policy alternatives to the status quo. In a *New York Times* editorial,[7] David Brooks expressed this view best, arguing that there is a disconnect between the "conservative policy johnnies and the Republican politicians" and saying that "because Republicans have no governing vision, they can't really replace the Obama vision with some alternative. They just accept the basic structure of Obamacare and cut it back some." We note that this is very different from the mid-1990s, when Republican elites crafted a conservative alternative to "Clintoncare" and thus differentiated their position relative to the status quo at the time. Second, some have criticized the party for allocating too much of their legislative agenda to an ACA repeal, thus suppressing bills in other salient policy domains—including infrastructure, immigration, and trade. It is, of course, impossible to know the counterfactual: what laws the GOP would have enacted had it not held over fifty votes to repeal the ACA from 2011 to 2017. With Democrats controlling the Senate until 2015 and Obama in the White House until 2017, perhaps only minor Republican priorities could have been enacted into law. Yet it is undeniable that the doomed ACA repeal effort in 2017 cost the party at least one landmark law given the failed use of a reconciliation bill, a powerful tool that prevents filibusters, but which the Budget Act allows only once per year.

On the other side of the aisle, some have critiqued Democrats for not doing enough to differentiate themselves from the GOP on issues that benefit the working class. For example, Robert Reich[8] points out that in recent decades, Democratic presidents have paid more attention to Wall Street and upper-middle-class households and "[standing] by as corporations hammered trade unions." Reich, Thomas Frank,[9] and other prominent liberals have noted the Democratic Party's relative silence on repealing section 14(b) of Taft-Hartley, the 1947 law that permitted state "right-to-work" laws. One would think repealing Taft-Hartley would be a constant cause for Democrats: not only did its passage coincide with a dramatic decline in union membership, but recent research indicates that Democrats lost as much as 3.5% of the vote in states with right-to-work laws (Feigenbaum, Hertel-Fernandez, and Williamson 2018). Yet in the sixty years since, the Democratic Party has consistently prioritized other agenda items, with a Taft-Hartley repeal always an afterthought. Both the Great Society programs in 1965 and the Panama Canal Treaty in 1978 took center stage over Taft-Hartley repeal bills that subsequently died in the Senate. Observers have argued that the decision to not take a stronger stance on labor issues has contributed to the rise of inequality in right-to-work states (Bucci 2018) and led to Donald Trump's success with union households in 2016 (Noah 2017). In response to these trends, the top Democrats in Congress—House minority leader Nancy Pelosi and Senate minority leader Chuck Schumer—unveiled their "Better Deal" initiative in an attempt to reconnect with working-class voters. In a 2017 op-ed announcing the initiative, Schumer echoed the points above, saying, "Democrats have too often hesitated from taking on those misguided policies directly and unflinchingly—so much so that many Americans don't know what we stand for."[10] Yet as the party has done since the 1970s, it seems poised to focus on creating new laws to try to appeal to the working class—a $1 trillion infrastructure program, a $15 minimum wage, paid family leave, etc.—rather than work to undo existing laws.

Repeals, Political Conflict, and Public Approval

In their influential books, Hibbing and Theiss-Morse (1995, 2002) show that Americans generally dislike political conflict—even though it is central to democratic governance—and that conflict is important to understanding why Americans disapprove of Congress as an institution (see also Butler and Powell 2014; Doherty 2015; Flynn and Harbridge 2016). Although one's party affiliation mediates this relationship and Americans often misjudge the level of policy disagreement among political actors, the basic finding is that conflict results in less approval, especially when it renders Congress unable to respond to pressing national issues (see also Adler and Wilkerson 2012) or lawmakers exercising their own personal judgment (Hibbing and Theiss-Morse 1995).

In the context of this body of research, repeals may play an underappreciated role in shaping the public's attitude toward Congress, the two-party system, and democracy in general, given the conflictual partisan nature of efforts to undo landmark laws. Although the literature does not distinguish between repeals and other legislative efforts, the linkage is intuitive, given our findings in this book. In a review article about political conflict and public approval, Hibbing and Theiss-Morse (1998) write, "People believe the political process has been commandeered by narrow special interests and by political parties whose sole aim is to *contradict* the other political party" (1998; emphasis added). Needless to say, a repeal is the ultimate way to "contradict" your rival. While Congress may respond to pressing national issues by enacting new laws or amending others (Adler and Wilkerson 2012), actions that should increase the institution's approval rating, Theiss-Morse, Barton, and Wagner (2015) suggest that repeals—specifically the ACA repeal effort—may magnify perceptions of the extent of conflict in Congress and thus lower approval.

Extending the discussion of repeals, political conflict, and congressional approval, there may be secondary effects that perpetuate these dynamics and make conflict over existing statutes self-reinforcing and thus difficult to break in perpetual cycles of party conflict (Dodd 1986a, 1986b, 2015). We see three additional effects, given extant research. Although we do not claim that repeals are leading *causes* of these processes, we think they may play an underappreciated role in them.

First, Lee (2009) shows that as the parties become more ideologically cohesive, they also seek to arrange the legislative agenda in a way that emphasizes the policy differences between the parties. As we discussed above, repeals represent a clear avenue for the parties to differentiate themselves on policy matters in a highly salient way. In this respect, while Congress may operate effectively under the radar on low-salience bills (Adler and Wilkerson 2012), on battles over high-salience issues, a party's effort to undo its rival's signature accomplishments may attract widespread media attention and lock the parties into a decades-long back-and-forth over the status quo in an effort to gain an electoral upper hand. Protracted legislative disputes that span multiple congressional sessions are especially likely on the conservative end of the spectrum (Grossmann and Hopkins 2016).

Second, partisan fighting over repeals may play a role in the rising number of political independents. As Klar and Krupnikov (2016) write, to identify as a partisan is to affiliate oneself with "disagreement, fighting, and gridlock" (8). By contrast, independents are commonly seen as "constructive and positive." Because repeals are a central focal point on partisan fighting—the attempts of one party to undo the actions of the other—they may drive Americans away from the parties and further increase the number of Americans who do not affiliate with either party. Paradoxically, in party cycles when repeals are most common, continued conflict over previously enacted laws—itself an attempt to energize its voters in the short term—may drive more voters away from the parties over the long term.

And third, the emphasis on repeals, rather than on achieving programmatic policies, may also be fueling negative partisanship. The phenomenon of voters developing increasingly negative feelings for the opposition party is unique to the contemporary context and has risen consistently since the 1980s (Abramowitz and Webster 2016, 2018; Huddy, Mason, and Aarøe 2015; Mason 2015). Because the emotionally driven reactions to partisanship may provide fertile ground for politicians to exploit, some voters may reward the party for attempting to undo the opposition's accomplishments. If party elites send signals that the opposition party's enactments are "bad" for the country, and given the way voters readily respond to party cues (Broockman and Butler 2017; Carsey and Layman 2006), the consequence may be that repeals, and the partisan rhetoric around them, encourage this negative partisanship in a unique way that promoting a positive agenda does not.

Repeals, Reform Efforts, and Legislative Capacity

We have argued that an underappreciated aspect of legislative behavior stems from a desire to reverse existing legislation rather than simply enact new laws or solve emerging problems. Although repeals, and the aversion to treating previous enactments as "settled law," have long been a feature of American politics, it is possible that the contemporary focus on repealing legislation is linked—both as a cause and consequence—to a shift in Congress's legislative capacity.

Extending the discussion above, the decrease in congressional approval that can arise from contentious repeal efforts may subsequently fuel calls for legislative reforms that weaken the institution's governing structure. Examples might include calls for term limits to limit lawmakers' reelection prospects (Karp 1995) or reduced donations to congressional campaign committees in favor of outside groups (La Raja and Schaffner 2015). At the same time, if repeals are indeed partisan contests over the status quo, as we have argued, lawmakers may pursue reforms that enhance the party's capacity to enact short-term policy goals (Binder 1997) at the expense of the institution's overall performance. Examples might include efforts to centralize power in the hands of party leaders, including fewer "regular order" procedures (Bendix 2016), reduced staff (Clarke n.d.), less committee autonomy and specialization (Krehbiel 1992; Polsby 1968), and efforts to avoid conference committees (Ryan 2011, 2018). Similarly, leadership's capacity to deprive members of the rank-and-file information about pending legislation—that is, keeping members "in the dark"—maintains a strong partisan agenda at the expense of more collaborate decision making (Curry 2015). Notably, these examples dovetail with our finding that the key factor in successful repeal efforts is the ideological cohesion of the majority and leaders' ability to set the agenda in a decisive way and thus overcome the unique barriers to repeal. Paradoxically, these reforms further incentivize the radical warfare approaches and disincentivize politicians to pursue compromise (Thomsen 2017).

Uniquely important in our view are changes in the way that Congress collects and uses information. As we mentioned in the chapter 3, and as Baumgartner and Jones (2015) detail extensively, the search for information tends to lead to the discovery of additional problems that the government could solve. Beginning under Ronald Reagan in the 1980s, the government began reducing its analytic capacity and its corresponding information search. Newt Gingrich helped accelerate these reforms when Republicans took over Congress in 1995, cutting the capacity of both analytic agencies and legislative committees, with the intention of bringing the preferences of his rank and file into line (Baumgartner and Jones 2015; Theriault 2013). Moreover, Baumgartner and Jones (2015) note that even under administrations that were more supportive of analytic agencies, the focus is still on party programs rather than on objective analysis and information. On these points, it is hard to overlook that the Gingrich-led Congresses were among the most repeal-active since Reconstruction.

Simply put, we suggest that these trends are related: the contemporary preoccupation with repealing legislation may be linked as both cause and consequence to the diminished capacity for information and analysis, especially on the Republican side of the aisle. In other words, given a lack of capacity to identify new problems, the party leadership is satisfied to maintain focus on older problems, especially when doing so is electorally beneficial, and when the party leadership is riding an electoral wave into power, it will work to repeal the opposition's laws. If the government's approach to collecting information and formulating analyses were expanded and improved, coupled with greater institutional capacity as a whole, it is possible that party leaders may allocate more agenda space to these new policy proposals and less space to relitigating old grievances. Yet as we have noted previously, the incentives to do so are asymmetric, and we do not expect liberals and conservatives to view these issues as equally deserving of attention (Grossmann and Hopkins 2016). In this respect, the parties today may be "stuck" in broader cycles of partisan contestation (Dodd 2015), bound not only to relitigate the same policy grievances but to fight over institutional structures and legislative procedures as well.

EXTENSIONS

Constitutional Amendments and Nullification

Until this point, we have not addressed the most famous repeal in American history: the repeal of the Eighteenth Amendment by the Twenty-First

Amendment. Enacted in 1919, the Eighteenth Amendment, which prohibited the manufacture and importation of alcohol, received large bipartisan majorities in both chambers of Congress before ratification by thirty-six of the forty-eight states in the Union.[11] A number of problems emerged while prohibition was in effect that precipitated the Eighteenth Amendment's repeal: the illegal manufacture of liquor, the rise of organized crime, and the Great Depression (see Blocker 2006). Proponents of the Twenty-First Amendment rightly cited the problem-solving nature of their action, saying repeal would "end once and for all the spectacle that has made for lawlessness, for loss of revenue, for loss of employment, and for unwarrantable restrictions upon state rights as well as individual freedom."[12]

We do not discuss the Twenty-First Amendment's repeal of the Eighteenth Amendment as trivia or a relic of a bygone era. Rather, over the previous decade, prominent politicians and political activists have made a concerted effort to repeal a handful of constitutional amendments. Former Arkansas governor Mike Huckabee has specifically called for a repeal of the Seventeenth Amendment, which led to the direct election of US Senators, on the grounds that it would return power to the states. Similarly, former Texas governor Rick Perry criticized the Sixteenth Amendment, which eased Congress's ability to implement a personal income tax. Perry (2010) called the amendment the "great milestone on the road to serfdom" (41) and advocated its repeal. Finally, on the 2016 campaign trail, Donald Trump called for an end to "birthright citizenship," the practice of conferring citizenship to all persons born in the United States, which would require repealing a portion of the Fourteenth Amendment.

It is relatively easy to dismiss these calls as provocative, mere grandstanding, and outside the mainstream. On the contrary, Huckabee and Perry were prominent presidential candidates for the Republican nomination, while Donald Trump secured the nomination and won the presidency. Moreover, the growing number of Republican state "trifectas"—or states where one party holds a majority in the lower house, upper house, and governor's mansion—has approached the minimum number of states necessary to use an Article V "Convention of the States" to propose constitutional amendments. Although the precise figures vary, one estimate is that twenty-eight states have completed the requirements for such a convention at this time. Notably, this amendment convention has been supported by the Heritage Foundation,[13] former Oklahoma senator Tom Coburn (2017), and retired Supreme Court Justice John Paul Stevens (2014). Moreover, while this call for a convention to change the framework of the government may seem unfamiliar to federal observers, state legislatures routinely amend their constitutions, often making legislative—rather than administrative—changes to them. Thus, while these calls may seem radical, they are not unprecedented in the scheme of constitutional revisionism in the United States.

In a similar vein, states have recently begun to assert the doctrine of nullification, which is the legal theory that states have the ability to invalidate national actions that a state considers unconstitutional. Although there are a variety of specific forms of nullification bills (see Dinan 2011), they roughly approximate an intergovernmental repeal. As Olson, Callaghan, and Karch (2017) show, nullification bills span the ideological spectrum but are more likely to be introduced among Republican state legislatures. Importantly, Olson, Callaghan, and Karch (2017) show that these proposals are evidence of partisan conflict across levels of government (what is often called "partisan federalism") as Republican state legislatures were more likely to introduce these nullification bills when Democrats controlled Congress.

Applying our results to these topics, we see some obvious similarities. First, we suggest that there is likely a wide gulf between constitutional amendments and nullification efforts actually *succeeding* and the partisan value for *calling* for these outcomes. In a sense, calls for an Article V convention, like efforts to nullify federal laws, are similar to the sponsorship of repeal bills that are unlikely to pass. As we have argued, a repeal bill's value is in messaging when it has no chance of becoming law. In our results, we found that when a party wins control of Congress, and thus its bills are more likely to pass, the number of repeal bills introduced drops. We see parallels in the fact that the most fervent calls for repealing constitutional amendments and nullifying federal laws comes from the political right, yet such efforts do not often succeed. One implication is that even though twenty-eight states have called for a convention of the states, and despite the fifteen hundred nullification proposals from 2010 to 2016, the outcome of these efforts is uncertain. Despite these similarities, there are certainly differences between repeals and these efforts, and as the emerging literature on topics like contemporary state nullification develops, we look forward to understanding more about how they relate.

Repeals and the Electoral Connection

As Mayhew (1974) reminds us, the reelection imperative is a powerful force in legislative behavior, and as such, it is worth expanding on the role of the electorate in repeals (Aldrich 1995; Bawn et al. 2012; Koger and Lebo 2017;

Lee 2016; Rohde 1991). Briefly, there are two specific results in our book worth mentioning in this regard: In chapter 5, we found that when the public's mood is more conservative, lawmakers are more likely to sponsor repeals, which suggests that there are electoral benefits for such behavior. Similarly, in chapter 4, we found that members with Republican-leaning constituents tend to sponsor more repeals than their counterparts.

We believe two extensions naturally follow from these findings. First, these results imply that liberal and conservative constituents will evaluate policy proposals differently when framed as a "new enactment" or a "repeal." While liberal constituents may see little difference in the appeal of new legislation and repeals, we would expect conservatives to be more favorable to the repeal condition and less favorable to the creation of a new law, all else being equal. Second, this also suggests that there are asymmetric electoral incentives to the promotion of repeals bills. Nonetheless, the specific incentives are not clear: Do legislators representing conservative districts receive an electoral bonus for sponsoring repeals bills, relative to their liberal counterparts? Do they receive funds from outside groups that they otherwise would not? Are they able to quash a primary challenger more effectively? More work is needed to effectively disentangle the electoral implications of repeals for legislative behavior, as well as how ideology shapes *citizens'* preferences for creating and repealing laws.

Laws Targeted for Repeal

A question that we have left largely unaddressed is why some laws are bigger targets for repeal than others are. Irrespective of the characteristics of the Congresses that enacted them, or of the subsequent Congresses that decide their fate, an enormous volume of laws exist that *could* be repealed at any given time. Why is it that some laws draw the focus of members and motivate them enough to sponsor a repeal bill, while others do not?

In the book, we are unable to address this question explicitly for a few reasons. First, the size and scope of our main data set—containing every major law enacted since the end of Reconstruction—makes it difficult to take a granular look at law-level dynamics. Second, and relatedly, our primary focus is on Congress as an institution and legislative politics in general rather than the durability of the law. And third, while we do examine a closely related topic—repeal bills introduced by members—a proper analysis of repeal targets would require a data set of the repeals members sponsor as well as those laws they do *not* target for repeal.

Identifying the distinctive characteristics of bills that are targeted for repeal is a worthwhile area for future research, and we think our results provide a few tentative clues about the basic dynamics of this process. In particular, it seems certain that a lawmaker's decision to target a law for repeal is directly related to its policy content and consequently the characteristics of party conflict on that issue domain. As we noted in chapter 3, laws in some policy domains are quite durable, while others—particularly macroeconomic laws—are the least durable.[14] We believe the most likely explanation for this is the simple fact that macroeconomics—and questions about the government's role regulating the economy—is the leading point of ideological conflict in the American two-party system (Poole and Rosenthal 1997). Similarly, we do not believe this trend reflects problem-solving motivations. Again, table D4 in the appendix D shows that repeals in the macroeconomic domain are unrelated to objective problems like spikes in the debt-to-GDP ratio or the number of bank failures.

We see similar trends when other issues motivate partisan or ideological conflict in Congress. The issue of civil rights upset the dimensionality of conflict in two major eras: Reconstruction and the post–World War II periods. And at both times, civil rights–oriented repeal activity increased. Other important examples exist as well—including conflict over monetary policy in the late 1800s and 1930s and labor rights in the post–World War II period—with the common theme of policy contestation in the two-party system. Returning to an idea introduced earlier in this chapter, repeals may play an underappreciated but powerful role in *how* the parties differentiate themselves on important issues. Yet as we noted, our book has only scratched the surface of this topic and a more rigorous examination is needed.

Toward a Unified Theory of Statutory Revision

Finally, extensions of our research may explore statutory revision more broadly than we have in this book. As we noted at the outset, only a handful of authors have examined when and why lawmakers revisit prior enactments. Among this group, however, researchers are parochial in their focus, examining various kinds of revision in isolation: the survivability of federal programs and reauthorization efforts (Adler and Wilkerson 2012; Berry, Burden, and Howell 2010; Carpenter and Lewis 2004; Corder 2004), the maintenance of general interest reforms (Leighton and López 2012; Patashnik 2008), and the passage of amendments (Adler and Wilkerson 2012; Maltzman and Shipan 2008). We note that this point applies equally to our research on repeals (Ragusa 2010; Ragusa and Birkhead

2015; Ragusa 2017). With this "initial wave" of statutory revision studies in place, the broader literature would benefit from a comprehensive theory on how these various actions relate to one another and why lawmakers opt for one path of policy revision or another.

We take a very modest step in that direction here. We developed a theory regarding why repeals differ from other enactments—including the creation of new laws and amendments—arguing that one of the defining features of repeals is that they are uniquely difficult to pass. We made this argument on three grounds: the constrained negotiating environment, increased path dependency, and conflict over party brands. In this respect, while a repeal is "just another law" and is governed by the same constitutional requirements, institutional structures, and legislative procedures as other forms of legislation, our general knowledge of the legislative process is insufficient to understand when and why repeals occur.

At the same time, our theoretical contribution is woefully incomplete in the broader landscape of legislative efforts to revise prior enactments. For example, the unique challenges of enacting a repeal is certainly not the only way they differ from other enactments, nor is repeal the only option for a policy's opponents. Even though repeals are "different," as we have repeatedly claimed, repeals have much in common with amendments, which can effectively undo laws in a similar way. Alternatively, amendments or changes in funding levels can weaken as well as *strengthen* laws, with the latter being uncharacteristic of repeals. Lastly, even so-called new laws shape the functioning of existing laws in incredibly complex ways, a fact that the literature has largely sidestepped (but see Clinton 2012 for an exception). Developing a comprehensive theory of statutory revision—one that links these disparate forms of revision and takes seriously their similarities and differences—would be a boon for the literature. After all, treating all bills as if they are the result of the same fundamental dynamics limits both the empirical estimates and the theoretical implications of the scholarship.

As a compliment to efforts to create a unified theory of statutory revision, a common data set that catalogs these forms of revision would be an enormous benefit to researchers. In the studies cited above, various data sets and methodologies have been used: case studies (Patashnik 2008), legal and governmental reference volumes (Berry, Burden, and Howell, 2010; Carpenter and Lewis 2004; Maltzman and Shipan 2008; Ragusa 2010), bills and policy subtopics (Adler and Wilkerson 2012), and the judgment of journalists and policy experts (Ragusa and Birkhead 2015). Once again, we undertook a modest effort in this direction by cataloging bills based on keywords in their title—"repeal," "amendment," "reauthorize," and so on—yet this is certainly an imprecise measurement strategy. No doubt the advances in natural language processing offer promise in this area. After all, the question of how laws relate to one another is a legal one concerning complex statutory language. Whatever the precise measurement strategy, a data set that isolates multiple forms of statutory revision across bills, thus cataloging them in a common way, would be a considerable contribution to various fields and disciplines.

FINAL THOUGHTS

Our book is the first to examine repeals enacted by Congress. While the dynamics of law creation have garnered an overwhelming amount of attention, we show that law creation and law repeal are not mirror opposites. Aided by an explicit theory of how repeals are different from other types of enactments and a database of major repeals dating back to 1877, we answer fundamental questions about when and why repeals occur. Our overarching claim is that repeals are best understood as long-term contests between the parties over the status quo and in pursuit of electoral supremacy. In particular, we argue that because they are exceptionally difficult to enact, repeals are most likely to succeed when a party wins election after a long period out of power, and an ideologically cohesive rank and file empower their party leaders to expedite efforts to undo prior enactments.

By moving beyond a focus on enactments to examining statutory revision, scholarship in this mold can broaden our understanding of the contours of legislative organization, behavior, and outcomes. In the literature, our claims fit with scholars who emphasize the centrality of partisanship in understanding how legislatures operate. Perhaps most importantly, where most of the work in this camp explores electoral and institutional partisan forces *separately*, we join with an emerging group (Rohde, Stiglitz, and Weingast 2013; Lee 2016; Koger and Lebo 2017) who marry the relationship between the party's electoral arena and its legislative arena.

Despite our main conclusions, we acknowledge the multifaceted relationship between parties and statutory revision. Adler and Wilkerson (2012) show that the dynamics of reauthorizations and amendments have a distinctly nonpartisan undercurrent that had been underappreciated in most studies. Similarly, Patashnik (2008) shows that the sustainability of government reforms is not driven by party politics, as most studies of bill passage show, but are instead explained by a complex set of characteristics, from reconfiguration of coalitional patterns to the response to market forces. Given these conclusions, we once again reiterate that greater work is needed in this emerging area and, as we argued above, future work should explore how the various forms of statutory revision have different theoretical dynamics than other forms of legislation.

We think continued work on statutory revision is needed not only for theoretical reasons but also because the topic is likely to remain salient for decades. First, the continued rightward and/or partisan change in the GOP should only increase future repeal efforts. As just one example, Republican lawmakers are likely to focus on repealing core elements of the Dodd-Frank financial reform legislation: one of the *other* landmark laws enacted during Obama's first two years in office. Likewise, with the passage of the GOP's historic tax reform bill in 2017—which is projected to add $1.4 trillion to the deficit in the next ten years—there will be growing calls to reign in federal spending on entitlement programs. While the most prominent of these revisions will be efforts to defund entitlement programs, repeals will no doubt target key elements of other programs as well. Second, on the Democratic side, with calls for the party to refocus on the working class in the aftermath of Trump's election, efforts to repeal Taft-Hartley may increase in the future. And third, the topic of statutory revision is likely to remain salient for decades given the continued growth of federal programs and layering of new laws on top of one another. As Baumgartner and Jones (2015) show, since World War II the federal government has "broadened," or become involved in a host of policy areas that it had not previously pursued (see also Jones, Theriault, and Whyman 2019). From a numerical standpoint, this broadening increases the volume of statutes that partisans can target for repeal while also increasing the number of laws that may become broken and need reauthorization, amendments, repeals, etc.

Although we do not have a crystal ball, we are confident that no matter what the future brings, it is a certainty that repeals will remain an important topic for academics and nonacademics alike. For as long as Congress creates laws, future Congresses will work to repeal them. In other words, *media vita in morte sumus*: in the midst of life we are in death.

ACKNOWLEDGMENTS

Like any book, ours is the product of many factors: thoughtful feedback, ample encouragement, long hours, a little ingenuity, and plenty of good fortune. Our project began with a research design written in 2005 during Jordan's first-year graduate institutions seminar when few journalists, politicians, and academics were interested in repeals. By the time of that paper's publication in 2010, repeals were thrust to the forefront of American politics when Democrats repealed Don't Ask, Don't Tell and Republicans began their efforts to repeal the newly enacted Affordable Care Act. Another bit of good fortune was our chance meeting at the 2007 Inter-University Consortium for Political and Social Research summer program at the University of Michigan. Staying in touch over the years, we forged a friendship, often exchanging research ideas via email and in person at conferences. A product of those conversations was a decision to write a second paper on repeals, which we published together in 2015 at the height of the GOP's ACA repeal efforts. And, in yet another stroke of good luck, Nate convinced Jordan to write a book after the second paper was published. Feeling as though we had more to say, we decided to give it a go.

In addition to our good fortune, we have received considerable support and feedback from various individuals, incurring many debts along the way.

Our departments at the College of Charleston and Kansas State University have been incredibly supportive places to do work. Jordan thanks Gibbs Knotts for being a friend, mentor, and supportive department chair. He also thanks his colleagues who commented on various aspects of this project: Karyn Amira, Chris Day, Phil Jos, Briana McGinnis, Matt Nowlin, and Claire Wofford. Nate has benefited tremendously from his colleagues but would particularly like to thank Jeff Pickering and Sam Bell, who as department heads have offered ample support and advice.

Both David Rohde and Larry Dodd deserve special recognition. David Rohde provided extensive feedback along the way, including in the earliest stages of this project, most notably prior to the publication of our 2015 article. He has been a source of patience and encouragement throughout. Larry Dodd provided a critical piece of advice that we build a data set of repeals dating back to 1877 in an effort to obtain variation in key historical factors. Without his input, and continued feedback, our project would not have gotten off the ground.

We also have benefited from a generous group of scholars who were kind enough to read sections of this book and provide feedback. We are particularly grateful to Scott Adler, Jim Curry, Jeff Harden, Tom Holbrook, Justin Kirkland, Gibbs Knotts, Greg Koger, Jon Rogowski, Josh Ryan, and Jason Windett.

We are fortunate to have presented various iterations of this work at a number of institutions, including the University of Colorado, the College of New Jersey, Loyola University Chicago, as well as our home institutions. We received helpful and critical advice from Scott Adler, Dan Bowen, Amanda Bryan, David Doherty, Tao Dumas, John Griffin, Richard Maitland, Peter Schraeder, and Anand Sokhey. These visits, as well as conference presentations at the American Political Science Association, Midwest Political Science Association, the Public Choice Society, and Southern Political Science Association have all been enormously helpful in developing this project. Thanks in particular go to discussants David Bridge, Neil Chaturvedi, Josh Clinton, Mike Crespin, Chris Donnelly, David Karol, Vernan Lewis, Michael Lynch, and Ryan Williamson.

We were lucky to present the entire manuscript at two workshops, and the detailed and extensive feedback was incredibly helpful. First, at the Social Science Research Council's "Negotiating Agreement in Congress" workshop in Brooklyn, New York. Thanks to the three facilitators for organizing the workshop: Jan Mansbridge, Frances Lee, and Gavin Kilduff. Thanks also to the other workshop participants: Daniel Butler, Michael Crespin, Laurel Harbridge Yong, Russell Mills, Josh Ryan, Jordan Tama, and Jennifer Wessel. Second, at a panel during the Public Choice Society meeting in Charleston, South Carolina. Thanks to Pete Calcagno for organizing the panel, and many thanks to Seth McKee, Irwin Morris, and William Shugart, who served as discussants.

Our project was aided by substantial funding from two organizations: the Social Science Research Council (SSRC) and the Center for Public

Choice and Market Process (CPMP) at the College of Charleston. Special thanks go to Sarah Binder, Kerry Haynie, Frances Lee, Jane Mansbridge, Nolan McCarty, and Christopher Parker for serving on the SSRC grant selection committee and CPMP director Pete Calcagno. This book was aided tremendously because of the support of these organizations and individuals, and we owe them an enormous debt of gratitude.

For data provision, we are indebted to Josh Clinton and John Lapinski for their archive of significant legislation from 1877 to 1994. We are similarly grateful for Scott Adler and John Wilkerson's Congressional Bills Project, the Policy Agendas Project archive, and Mike Crespin, Jason Roberts, and David Rohde's Political Institutions and Public Choice Roll-Call Database. And like many projects on Congress, ours would have been nearly impossible had it not been for Keith Poole's VoteView archive. Thanks also to the many College of Charleston students who helped compile the database of repeals.

As we mentioned above, we laid the foundation for this work with our 2015 article, "Parties, Preferences and Congressional Organization: Explaining Repeals in Congress from 1877–2012," *Political Research Quarterly* 68(4):745–59, and in Jordan's 2010 article, "The Lifecycle of Public Policy: An Event History Analysis of Repeals to Landmark Legislative Enactments, 1951–2006," *American Politics Research* 38(6):1015–51. In those articles the anonymous reviewers and the guidance from editors Jeanette Mendez, Jason Maloy, and Jim Gimpel (respectively) have helped us sharpen and broaden our thinking about this topic.

Last, but certainly not least, our families have been a source of constant support, and we are lucky to have thoughtful—and understanding—partners. Nate is grateful to Shannon for her encouragement and patience throughout, and for all the long hours watching the monsters while writing the book. He is also thankful for Ethan, Emma, Eli, and Everett and all the Nerf gun battles, time spent cooking, and Minecraft tutorials when not at work. Jordan thanks Christine for her many sacrifices on behalf of this book: household chores, movie nights, and weekends, just to name a few. He also thanks his one-year-old twins—Myles and June—for the long naps that provided the time to complete the manuscript.

APPENDIX A

BILL PASSAGE ANALYSIS

At the outset of the data collection effort we sought to identify repeal bills in the same manner used to compile our list of enacted repeals: by culling the contemporaneous and retrospective sources of legislative activity for mentions of notable repeal efforts that ultimately failed. Upon reexamining our primary source material, we found very few mentions of attempted—but ultimately unsuccessful—repeal efforts. Undoubtedly, journalists and policy experts focus on bills that become law, not those that were introduced but died in committee, failed on the floor, died in the other chamber, etc. Simply put, the sample size would be too low to permit any kind of meaningful analysis.

Another challenge we faced was how to operationalize repeal bills. On the one hand, it is rare for a bill's only purpose to be the repeal of a previously enacted law. Although full repeal bills with no new statutory content do indeed exist, the practice was much more common 1800s. On the other hand, many laws, perhaps most, contain some repealing provisions, making the full text of a bill an imperfect data source as well. As noted elsewhere, repeals are part of the normal process of updating the nation's statutes and are therefore very common. Rather than identify the universe of all repeal efforts, which would contain many trivial statutory changes, we wanted to focus on those where repeal was a *major* component of the bill.

We therefore utilized the keyword methodology described in the body of chapter 1. Simply put, our approach of using bill titles balances both of the above concerns: providing a sufficient sample size while also restricting the focus to cases where repeal was a key aspect of the bill under consideration. An additional advantage is that this approach allows us to compare repeal bills to other bill types—amendments, reauthorizations, and appropriations bills—and make direct comparisons. A downside is that the bills we classify no doubt contain a mix of amendments, repeals, and new statutory text. Again, however, because the titles we use are brief summaries of a bill's content, the phrases "A bill to repeal . . . ," "A bill to amend . . . ," etc. reveal key information about a bill's *primary* type.

We have seven control variables in the bill passage models that do not receive discussion in the body of the book. *Committee chair* is a 1/0 for whether the bill's sponsor chaired any committee. We expect a positive effect given the power of committee chairpersons.[1] *Chamber median distance* is the sponsor's ideological distance from chamber median (Krehbiel 1998). We expect a negative effect, indicating that extremists have a harder time attracting support for their proposals. *Chamber polarization* is the distance between the median Democrat and the median Republican in the chamber.[2] We expect a positive effect in the House model, as polarization helps the majority act in a decisive manner (Rohde 1991), and a negative effect in the Senate model, as polarization increases gridlock in the sixty-vote chamber (Sinclair 2002). *Bicameral distance* is the distance between the House and Senate medians. We expect a negative effect in all three models, as the gap between the chambers hurts their capacity to resolve differences (Binder 1999, 2003). *Congress workload* is the total number of bills sponsored in both chambers and *issue area workload* is a count of the number of bills introduced in the bill's policy domain.[3] We expect negative effects on both, indicating that a high workload reduces the chances of an individual bill's passage. *Issue attention* is the total number of hearings in the bill's policy domain and is often used as a measure of Congress's attention to policy problems.[4] We expect a positive effect on this variable, indicating that bills in active domains are more likely to pass (Adler and Wilkerson 2012). Lastly, we have a series of 1/0 variables for the bill's specific policy content.[5]

Tables A1 & A2 present the models described in chapter 1. Because the dependent variable is a dichotomous measure indicating whether a bill passed, positive coefficients indicate a higher probability of passage and negative coefficients indicate a lower probability of passage. Our primary independent variables—representing a bill's type—are described in the body of the chapter. Models 1–3 in table A1 contain the analysis of bills with a "high chance of passage," which focuses on bills sponsored by a member of the majority and those that had a large number of cosponsors. Because we restrict the sample to bills with a large number of cosponsors,

TABLE A1. Models of Bill Passages (High Chance of Passage)

Variables	Model 1 House Bills Coefficient	SE	Model 2 Senate Bills Coefficient	SE	Model 3 All Bills Coefficient	SE
Bill Type						
Repeal	−0.81***	(0.26)	−2.41**	(1.01)	−1.33***	(0.51)
Amendment	−0.55***	(0.07)	−0.45***	(0.09)	−0.48***	(0.08)
Appropriation	0.24	(0.19)	0.12	(0.25)	0.26	(0.21)
Reauthorization	0.33*	(0.17)	0.53***	(0.17)	0.72***	(0.16)
Controls						
Committee Chair	0.88***	(0.08)	0.06	(0.09)	0.42***	(0.09)
Chamber Median Distance	−0.12	(0.21)	1.13***	(0.35)	0.34	(0.26)
Chamber Polarization	2.21***	(0.48)	−3.55***	(0.69)	−0.96*	(0.52)
Bicameral Distance	0.28	(0.28)	−1.37***	(0.45)	−0.88**	(0.35)
Congress Workload	−0.05*	(0.03)	0.02	(0.01)	0.06***	(0.01)
Issue Area Workload	0.31	(0.38)	−0.51	(0.75)	0.25	(0.30)
Issue Attention	1.10	(1.05)	−1.73	(1.63)	−2.86***	(0.98)
Policy Domain						
Macroeconomics	−0.87***	(0.23)	−4.15***	(1.03)	−2.37***	(0.48)
Civil Rights	−0.16	(0.24)	−0.74**	(0.35)	−0.38	(0.26)
Health	−1.22***	(0.19)	−0.80***	(0.22)	−0.66***	(0.20)
Agriculture	−0.61**	(0.29)	−1.02***	(0.36)	−0.55*	(0.30)
Labor	−0.91***	(0.21)	−1.75***	(0.35)	−1.48***	(0.28)
Education	−0.71***	(0.22)	−1.28***	(0.34)	−0.96***	(0.26)
Environment	−0.83***	(0.22)	−0.46	(0.28)	−0.57**	(0.24)
Energy	−0.79***	(0.24)	−0.85***	(0.30)	−0.79***	(0.28)
Transportation	−0.44*	(0.23)	−0.70**	(0.34)	−0.31	(0.26)
Law and Crime	−0.51***	(0.19)	−0.25	(0.26)	−0.39*	(0.22)
Social Welfare	−1.00***	(0.27)	−1.45***	(0.36)	−1.23***	(0.31)
Housing	−0.56*	(0.30)	−1.50***	(0.45)	−1.46***	(0.43)
Banking and Commerce	−0.69***	(0.21)	−0.31	(0.25)	−0.33	(0.22)
Defense	−0.66***	(0.22)	−0.59**	(0.27)	0.09	(0.21)
Technology	0.00	(0.27)	−0.40	(0.36)	−0.51	(0.32)
Foreign Trade	−0.63**	(0.26)	−1.10***	(0.35)	−1.46***	(0.38)
International Affairs	−0.22	(0.25)	−0.85**	(0.34)	0.18	(0.24)
Government Operations	−0.13	(0.18)	0.13	(0.27)	0.66***	(0.19)
Constant	−1.69***	(0.34)	0.89*	(0.47)	−1.96***	(0.37)
Observations	7,202		3,946		11,148	

TABLE A2. Models of Bill Passages (All Bills)

Variables	Model 4 House Bills Coefficient	SE	Model 5 Senate Bills Coefficient	SE	Model 6 All Bills Coefficient	SE
Bill Type						
Repeal	−0.58***	(0.07)	−0.30**	(0.12)	−0.47***	(0.08)
Amendment	−0.20***	(0.02)	−0.19***	(0.02)	−0.23***	(0.02)
Appropriation	1.27***	(0.03)	0.70***	(0.05)	1.11***	(0.03)
Reauthorization	0.89***	(0.04)	0.85***	(0.04)	0.91***	(0.04)
Controls						
Committee Chair	1.07***	(0.02)	0.35***	(0.03)	0.72***	(0.02)
Majority Party Sponsor	0.89***	(0.02)	0.61***	(0.03)	0.78***	(0.02)
Chamber Median Distance	−0.55***	(0.05)	−0.36***	(0.07)	−0.31***	(0.05)
Chamber Polarization	1.12***	(0.08)	−2.38***	(0.12)	−2.47***	(0.09)
Bicameral Distance	−0.13	(0.08)	−1.15***	(0.13)	−0.24**	(0.10)
Congress Workload	−0.13	(0.08)	−1.15***	(0.13)	−0.24**	(0.10)
Issue Area Workload	−0.06***	(0.00)	−0.02***	(0.00)	−0.04***	(0.00)
Issue Attention	−0.47***	(0.03)	−0.51***	(0.12)	−0.51***	(0.02)
Policy Domain						
Macroeconomics	−1.33***	(0.05)	−2.26***	(0.11)	−1.40***	(0.05)
Civil Rights	−1.70***	(0.07)	−1.31***	(0.10)	−1.85***	(0.09)
Health	−1.51***	(0.04)	−1.34***	(0.06)	−1.52***	(0.05)
Agriculture	−1.23***	(0.05)	−0.85***	(0.07)	−0.97***	(0.05)
Labor	−1.69***	(0.05)	−1.63***	(0.09)	−1.74***	(0.06)
Education	−1.56***	(0.05)	−1.48***	(0.08)	−1.53***	(0.06)
Environment	−1.16***	(0.04)	−0.92***	(0.07)	−1.15***	(0.05)
Energy	−1.34***	(0.05)	−1.05***	(0.07)	−1.33***	(0.06)
Transportation	−0.95***	(0.04)	−0.68***	(0.05)	−0.84***	(0.04)
Law and Crime	−1.02***	(0.04)	−0.69***	(0.06)	−1.06***	(0.04)
Social Welfare	−1.93***	(0.06)	−1.74***	(0.10)	−1.82***	(0.07)
Housing	−1.43***	(0.06)	−1.31***	(0.10)	−1.68***	(0.08)
Banking and Commerce	−1.00***	(0.04)	−0.72***	(0.05)	−1.05***	(0.04)
Defense	−0.78***	(0.03)	−0.72***	(0.05)	−0.63***	(0.03)
Technology	−1.01***	(0.06)	−0.69***	(0.08)	−1.13***	(0.07)
Foreign Trade	−1.43***	(0.05)	−2.36***	(0.09)	−1.50***	(0.05)
International Affairs	−0.90***	(0.05)	−0.72***	(0.07)	−0.84***	(0.05)
Government Operations	−0.21***	(0.03)	−0.21***	(0.06)	−0.10***	(0.03)
Constant	−1.80***	(0.06)	−0.33***	(0.09)	−1.12***	(0.06)
Observations	280,917		98,368		379,285	

the time span is the 93rd to 114th Congresses (1973–2017), when cosponsor data are available. Models 4–6 in table A2 contain the analysis of "all bills," with no restrictions in place, making the time span the 80th to 114th Congresses (1947–2017). In the models in table A2, we included an extra control for whether the sponsor is a member of the chamber's majority. We expect a positive effect on the coefficient for *majority party sponsor*.

In tables A1 and A2, the bill type results are as expected and consistent with our theoretical discussion in chapter 1. Whether we look at bills with a high chance of passage since 1973, as we do in table A1, or all bills introduced since 1947, as we do in table A2, repeal bills are the least likely to pass either chamber and be enacted into law. In the body of the chapter we do not report the all bills analysis due to space constraints. However, compared to amendments, which once again are the second-least likely to pass, repeals are 36% less likely to pass the House, 15% less likely to pass the Senate, and 28% less likely to be enacted into law. Finally, the control variables perform as expected.[6]

APPENDIX B

BAYESIAN ITEM RESPONSE MODEL

We adapt our methodology in chapter 2 from Clinton and Lapinski's (2006) approach to measuring legislative accomplishment, with contemporaneous and retrospective raters "voting" in favor of each piece of legislation as a way of operationalizing a repeal's underlying significance. Our database consists of an N × K matrix, with N being each piece of legislation mentioned and K being the votes by the sources on each piece's significance. We adopt a two-parameter model, allowing each rater to have different difficulty and discrimination parameters. Such a technique is important, as it allows us to determine if some raters have higher standards relative to the others (difficulty) and if a rater often distinguishes between more significant and less significant legislation (discrimination).

As noted in the text we incorporate additional information in the estimation strategy: (1) the number of mentions the repeal received contemporaneously in the *Washington Post* and *New York Times* at the time of its repeal;[1] (2) a word count of the amount of text that discussed the repeal in each source (contemporaneous or retrospective) that mentioned the repeal; (3) the proportion of mentions by the contemporaneous and retrospective raters; and (4) the individual estimates of the enacting and repealing bill's significance from Clinton and Lapinski. With this additional information we estimate informed priors of legislative significance as a latent trait. We adopt uninformative priors for all other unobserved parameters.

Formally:

$$\Pr(Y_{ij} = 1) = \frac{exp\{a_i(\Theta_j - b_i)\}}{1 + exp\{a_i(\Theta_j - b_i)\}}$$

The prior on the significance of the repeal (Θ) is given by the following model:

$$\Theta_j \sim (\mu_j,\ 1)$$

And the prior's mean is estimated in the following manner:

$$\mu_j = \kappa 0 + \kappa 1(NYT\ mentions) + \kappa 2(WP\ mentions) + \kappa 3(CL\ Repealing\ Sig) + \kappa 4(CL\ Repealed\ Sig) + \kappa 5(Retro\ \%) + \kappa 6(Contemporaneus\ \%) + \zeta t$$

The remaining priors are specified as follows:

$$\ln(a_i) \sim N(\mu_a,\ \sigma_a^2)$$
$$b_i \sim N(\mu_b,\ \sigma_b^2)$$
$$\mu_a,\ \mu_b \sim N(0,\ 1)$$
$$\sigma_a^2,\ \sigma_b^2 \sim \mathrm{Gamma}(1,\ 1)$$

We utilized the Bayesian 2pl model using the "bayesmh" algorithm in Stata 14.1. In the estimation routine the sampler had 5 million steps, with a burn-in of ten thousand steps, and thinned to every fifth step, resulting in one million steps. In the estimation the average efficiency of the MH sampler is 32.7%, which is well within the 15–50% recommended by Roberts and Rosenthal (2001).

APPENDIX C

REPEAL INTRODUCTION ANALYSIS

Our dependent variable is a count of the number of repeal bills a member of the House or Senate sponsored in a given two-year Congress from the 83rd Congress to the 114th Congress (1953–2017). As noted in appendix A, our data came from Adler and Wilkerson's Congressional Bills Project database. Like many count variables in the social sciences, the response exhibits overdispersion (in other words, it has high variance caused by a large number of zeroes and a handful of very large counts). In our case, 75% of lawmakers sponsor zero repeals in a given Congress, 18% sponsor one repeal, 5% sponsor two repeals, and the rest sponsor three or more repeals (with the largest observation being sixteen sponsored repeals in one Congress).

We therefore estimate two negative binomial count models.[1] Although some statistics texts recommend a zero-inflated specification, such models are typically used when excess zeroes arise because observations *cannot* assume a value other than zero (which is not the case here, as any member, for any reason, can introduce any bill). In this respect, we follow Long and Freese (2005), who write, "When fitting a series of models with no theoretical rationale, it is easy to over fit the data" (409). We note, however, that a zero-inflated model produces comparable results. Lastly, because our data consist of multiple observations per lawmaker, the response violates the independence assumption, as each member has a baseline level of repeal introductions, irrespective of the fixed effects in the model. We therefore estimated negative binomial mixed effects count models with random intercepts for each member.

Our main independent variables come from a variety of sources and receive a full discussion in their respective chapters. From Adler and

TABLE C1. Models of Repeal Sponsorship (Main)

Variables	Model 1 Coefficient	SE	Model 2 Coefficient	SE
Preferences				
Conservatism	1.75***	(0.12)	2.05***	(0.19)
Ideological Extremism	1.74***	(0.22)	1.64***	(0.21)
Polarization	0.44***	(0.10)	0.52***	(0.13)
Public Mood	0.98***	(0.004)	0.98***	(0.004)
Parties				
Majority Party	0.96	(0.04)	0.99	(0.04)
Unified Government	1.02	(0.03)	0.99	(0.03)
Ideological Cohesion	1.58	(1.11)	1.49	(1.03)
Historical Minority Status	1.02**	(0.01)	1.02**	(0.01)
District/State Partisanship	0.996**	(0.002)	0.996*	(0.002)
Safe Seat	1.003	(0.002)	1.003	(0.002)
Interaction				
Conservatism * Majority	—	—	0.79**	(0.07)
Controls				
Senator	0.70***	(0.04)	0.70***	(0.04)
Committee Chair	0.90*	(0.06)	0.89*	(0.06)
Terms in Congress	1.00	(0.00)	1.00	(0.00)
Member Sponsorship	2.64***	(0.07)	2.63***	(0.07)
Congress Sponsorship	0.76***	(0.05)	1.00***	(0.00)
Constant	0.61	(0.45)	0.06***	(0.02)
Observations	16,832		16,832	
Groups (Random Intercepts)	2,814		2,814	

Dependent variable is a count of the number of repeal bills a lawmaker sponsored in a given Congress. Negative binomial mixed effects model. Coefficients reported as incident rate ratios. Coefficients > 1 indicate a positive effect, while coefficients < 1 indicate a negative effect. *** $p < 0.01$, ** $p < 0.05$, * $p < 0.1$

Wilkerson's data set, we obtain the sponsor's party affiliation and ideology. Our measure of public mood came from James Stimson's website.[2] We measured polarization using to Poole's (1997) NOMINATE scores. However, we also include a number of control variables that are unique to the analysis of repeal sponsorship and therefore do not receive discussion in the body of the manuscript. *Senator* records whether the lawmaker is in the Senate, *committee chair* records whether he or she chaired any committee, *member sponsorship* is the total number of bills the member sponsored, and *Congress sponsorship* the total number of bills sponsored by all members in a two-year Congress. Each of these variables came from Adler and Wilkerson's data set. Finally, we include a variable *terms in Congress*, which is a count of the number of two-year terms in either chamber. We obtained this variable from Keith Poole and Howard Rosenthal's (1997) NOMINATE data set. All remaining variables were created by the authors.

In the table below, we report two models. Model 1 is the "main" model that we describe in the chapters 4 and 5. Model 2 is a "supplementary" model that contains an interaction term *conservatism * majority* testing if the repealing behavior of conservatives depends on whether they are in the majority or minority. We discuss this additional hypothesis in chapter 5. In model 2, the interaction term is significant and in the direction described in the body of the chapter.

A few control variables do not receive discussion in the body of the manuscript but are nonetheless significant. In the analysis, we find that lawmakers who sponsor a greater number of bills overall (*member sponsorship*) in turn sponsor more repeals. Although not surprising, this variable ensures that the other results are unique to repeal sponsorship and do not simply reflect general sponsorship dynamics. A variable for the total number of bills sponsored in a session (*Congress sponsorship*) is negative and significant. We include this variable to account for changing sponsorship/cosponsorship dynamics over time. As Adler and Wilkerson note on their website, when cosponsorship became more prominent in the 1970s, members shifted strategies and began sponsoring fewer bills.[3] In this respect, the negative effect indicates that sponsorship by *other* members—which in turn increases the overall rate of cosponsorship—reduces repeal sponsorship in the aggregate. We also find that senators (*senator*) and committee chairpersons (*committee chair*) sponsor fewer repeal bills. We attribute the lower rate of repeal sponsorship among senators to the chamber's more collegial character and representatives' greater electoral pressure and the negative effect for committee chairpersons to their greater focus on the creation of new laws.

APPENDIX D

MAIN SURVIVAL ANALYSIS

Our primary database of repeals identifies two laws: the enacting law and the repealing law. In the data set, laws are arranged longitudinally, spanning the period from the first Congress after passage to the time of its repeal. Our time series begins in 1877 at the opening of the 45th Congress and ends in 2011 at the close of the 111th Congress. No landmark repeals were identified in the 112th Congress, so after the 111th Congress, all nonrepealed laws are right censored. Of the 111 repeals in our primary database, 10 were enacted before 1877 and cannot be included due to the lack of independent variables prior to that point. Likewise, three repeals occurred in the same Congress that enacted the law and thus have no variation in many of the predictors.

Given the structure of our data, we use survival analysis to assess whether law i experienced a major repeal in Congress t after passage. We note that this approach is standard practice in research on statutory and program durability (Adler and Wilkerson 2012; Berry, Burden, and Howell 2010; Corder 2004; Maltzman and Shipan 2008; Thrower 2017) and is the approach we use in our previous work (Ragusa 2010; Ragusa and Birkhead 2015). However, our specific modeling strategy in this book differs in two ways.

First, unlike our 2015 article, which examined only repealed laws, the population under examination in this book consists of all significant laws.[1] We define significant laws as those in the top 10% of the distribution. We do so using Clinton and Lapinski's (2006) measure of legislative accomplishment, which scales the importance of every public law enacted from 1877 to 1994. For the period after 1994, which was not covered by

Clinton and Lapinski, we substitute the Policy Agendas Project article length variable, which records the amount of media coverage for a bill and is widely used as a measure of important legislative items. We do so by, first, creating a linear model that relates the *Congressional Quarterly* article length variable to Clinton and Lapinski's measure where they overlap and, second, estimating a bridged measure for all laws enacted after 1994. We note that this method of linear projection onto a common space has been used in ideal point estimation (Shor and McCarty 2011; Windett, Harden, and Hall 2015). As discussed in chapter 2 of the main manuscript, restricting the analysis to enacted laws in the top 10% removes fourteen repeals from the analysis.

Second, we estimate a parametric survival model in this book, while our earlier work utilized a semiparametric Cox model. As noted in our 2015 article, an advantage of semiparametric models, like the Cox, is that the researcher does not need to specify the functional form of the underlying hazard. However, in this case, we have clear information about what that hazard looks like. First, a number of studies of legal and program durability have identified the same underlying hazard shape (Berry, Burden, and Howell 2010; Corder 2004; Ragusa 2010; Ragusa and Birkhead 2015). Second, the nonmonotonic hazard reported in chapter 2 looks much like a log-logistic or log-normal function. Further, in that chapter we noted that there were theoretical reasons to expect the repeal hazard to be nonmonotonic. As Box-Steffensmeier and Jones (2004) say, "The appeal of the [parametric] models is highest when there is a strong theoretical reason to expect one distribution over another" (38). In addition to its theoretical fit, a parametric model provides estimates that are more precise over semiparametric models (Box-Steffensmeier and Jones 2004).

Following these recommendations, we tested multiple parametric survival models and computed fit statistics to identify the best performing model (Blossfeld, Golsch, and Rohwer 2007; Cleves, Gould, and Marchenko 2016). We tested the log-normal, log-logistic, and Weibull. In these preliminary analyses we found that the log-normal performed best, followed by the log-logistic and Weibull.[2] All models reported in the book were therefore estimated using a log-normal parametric survival model. It is no surprise that the log-normal and log-logistic come in first and second given the nonmonotone hazard reported in chapter 2. Likewise, all three outperform the Cox model by a wide margin, according to fit statistics.[3]

In the results tables in this appendix, we report coefficients rather than hazard ratios. Because the coefficients do not have a straightforward interpretation in log-normal parametric survival models, in each chapter we

TABLE D1. Model of Repeal (Main Analysis)

Variables	Model 1 Coefficient	SE
Parties		
Unified at Enactment	−0.05	(0.14)
Unified at Subsequent	−0.31*	(0.17)
Enacting Party Seat Change	0.01	(0.01)
Conditional Party Government (CPG)	1.19***	(0.42)
Historical Minority Status	0.08	(0.05)
CPG * Minority Status	−0.21***	(0.07)
Preferences		
Cloture Era	0.41	(0.26)
Exposed Space	1.11***	(0.36)
Cloture * Exposed Space	−1.96**	(0.97)
Coalition Degradation	−3.55***	(0.32)
Conservative Shift	−0.67	(0.56)
Conservative Congress	−0.66	(0.68)
Sponsor Conservatism	−0.15	(0.22)
Bicameral Distance	0.07	(0.86)
Problem Solving		
Issue Attention	0.11	(0.81)
Controls		
Senate Bill	0.34**	(0.16)
Passage Margin	0.46*	(0.24)
Bill Complexity	0.11	(0.07)
Bill Significance	−0.35***	(0.05)
Environment	0.61**	(−0.28)
Social	0.50**	(−0.20)
Agriculture	0.33	(−0.29)
Science and Technology	0.28	(−0.40)
Law and Crime	0.18	(−0.23)
Defense	0.06	(−0.15)
Foreign Trade	0.06	(−0.24)
Energy	−0.04	(−0.26)
International Affairs	−0.10	(−0.18)

(*continued*)

TABLE D1. (continued)

Variables	Model 1 Coefficient	SE
Banking and Commerce	−0.11	(−0.14)
Transportation	−0.22	(−0.18)
Civil Rights	−0.25	(−0.44)
Immigration	−0.33	(−0.36)
Macroeconomics	−0.53***	(−0.16)
War Law	−1.25***	(−0.25)
Constant	6.90***	(0.71)
Observations	86,987	
Laws (top 10%)	3,381	

Response records whether law i was repealed in Congress t after passage. Log-normal parametric survival model. Coefficients > 0 indicate greater survivability (fewer repeals), while coefficients < 0 indicate less survivability (greater repeals). *** $p < 0.01$, ** $p < 0.05$, * $p < 0.1$

present survival curves for specific covariate patterns. In the tables, negative coefficients indicate less survivability (i.e., a greater risk of repeal), while positive coefficient indicate greater survivability (i.e., a lower risk of repeal). We group the main variables into three clusters, each of which receives separate treatment in a chapter in the book: parties, preferences, and problem solving. Our main model, model 1, is reported in table D1. In the supplementary models, models 2–12, we included all policy domain controls in the analysis but do not report them in the table due to space constraints.

We include three control variables that are not discussed in detail in the chapters because they do not fit cleanly into any of the three theoretical categories. *Passage margin* is the percentage of lawmakers voting for the law at the time of passage averaged for both chambers. Our data came from the Political Institutions and Public Choice (PIPC) Roll-Call Database and the Swift et al. Database of Congressional Historical Statistics.[4] In model 1, the coefficient is positive and significant, indicating that bills passed with large margins are more likely to survive repeals. We discuss the cause of this effect in chapter 4, as further analysis reveals it has roots in partisan conflict.

We also have a variable *bill significance* that is the significance of the enacted law using the methodology and data described elsewhere. In model 1, the coefficient is negative and significant, indicating that the most significant of the top 10% of laws in our analysis (for example, those in the top 1%) are more likely to be repealed than important but less significant laws (for example, those in the top 9%). We conducted a long list of secondary analyses to try to identify the underlying dynamics of this effect, as there are good reasons why such a result would fit any of the "three Ps" comprising our empirical chapters: problem solving, parties, or preferences. Yet we were unable to find a clear and consistent interpretation of this effect. Our suspicion is that the most likely explanation has to do with the scarcity of the legislative agenda. Given the variety of impediments to passing a repeal, party leaders may be unwilling to dedicate precious agenda space and spend political capital in an effort to repeal a notable, but not landmark, bill. An alternative explanation is that the effect may simply mirror the process motivating our data collection effort. Because our focus is on the most significant repeals in history, it follows that the laws motivating the repeal are uniquely significant as well. In other words, we think it is very possible that there is no substantive cause of this effect.

Finally, we have a control variable *bill complexity* that is the number of characters (divided by one hundred) in a bill's description. Conceivably, bills with longer descriptions contain a greater range of policy content and/or provisions and may therefore face a greater risk of repeal due to the simple fact that there is more statutory content to repeal in the first place. However, this effect is insignificant in the model. In our earlier work (Ragusa 2010), we found a significant positive effect linking the number of bill provisions and the likelihood of repeal, though this different result is likely due to the different data set, as Ragusa (2010) analyzes repeals using the US Code.

CHAPTER 3: SUPPLEMENTARY ANALYSES

MEASURING BILL QUALITY

As noted in the body of the chapter, bill quality is certainly central to discussions of problem solving. Where spikes in issue attention may indicate a problem in an issue domain that requires legislative action, there are intuitive reasons why the quality of legislation explains repeal as well. First, good legislation may fix the problem it was intended to solve, thus reducing the need for future legislative activity in that domain. Second, high-quality legislation may be less likely to contain defective statutes that compel lawmakers to revisit the law. And third, lawmakers who craft good legislation may anticipate future problems and thus prevent the law's statutes from becoming outmoded or obsolete.

Despite this, it has been described as a "fool's errand" to try to distinguish between good and bad laws in an objective manner (Sinclair 2008, 82). Even among the few studies that have tried to measure bill quality, there is far from a consensus on best practices. For example, Bendix (2016) used unsigned newspaper editorials for a twenty-year period while Iaryczower, Katz, and Saiegh (2012) used a bill's vote margin. Naturally, both have limitations for our purposes. Newspaper editorials are simply unfeasible given the time frame of our analysis, while the vote margin may be associated with a range of historically contingent factors: the size of the majority and party polarization, just to name a few.

Another logical approach is to measure the extent of deliberation in Congress, although even this seemingly straightforward concept poses a series of challenges (Lascher 1996). While floor debate may seem like an obvious metric, the fact is that, by the time a bill reaches the floor, the vast bulk of the its statutory content is set. In fact, if a bill reaches the floor under a closed rule blocking all amendments, the entire bill is beyond revision. Because debate proceeds even under closed rules, it can be asked whether debate is "deliberative" at all (see Quirk 1993). Committee hearings, by comparison, occur earlier in the legislative process and involve the testimony of experts. Yet like floor debate, an open question is whether committee members reach their decision irrespective of what was said in the hearing. Perhaps more importantly, committees consist of a tiny fraction of the chamber's overall membership, calling into question the aggregate deliberative value of hearings (see Solomon and Wolfensberger 1994). Notably, this critique applies equally, if not more, to committee markup. In most markups—when the committee alters the introduced bill—the committee chairperson has tremendous power over the statutory changes considered (Deering and Smith 1997). Finally, amendments are of limited value because they are offered after the legislation is already written and, in many cases, are brought forward by the minority party for strategic ends.

Although we cannot measure bill quality in a suitable way, a control variable in our analysis is tangentially related to the underlying construct. Our variable *Senate bill* is simply a 1/0 for whether the bill was introduced in the upper chamber. It is significant in the analysis. Although this is an exceptionally blunt measure, the Constitution's architects certainly believed the Senate would be the more deliberative chamber and would therefore pass "sound" legislation. A brief review of Federalist No. 62 reveals Madison's thoughts on this matter. First, senators possess a "greater extent of information and stability of character" than their counterparts in the House. Second, the smaller Senate would be less susceptible to "the impulse of sudden and violent passions." And third, because they serve six-year terms, senators would possess "due acquaintance with the objects and principles of legislation" and would therefore devote themselves to "a study of the laws." Nevertheless, whether this is an imprecise measure of bill quality or simply one that captures broader bicameral differences, we include it as a control in the analysis.

Measuring Issue Attention

As noted in chapter 3, our measure of issue attention is based on the number of bills enacted in a given policy domain per Congress. Fortunately, Clinton and Lapinski's (2006) database of legislative accomplishment contains all enacted bills along with their descriptions from 1877 to 1946, while Adler and Wilkerson's (2012) Congressional Bills Project database contains the same from 1947 to 2016. Using these bill descriptions, which have an average of twenty-three words, we use a two-step process to catalog the content of all laws enacted from 1877 to 2011.

First, we go through each issue domain listed in the Policy Agendas Project topic codebook and hand-code keywords used in each issue area. For example, in the health domain, the Policy Agendas Project lists the following examples: "health care," "health insurance," "drug safety," "hospitals," "health center," "mental health," "alcohol abuse," and a few dozen others. Using these hand-coded dictionaries, a program we wrote culls the roughly 45,500 enacted bill descriptions and classifies each bill's policy content. As one example, our approach identifies HR 6675 in the 89th Congress (1965–67) as belonging to the health policy domain. Looking at the description, we can see that this was the law creating Medicare in 1965: "To provide a hospital insurance program for the aged under the Social Security Act with a supplementary health benefits program and an expanded program of medical assistance, to increase benefits under the Old-Age, Survivors, and Disability Insurance System, to improve the Federal-State public assistance programs, and for other purposes."

Due to inherent limitations with the keyword analysis (Quinn et al. 2010), as a second step we also used a supervised machine learning algorithm via RTextTools to classify bills not categorized in the first step.[5]

TABLE D2: VALIDATING ISSUE ATTENTION

Correlation with Indicators (1877–2011)		Correlation with Policy Agendas Project Hearings Data (1947–2011)		Issue Areas (1877–2011)
Policy Domain	Correlation	Policy Domain	Correlation	Total Bills
Defense	0.71	Health	0.82	208 (5.8%)
Macroeconomics	0.46	Macroeconomics	0.76	608 (17.0%)
Banking and Commerce	0.29	Environment	0.72	589 (16.5%)
		International Affairs	0.66	307 (8.6%)
Average	0.49	Social Welfare	0.64	634 (17.7%)
Adjusted Average	0.66	Law and Crime	0.63	224 (6.3%)
		Education	0.62	173 (4.8%)
		Energy	0.61	158 (4.4%)
		Science and Technology	0.42	186 (5.2%)
		Banking and Commerce	0.40	893 (25.0%)
		Immigration	0.32	39 (1.1%)
		Labor	0.30	297 (8.3%)
		Transportation	0.29	339 (9.5%)
		Community Development	0.23	127 (3.6%)
		Foreign Trade	0.19	206 (5.8%)
		Defense	0.06	718 (20.1%)
		Agriculture	−0.03	314 (8.8%)
		Civil Rights	−0.32	100 (2.8%)
		Average	0.41	
		Adjusted Average	0.47	

We created the training corpus from the Congressional Bills Project using its bill classifications and titles and applied this to the virgin data of bill titles. Following Collingwood and Wilkerson (2012), we estimated nine algorithms and used ensemble consensus agreement methods to make the ultimate classification. When we had the consensus of five algorithms, we attained coverage of 73% of the data with 88% reliability.

TABLE D3. Model of Repeal (Supplementary Analyses—Relative Issue Attention)

Variables	Model 2 Coefficient	SE
Parties		
Unified at Enactment	−0.06	(0.14)
Unified at Subsequent	−0.31*	(0.17)
Enacting Party Seat Change	0.01	(0.01)
Conditional Party Government (CPG)	1.31***	(0.44)
Historical Minority Status	0.08	(0.05)
CPG * Minority Status	−0.21***	(0.07)
Preferences		
Cloture Era	0.47*	(0.27)
Exposed Space	1.18***	(0.37)
Cloture * Exposed Space	−1.95**	(0.94)
Coalition Degradation	−3.53***	(0.32)
Conservative Shift	−0.63	(0.56)
Conservative Congress	−0.79	(0.68)
Sponsor Conservatism	−0.15	(0.22)
Bicameral Distance	0.06	(0.86)
Problem Solving		
Relative Issue Attention	−0.05	(0.04)
Controls		
Senate Bill	0.34**	(0.16)
Passage Margin	0.45*	(0.25)
Bill Complexity	0.11	(0.07)
Bill Significance	−0.35***	(0.05)
Policy Controls (Not Reported)	–	–
Constant	6.77***	(0.73)
Observations	86,987	
Laws (top 10%)	3,381	

Response records whether law i was repealed in Congress t after passage. Log-normal parametric survival model. Coefficients > 0 indicate greater survivability (fewer repeals) while coefficients < 0 indicate less survivability (greater repeals). *** $p < 0.01$, ** $p < 0.05$, * $p < 0.1$

TABLE D4. Model of Repeal (Supplementary Analyses—Objective Problems)

Variables	Model 3 Coefficient	SE	Model 4 Coefficient	SE	Model 5 Coefficient	SE
Parties						
Unified at Enactment	-0.06	(0.14)	0.03	(0.11)	-0.04	(0.13)
Unified at Subsequent	-0.39**	(0.18)	-0.47***	(0.14)	-0.20	(0.16)
Enacting Party Seat Change	0.01	(0.01)	0.01	(0.01)	0.00	(0.01)
Conditional Party Government (CPG)	1.31***	(0.43)	1.35***	(0.41)	1.49***	(0.42)
Historical Minority Status	0.10*	(0.05)	0.02	(0.05)	0.14**	(0.06)
CPG * Minority Status	-0.23***	(0.07)	-0.16**	(0.06)	-0.27***	(0.07)
Preferences						
Cloture Era	0.38	(0.27)	-0.23	(0.25)	0.58**	(0.28)
Exposed Space	1.09***	(0.36)	0.55*	(0.29)	1.32***	(0.37)
Cloture * Exposed Space	-1.81*	(0.98)	-0.45	(0.81)	-2.44**	(0.98)
Coalition Degradation	-3.56***	(0.32)	-3.44***	(0.25)	-3.55***	(0.31)
Conservative Shift	-0.67	(0.57)	-0.71	(0.44)	-1.03**	(0.51)
Conservative Congress	-0.84	(0.69)	-0.94*	(0.52)	-0.44	(0.63)
Sponsor Conservatism	-0.15	(0.23)	-0.18	(0.19)	-0.17	(0.21)
Bicameral Distance	0.18	(0.87)	0.78	(0.73)	0.32	(0.87)
Problem Solving						
Issue Attention	0.07	(0.77)	0.07	(0.63)	0.05	(0.76)
Defense	0.07	(0.16)				

	Model 1		Model 2		Model 3	
Deaths in War	0.02	(0.01)				
Defense * Deaths in War	-0.01	(0.01)				
Macroeconomics			-0.64**	(0.32)		
Debt-to-GDP Ratio			0.01***	(0.00)		
Macroeconomics * Debt-to-GDP			0.01	(0.01)		
Banking and Commerce					-0.13	(0.13)
Bank Failures					-0.03***	(0.01)
Banking * Bank Failures					0.01	(0.01)
Controls						
Senate Bill	0.35**	(0.16)	0.27**	(0.12)	0.30**	(0.14)
Passage Margin	0.44*	(0.24)	0.32*	(0.18)	0.38	(0.23)
Bill Complexity	0.11	(0.07)	0.09*	(0.05)	0.10	(0.06)
Bill Significance	-0.36***	(0.05)	-0.26***	(0.04)	-0.32***	(0.05)
Policy Controls (Not Reported)						
Constant	6.89***	(0.70)	5.67***	(0.53)	6.17***	(0.71)
Observations	86,987		86,987		86,987	
Laws (top 10%)	3,381		3,381		3,381	

Response records whether law i was repealed in Congress t after passage. Log-normal parametric survival model. Coefficients > 0 indicate greater survivability (fewer repeals) while coefficients < 0 indicate less survivability (greater repeals). *** $p < 0.01$, ** $p < 0.05$, * $p < 0.1$

In the body of the chapter we briefly mentioned efforts to validate our measure of issue attention. First, we selected three domains with objective problems that can be measured since 1877: defense (deaths in war), macroeconomics (the debt-to-GDP ratio), and banking and commerce (bank failures). Table D2 presents the results. Over the entire time period, we find correlations ranging from "strong" to "moderate" according to Cohen's (1988) scale. Deaths in war correlate with defense attention at 0.71 ($p < .01$), the debt-to-GDP ratio correlates with macroeconomics attention at 0.46 ($p < .01$), and bank failures correlate with banking and commerce attention at 0.29 ($p < .05$). If we invoke some intuitive refinements to the calculation,[6] the adjusted correlations jump to 0.79, 0.51, and 0.68.

Second, we correlated our measure of policy attention with Baumgartner and Jones's preferred measure of issue attention: congressional hearings.[7] Table D2 presents these results as well. Of the eighteen policy domains used in the analysis, sixteen, or 89%, are positive. According to Cohen's (1988) scale, eight have "strong" positive correlations ($p > .50$), four have "moderate" positive correlations ($p > .30$), and three have "weak" positive correlations ($p > .10$). Only two have "no correlation" ($p < |.10|$) and one, civil rights, has a "moderate" negative correlation ($p < .30$). As Jones and Baumgartner (2004) note, there are good reasons why civil rights would have a negative correlation between the number of hearings and bill passage.[8] Likewise, we believe there are good reasons why the defense correlation is nearly zero.[9] If we remove civil rights and defense, given their unique nature, the adjusted correlation is 0.47.

Supplementary Models

Models 2–8 in tables D3–D6 are described in detail in the body of chapter 3. Model 2 contains the measure of relative issue attention. Our measure of relative issue attention converts the raw estimates used in the main model to z scores. Models 3–5 contain interaction terms between the three measures of objective problems (deaths in war, recessions, and bank failures) and the corresponding policy domain (defense, macroeconomics, and banking and commerce). Model 6 contains our measure of technological advancement interacted with laws that contain a technological component. And models 7 and 8 present our analysis of hearings data and issue attention omitting miscellaneous cases, respectively. As noted chapter 3, we find no evidence to support the problem-solving theory in these supplementary analyses.

TABLE D5. Model of Repeal (Supplementary Analyses—Technological Advancement)

	Model 6	
	Coefficient	SE
Parties		
Unified at Enactment	−0.09	(0.14)
Unified at Subsequent	−0.43***	(0.16)
Enacting Party Seat Change	0.01	(0.01)
Conditional Party Government (CPG)	1.49***	(0.47)
Historical Minority Status	0.10*	(0.05)
CPG * Minority Status	−0.23***	(0.07)
Preferences		
Cloture Era	0.29	(0.26)
Exposed Space	1.00***	(0.36)
Cloture * Exposed Space	−1.61*	(0.93)
Coalition Degradation	−3.60***	(0.31)
Conservative Shift	−0.73	(0.55)
Conservative Congress	−0.99	(0.70)
Sponsor Conservatism	−0.20	(0.23)
Bicameral Distance	0.44	(0.87)
Problem Solving		
Issue Attention	−0.04	(0.75)
Technological Advancement	−0.11	(0.22)
Technology	2.29*	(1.17)
Technology * Advancement	0.55	(2.71)
Controls		
Senate Bill	0.33**	(0.15)
Passage Margin	0.38	(0.25)
Bill Complexity	0.09	(0.06)
Bill Significance	−0.35***	(0.05)
Policy Controls (Not Reported)		
Constant	6.73***	(0.70)
Observations	86,708	
Laws (top 10%)	3,380	

Response records whether law i was repealed in Congress t after passage. Log-normal parametric survival model. Coefficients > 0 indicate greater survivability (fewer repeals) while coefficients < 0 indicate less survivability (greater repeals). *** $p < 0.01$, ** $p < 0.05$, * $p < 0.1$

TABLE D6. Model of Repeal (Supplementary Analyses—Hearings and Miscellaneous Cases)

	Model 7		Model 8	
Variables	Coefficient	SE	Coefficient	SE
Parties				
Unified at Enactment	−0.18*	(0.10)	−0.09	(0.13)
Unified at Subsequent	−0.00	(0.16)	−0.31**	(0.15)
Enacting Party Seat Change	−0.02	(0.01)	0.01	(0.01)
Conditional Party Government (CPG)	0.59	(0.36)	1.00***	(0.37)
Historical Minority Status	−0.01	(0.07)	0.07	(0.05)
CPG * Minority Status	−0.03	(0.08)	−0.18***	(0.07)
Preferences				
Cloture Era	–	–	0.42*	(0.24)
Exposed Space	0.58	(1.05)	1.09***	(0.32)
Cloture * Exposed Space	–	–	−1.89**	(0.94)
Coalition Degradation	−3.05***	(0.18)	−3.57***	(0.29)
Conservative Shift	−0.75	(0.64)	−0.16	(0.58)
Conservative Congress	0.30	(0.75)	−0.88	(0.70)
Sponsor Conservatism	0.10	(0.25)	0.12	(0.26)
Bicameral Distance	−0.84	(0.62)	0.22	(0.71)
Problem Solving				
Issue Attention	–	–	−0.15	(0.79)
Hearings	0.01	(0.04)	–	–
Controls				
Senate Bill	0.25*	(0.13)	0.44***	(0.17)
Passage Margin	0.07	(0.15)	0.47*	(0.25)
Bill Complexity	0.12	(0.08)	0.09	(0.07)
Bill Significance	−0.19***	(0.04)	−0.34***	(0.05)
Policy Controls (Not Reported)	–		–	
Constant	5.57***	(0.56)	6.86***	(0.68)
Observations	38,102		74,629	
Laws (top 10%)	2,188		2,906	

Response records whether law i was repealed in Congress t after passage. Log-normal parametric survival model. Coefficients > 0 indicate greater survivability (fewer repeals) while coefficients < 0 indicate less survivability (greater repeals). *** $p < 0.01$, ** $p < 0.05$, * $p < 0.1$

CHAPTER 4: SUPPLEMENTARY ANALYSES

In model 9 in table D7, we take a closer look at the passage margin result. In the main analysis, in model 1, we find that bills enacted by large margins are more durable. We listed this variable (*passage margin*) in the control section because there are competing partisan and problem-solving explanations for this effect, and additional analysis was needed to assign it to one category. On the former, it may be that bills enacted by large margins are bipartisan and thus less likely to be targets for repeal in the future. On the latter, it may be that bills enacted by large margins are higher quality and thus less likely to need subsequent revisions. In the body of the chapter we discussed both options in detail and described the results lending support to the partisan explanation.

In this additional analysis the percentage of the minority voting for the bill (*minority passage margin*) is significant and positive, indicating that minority support increases a law's durability, while the percentage of the majority voting for the bill (*majority passage margin*) is marginally significant ($p = 0.07$) but *negative*, indicating that majority support decreases a law's durability. Simply put, this additional analysis, breaking down the raw passage margin into its constituent parts, indicates that partisan laws face a greater risk of repeal, irrespective of how many lawmakers voted for the bill.

In the main model, model 1, we use the raw passage margin due to the fact that data on the yeas/nays by party is only available starting with the 85th Congress (1957–59). Our data came from the PIPC Roll Call Dataset maintained by the Carl Albert Center. We matched each public law (via its bill number) to the final passage votes in the House[10] and Senate.[11] Our majority/minority passage variables are averages of the votes in both chambers.[12] Because our sample size was reduced by about 70%, with a significantly restricted time frame, we encountered a number of modeling challenges in the supplementary analysis, the most critical being a sharp reduction in the number of Congresses ($n = 26$) and limited Congress-level variation in the independent variables. For this reason, model 9 only includes variables with bill-level variation. We also add the caveat that the results are based on just nineteen repeals from 1957 to 2011.

CHAPTER 5: SUPPLEMENTARY ANALYSES

In the body of chapter 5, we report two supplementary models that explore the role of ideology in successful repeals. In model 10 in table D8, we

TABLE D7. Model of Repeal (Supplementary Analysis—Passage Margin)

	Model 9	
Variables	Coefficient	SE
Parties		
Unified at Enactment	−0.09	(0.12)
Enacting Party Seat Change	−0.04**	(0.01)
Preferences		
Coalition Degradation	−2.93***	(0.21)
Conservative Shift	−0.76*	(0.41)
Sponsor Conservatism	0.01	(0.19)
Problem Solving		
Issue Attention	−0.05	(0.88)
Controls		
Minority Passage Margin	0.37***	(0.10)
Majority Passage Margin	−0.79*	(0.44)
Senate Bill	0.28**	(0.13)
Bill Complexity	0.26***	(0.09)
Bill Significance	−0.23***	(0.06)
Policy Controls (Not Reported)		
Constant	6.24***	(0.74)
Observations	29,681	
Laws (top 10%)	1,915	

Response records whether law *i* was repealed in Congress *t* after passage. Log-normal parametric survival model. Coefficients > 0 indicate greater survivability (fewer repeals) while coefficients < 0 indicate less survivability (greater repeals). *** $p < 0.01$, ** $p < 0.05$, * $p < 0.1$

report a model with an interaction that tests whether conservatives repeal a greater share of legislation they ideologically oppose. In the model, the interaction *conservative Congress * sponsor* examines whether conservative Congresses target bills sponsored by liberal lawmakers. As noted in the chapter, this tests the possibility that conservatives do not target *all* bills equally, just liberal ones. Although intuitive, the extra interaction term is insignificant. In model 11, also in table D8, we restrict the time span to the post–New Deal era. Specifically, we limit the time span to the

TABLE D8. Model of Repeal (Supplementary Analyses—Sponsor Ideology and New Deal Era)

Variables	Model 10 Coefficient	SE	Model 11 Coefficient	SE
Parties				
Unified at Enactment	−0.05	(0.14)	−0.03	(0.13)
Unified at Subsequent	−0.31*	(0.17)	−0.15	(0.13)
Enacting Party Seat Change	0.01	(0.01)	−0.01	(0.01)
Conditional Party Government (CPG)	1.19***	(0.44)	0.95***	(0.37)
Historical Minority Status	0.08	(0.05)	0.03	(0.04)
CPG * Minority Status	−0.21***	(0.07)	−0.10**	(0.05)
Preferences				
Cloture Era	0.41	(0.26)	–	–
Exposed Space	1.11***	(0.36)	−0.28	(0.85)
Cloture * Exposed Space	−1.96**	(0.95)	–	–
Coalition Degradation	−3.55***	(0.32)	−3.20***	(0.22)
Conservative Shift	−0.66	(0.55)	−1.09*	(0.62)
Conservative Congress	−0.66	(0.68)	0.39	(0.77)
Sponsor Conservatism	−0.15	(0.22)	−0.22	(0.21)
Conservative Congress * Sponsor	−0.01	(1.19)	–	–
Bicameral Distance	0.07	(0.84)	0.19	(0.74)
Problem Solving				
Issue Attention	0.10	(0.80)	−0.52	(0.62)
Controls				
Senate Bill	0.34**	(0.16)	0.27**	(0.13)
Passage Margin	0.46*	(0.24)	0.34*	(0.20)
Bill Complexity	0.11	(0.07)	0.09	(0.07)
Bill Significance	−0.35***	(0.05)	−0.20***	(0.04)
Policy Controls (Not Reported)				
Constant	6.90***	(0.71)	5.81***	(0.50)
Observations	86,987		52,143	
Laws (top 10%)	3,381		2,628	

Response records whether law i was repealed in Congress t after passage. Log-normal parametric survival model. Coefficients > 0 indicate greater survivability (fewer repeals) while coefficients < 0 indicate less survivability (greater repeals). *** $p < 0.01$, ** $p < 0.05$, * $p < 0.1$

TABLE D9. Model of Repeal (Supplementary Analysis—Coalition Drift)

Variables	Model 12 Coefficient	SE
Parties		
Unified at Enactment	0.01	(0.07)
Unified at Subsequent	−0.08	(0.10)
Enacting Party Seat Change	0.01	(0.01)
Conditional Party Government (CPG)	0.72***	(0.26)
Historical Minority Status	0.06**	(0.03)
CPG * Minority Status	−0.12***	(0.04)
Preferences		
Cloture Era	0.04	(0.16)
Exposed Space	0.47**	(0.23)
Cloture * Exposed Space	−0.85	(0.60)
Coalition Degradation	−0.38	(0.53)
Conservative Shift	−0.47	(0.30)
Conservative Congress	0.02	(0.38)
Sponsor Conservatism	−0.17	(0.13)
Bicameral Distance	0.12	(0.41)
Problem Solving		
Issue Attention	0.18	(0.44)
Controls		
Senate Bill	0.19**	(0.09)
Passage Margin	0.26*	(0.14)
Bill Complexity	0.06	(0.04)
Bill Significance	−0.18***	(0.03)
Policy Controls (Not Reported)		
Time Controls		
1st Subsequent Congress	−3.04***	(0.49)
2nd Subsequent Congress	−2.22***	(0.41)
3rd Subsequent Congress	−1.77***	(0.33)
4th Subsequent Congress	−1.50***	(0.30)
5th Subsequent Congress	−1.29***	(0.27)
6th Subsequent Congress	−1.09***	(0.29)

TABLE D9. *(continued)*

Variables	Model 12 Coefficient	SE
7th Subsequent Congress	−0.96***	(0.25)
8th Subsequent Congress	−0.96***	(0.23)
9th Subsequent Congress	−0.81***	(0.22)
10th Subsequent Congress	−0.78***	(0.20)
11th Subsequent Congress	−0.88***	(0.15)
12th Subsequent Congress	−0.84***	(0.17)
13th Subsequent Congress	1.76***	(0.38)
Constant	5.36***	(0.37)
Observations	86,987	
Laws (top 10%)	3,381	

Response records whether law i was repealed in Congress t after passage. Log-normal parametric survival model. Coefficients > 0 indicate greater survivability (fewer repeals) while coefficients < 0 indicate less survivability (greater repeals). *** $p < 0.01$, ** $p < 0.05$, * $p < 0.1$

73rd Congress (1933–35) and on, which corresponds with FDR's first term. As Grossmann and Hopkins (2016) note, although the parties have evolved in a number of ways over the years, the asymmetric nature of the two parties is an enduring feature of the New Deal era. Yet in this supplementary analysis, the coefficients on two of the three variables testing this proposition (*conservative Congress* and *sponsor conservatism*) are insignificant. *Conservative shift* is marginally significant ($p = .08$) and negative, providing moderate evidence that laws exhibit less survivability in the post–New Deal era when Congress shifts to the right after enactment. All in all, we conclude that there is weak evidence—at best—to support the notion that conservatives are more successful in their repeal efforts.

Lastly, in model 12 in table D9, we take a closer look at the drift variable in the main model. Conceivably, the negative and significant effect indicates that bills are *less* likely to survive when a large percentage of the enacting coalition remains in Congress after enactment. Needless to say, this is the opposite of expectations. Yet one possibility is that this variable is simply picking up the normal temporal dynamics of repeal, where the raw data indicate that repeals are most likely in the first decade after passage and less likely decades after enactment. In the model reported below, we included a series of 1/0 variables for each subsequent Congress (up to and beyond the 13th, or twenty-five years after passage) to control for a law's initial instability and subsequent path dependency. Because of significant historical variation in how quickly the enacting Congress degrades, we can easily separate these two processes.[13] Looking at the results, we can see that the variable *coalition drift* is insignificant once we control these temporal effects. Although this failed to confirm the drift hypothesis (Horn and Shepsle 1989), it is no longer the opposite of expectations.

NOTES

CHAPTER ONE

1. See Jordan Fabian, "White House Scoffs at Obamacare Repeal Vote," TheHill.com, January 7, 2016, https://thehill.com/homenews/administration/265091-white-house-scoffs-at-obamacare-repeal-vote.

2. We created this figure by recording the frequency of the word "repeal" in articles that also contained the word "Congress" in the historical *New York Times*. We then aggregated the data in six-month intervals.

3. An obvious downside of this approach is that academics, policy experts, and journalists may use the term "repeal" to describe actions that are not literally repeals from a legal standpoint. For example, lawmakers may pass an amendment that effectively nullifies a law without striking the original text from the US Code.

4. See Obama's signing statement of April 14, 2011.

5. See HSS Secretary Sebelius's letter to Congress of October 14, 2011.

6. See President Donald Trump's State of the Union Address of January 30, 2019.

7. Although most journalists, lawmakers, and other political observers cite the GOP's Tax Cuts and Jobs Act (HR 1) as having repealed the individual mandate, the fact is that most of the individual mandate's statutory text remains in place. See PL 115-97 Section 11081, which reads: "(a) In General—Section 500A(c) is amended—(1) in paragraph (2)(B)(iii), by striking '2.5 percent' and inserting 'Zero percent,' and (2) in paragraph (3)—(A) by striking '$695 in subparagraph (A) and inserting '$0,' and (B) by striking subparagraph (D)." As we note in body of the chapter, we consider this a repeal on substantive grounds—given that it "nullified," "annulled," or "undid" a key element of the ACA—and discuss it as such in the book.

8. See chapter 15, "Unlimited Power of Majority in the United States, and Its Consequences."

9. See part III, lecture 21, "Of Reports of Judicial Decisions."

10. While McKelvey (1976), Schofield (1978), and McKelvey and Schofield (1987) suggest that stable equilibria are uncommon in multidimensional games, the actual set of solutions that are observed empirically are constrained to the uncovered set, or a rela-

tively small subset of possible outcomes (McKelvey 1986; Bianco, Jeliazkov, and Sened 2004; Bower-Bir et al. 2015). In behavioral psychology, when the number of options available expands from one to several, the choice process becomes easier (Grant and Schwartz 2011). Lastly, while some authors cite a phenomenon where a greater range of choices reduces actors' decision-making capacity, often called "choice paralysis," a recent meta-analysis found no consistent evidence of such paralysis (Scheibehenne, Greifeneder, and Todd 2010).

11. While the reversion point may have evolved over time as well—as in the case of inflation adjusting the meaning of a minimum-wage law—the implication is still that the reversion point is still a relatively familiar concept to lawmakers. Moreover, there are policy areas (such as immigration quotas) where the reversion point does not naturally evolve.

12. In contrast, the alternative scenario, where there are diffuse benefits to a potential repeal, with costs specific to a particular sector, is unlikely to see repeals. As LaPira and Thomas (2017) point out, political lobbyists work to stave off political threats, particularly for well-resourced organized interests. With diffuse benefits, the "for" constituency is unlikely to overcome this opposition in a system that already has a status quo bias, and thus the odds of policy reversal are low.

13. We define a "large" number of cosponsors as a standard deviation above the mean for that chamber (thirteen cosponsors in the Senate and thirty-nine cosponsors in the House). In the public law model we use the number of cosponsors in the originating chamber. Because the cosponsorship data are only available after the 92nd Congress, the model used to create figure 1.2 is restricted to the period from 1973 to 2016. In appendix A we report the results of an analysis for the full time period, from 1947 to 2016, that includes all bills irrespective of who sponsored it or the number of cosponsors. Our primary results are the same.

14. In the case of repeals and amendments, we used the keywords "repeal" and "amendment" exclusively. In the case of reauthorizations, we used the terms "reauthorize," "reauthorization," "to extend," and "to renew." And for appropriations bills, we use the keywords "appropriation" and "appropriate."

CHAPTER TWO

1. See the Policy Agendas Project databases.

2. Mayhew's session wraps are available in the appendix of *Divided We Govern* (1991, 2005) or on his personal web page: http://davidmayhew.commons.yale.edu/. Our extended session wraps are available at *future web address here.*

3. We restricted the search to adopted repeals and omit attempted repeals, as these are likely to be simple position-taking moves. We also omit significant amendments to existing policies, as tracking down and identifying which reauthorizations characterized dramatic shifts in scope would require a different search process. Focusing exclusively on repeals allows for a clearly defined dependent variable.

4. As an aside, we believe the relatively low number of enacting laws outside the top 10% further validates that our data set catalogs the most significant repeals in history.

5. We are unable to estimate the significance of all enacted pieces of legislation, as it is beyond the scope of this analysis. Clinton and Lapinski (2006) remains the comprehensive index of significant individual pieces of legislation.

6. Because Clinton and Lapinski's data set ends at the 103rd Congress, we simulated their estimates for laws from the 104th to the 111th Congresses. Using the *CQ Almanac* article size variable from the Policy Agendas Project, which is often used as a measure of a bill's significance, we map the Clinton and Lapinski significance estimates onto a common space and use linear projection to estimate the missing values. Although this is imperfect, linear projection is often used to "bridge" between two different scores (Shor and McCarty 2011; Windett, Harden, and Hall 2015), and given the downside of treating these observations as missing, we see this as a reasonable substitute. Data from the Policy Agendas Project are available at http://www.comparativeagendas.net/.

7. First, the National Maximum Speed Law had numerous cases of noncompliance, and second, Congress had begun to grant state exemption to the law in a 1987 spending bill. On the first point, see US Department of Transportation, National Highway Traffic Safety Technical Report, "The Effectiveness of the 55 MPH National Maximum Speed Limit as a Life Saving Benefit" (October 1980, DOT HS-805 694). On the second point, see Irvin Molotsky, "20 States to Win the Right to Set a 65 M.P.H. Speed," *New York Times*, December 29, 1987.

8. More broadly, this speaks to the point that each of these statutes exist in a particular context and that what is important in one context may be more so, less so, or equally so in the subsequent one. In this respect repeals depend on the statutes they replace but are not simply mirror images of the act. The National Maximum Speed Law was part of a suite of laws that dominated the country's attention for some time in 1973. When it was repealed in 1995, it did receive attention from highway safety advocates, but it did not dominate the country's attention the same way. By contrast, by 2009 the Gramm-Leach-Bliley Act, which repealed Glass-Steagall, made the act all the more notable in its absence than it would had it remained on the books.

9. Because the 1937 Neutrality Act permanently codified the provisions of the earlier acts (the 1935 and 36 acts contained sunset provisions), it counts as the enacting law in our database.

10. Specifically, we sum together the average significance estimate of each piece of legislation in Clinton and Lapinski's Top 3500 statutes for each Congress.

11. The significance of a Congress's laws are not a significant predictor of whether or not it passed any doomed statutes ($z = -1.14$, $p = 0.25$).

12. In addition, the 53rd Congress also repealed the McKinley Tariff.

13. See "Repeal of the Chinese Exclusion Act, 1943," Office of the Historian, US Department of State, https://history.state.gov/milestones/1937-1945/chinese-exclusion-act-repeal.

14. Specifically, we sum together the average significance estimate of each piece of legislation in Clinton and Lapinski's Top 3500 statutes for each Congress and add a scalar to ensure that all values are positive.

15. We focus on time as the number of Congresses after a bill is enacted. In investigating when a repeal occurs within a particular session of Congress, there is no consis-

tent pattern. Don't Ask, Don't Tell was repealed in the lame-duck session of Congress, after the elections took place but before the inauguration of the new class. By contrast, Grover Cleveland and Franklin Roosevelt called Congress into session early to repeal targeted legislation. Other major repeals, such as the Tax Reform Act of 1986 or the Chinese Exclusion Act of 1943, occurred in the midst of the congressional session.

16. Bianco (1994) describes one such instance of this in his discussion of the Medicare Catastrophic Coverage Act, which was passed in 1988 and repealed in 1989.

17. As we do in the main analyses in chapters 3–5, we define significant laws as those in the top 10% of all laws enacted since 1877 (Clinton and Lapinski 2006).

18. Given the theoretical reason to expect a curvilinear hazard rate (Ragusa 2010), as well as the observed hazard rate, we proceed with a log-logistic parametric survival model in our analytical sections. We discuss additional details in appendix B.

CHAPTER THREE

1. John Finney, "Senate Votes Again for Tonkin Repeal," *New York Times*, July 11, 1970, 7.

2. Eric Litke, "Paul Ryan Wrongly Claims Actuaries Have Determined Obamacare Is in a 'Death Spiral,'" PolitiFact,(January 18, 2017, http://www.politifact.com/wisconsin/statements/2017/jan/18/paul-ryan/paul-ryan-wrongly-claims-actuaries-have-determined/

3. See Congressional Budget Office cost estimate, "American Health Care Act," March 13, 2017.

4. Joseph Stiglitz, "Capitalist Fools," *Vanity Fair*, January 2009. We note that the Glass-Steagall repeal was largely bipartisan.

5. Following Jones and Baumgartner (2004), we did not include government operations and public lands in the analysis. As they put it, these two domains are largely "housekeeping in nature" (7). Our routine allows each enacted law to fall into multiple categories. For example, the USA Patriot Act is classified as belonging to international affairs, given its goal of curbing terrorist attacks, as well as law and crime, given its domestic surveillance provisions and criminal punishments. For all laws enacted from 1877 to 2011, 35% are classified into a single category, while 27% are classified into two domains. Roughly 17% cannot be classified (almost always because of inadequate bill descriptions) and are considered "miscellaneous." Similar miscellaneous categories have been used in comparable research. See for example Keith Poole's VoteView webpage, http://voteview.com/clacodes.htm.

6. We do so by standardizing each issue attention variable, subtracting the mean and dividing by the standard deviation.

7. In addition, two one-sided t tests indicate that this is a "precisely negligible" result (see Rainey 2014).

8. We interacted deaths in war with defense, the debt-to-GDP ratio with macroeconomics, and bank failures with banking and commerce. We also interacted bank failures with macroeconomics, given that bank failures correspond with poor macroeconomic conditions. We do not report the results of this analysis, but the interaction effect is insignificant as well.

9. We also tested an interaction term between macroeconomic laws and technological advancement. After all, technological advancements affect the economy's performance, while increased labor force productivity leads to a higher standard of living among citizens (Gordon 2016). We find an insignificant interaction term here as well.

10. A "war law" had to be enacted during wartime and contain the word "war" in the bill's description. We excluded "war department" and "secretary of war" to prevent administrative items from being classified as war laws. Likewise, we excluded references to the "war on poverty." In classifying periods of war, we included a reasonable time frame leading up to the war. Indeed, some war laws (like emergency "war taxes") were enacted before the United States' official entry into the conflict. For the Spanish-American War, we use the 55th Congress, when the war began and ended. For World War I, we use the 63rd Congress (when war broke out in Europe) to the 65th Congress (when the war ended). For World War II, we use the 75th Congress (corresponding with Germany's occupation of Czechoslovakia and the Japanese invasion of China) to the 79th Congress (when the war ended). For the Vietnam War, we use the 88th Congress (corresponding to the Gulf of Tonkin incident and Johnson's escalation) to the 92nd Congress (corresponding with Nixon's first term and the beginning of troop withdrawals).

11. One limitation with this analysis is the fact that the last time the United States mobilized for a massive scale requiring this sort of funding was the Vietnam War, which gives us relatively little purchase on understanding more contemporary politics.

12. Although the content of the two bills are nearly identical, the vote in the Senate is to proceed to the consideration of the bill. See vote 134, to consider S 3423, February 6, 1893.

13. One can't help but note that some lawmakers sought to repeal the Sherman Act on ideological and/or partisan grounds long before the Panic of 1893. First and foremost, although Grover Cleveland advocated repeal as a solution to the nation's economic woes, the fact is that Cleveland was a financial conservative and a champion of sound money. As a private citizen between his two terms as president, Cleveland opposed Harrison's decision to sign the Sherman Act and called free silver the "greatest peril" facing the nation (Haynes 2015, 180).

14. Quoted in Harvey (1896).

15. As Rogowski (2017) points out, the use of patronage was common in this era.

CHAPTER FOUR

1. Stuart M. Butler, "Assuring Affordable Health Care for All Americans," Heritage Foundation Report, October 1 1989, https://www.heritage.org/social-security/report/assuring-affordable-health-care-all-americans.

2. It should be noted that each study examines a separate aspect of statutory revision, so one possibility is that all three are correct in their own context.

3. We use first-dimension DW-NOMINATE scores. For simplicity we combined representatives and senators in the figure. Separate figures by chamber would show the same patterns.

4. We discuss how this variable was coded in the data and methods section.

5. While the analysis in chapter 1 begins in the 80th Congress, this analysis begins in the 83rd Congress due to data availability—as Stimson's public mood data begin in 1952.

6. Although this variable correlates highly with the measure of conditional party government used in the main analysis, there are subtle differences. Specifically, the measure we use here is the standard deviation in the distribution of first-dimension NOMINATE scores in the member's party, which is one of four components in the overall conditional party government index. We use this alternative because the overall index contains information on both parties, which would force us to aggregate the measure at the Congress level. For this analysis, because the time span is smaller and the focus is on the behavior of individual members, we wanted a less aggregated measure.

7. As in the main analysis, it records the number of House and Senate chambers (during a two-year Congress) the lawmaker's party was in the minority over the past decade.

8. Using Poole's DW-NOMINATE scores, we compute four values: (1) the gap between the median Democrat and median Republican, (2) the standard deviation of ideal points in the majority relative to the full chamber, (3) the percentage of explained variation resulting from regressing the member's ideal point on party affiliation, and (4) the proportion of overlap between the two parties' distribution of ideal points. Following Aldrich, Berger, and Rohde (2002) we then compute a single indicator that averages the data for both chambers using principal components analysis and a varimax rotation.

9. On this point, we cite Brambor, Clark, and Golder (2006) at length: "If a multiplicative interaction model is employed, it is nearly always necessary for the analyst to go beyond the traditional results table in order to convey quantities of interest such as the marginal effect of X on Y. . . . If the conditioning variable is continuous, the analyst must work a little harder. A simple figure can be used to succinctly illustrate the marginal effect of X and the corresponding standard errors across a substantively meaningful range of the modifying variable(s)" (74).

10. We do not report these estimates but are happy to make them available upon request. We note that the difference between these two individual effects is marginally significant ($p < .10$) but not at conventional levels ($p < .05$).

11. A test using the predicted median time to repeal is marginally significant ($p = .07$). We consider this a significant difference given the upper limit on a law's survivability. After all, the estimated likelihood of survival in the homogenous majority and mean time in minority condition at twenty-five subsequent Congresses is .9975, leaving little room for the homogenous and ascendant majority to have *greater* survivability.

12. We are unable to include these disaggregated vote totals in the full analysis because they are only available starting with the 85th Congress (1957–59).

13. In the model the majority passage margin variable has a p value of 0.06.

14. See the essays in Schram, Soss, and Fording (2003) for a thorough review.

15. In the case of the Family Assistance Plan, a family of four would receive $1,600 benefit that was to be taxed back at 50% above the first $720 of a family's income.

16. See table 10-26 in the US House of Representatives Ways and Means Committee's "Overview of Entitlement Programs: 1994 Green Book."

17. See Table 10-15 in the US House of Representatives Ways and Means Committee's "Overview of Entitlement Programs: 1994 Green Book."

18. See Kristina Peterson and Richard Rubin, "Intraparty Disputes Stall Republicans' Legislative Agenda," *Wall Street Journal*, June 27, 2017. .

CHAPTER FIVE

1. See "Bank Reform Bill Swiftly Approved," *New York Times*, June 14, 1933.

2. See "Testimony of Robert Kuttner," *Congressional Record*, October 2, 2007.

3. See Gillian B. White and Bourree Lam, "Could Reviving a Defunct Banking Rule Prevent a Future Crisis?," *Atlantic*, August 23, 2016.

4. See Oonagh McDonald, "The Repeal of the Glass-Steagall Act: Myth and Reality," Cato Institute Policy Analysis no. 804, November 16, 2016.

5. See Tyler Cowen, "Did the Gramm-Leach-Bliley Act Cause the Housing Bubble?," *Marginal Revolution* (blog), September 19, 2008, https://marginalrevolution.com/marginalrevolution/2008/09/did-the-gramm-l.html.

6. See William A. Niskanen, "The Clinton Regulatory Legacy," Cato Institute, Summer 2001.

7. These ideological changes do not occur on their own. Rather, they are nearly all the result of electoral replacement, with election results moving systematically in response to shifts in public opinion. As the public begins to favor more liberal policies, liberal politicians tend to be more successful than conservative ones (and vice versa). Thus we suggest that quite often, ideological changes in Congress reflect the ideological changes in the public's policy "mood."

8. As we note in our discussion of calculating the gridlock interval variable, in the postcloture Congresses (45th to 64th) we follow Heitshusen and Young (2006), who identify the gridlock interval as the entire range of preferences in the Senate, as much of the Senate's procedures in the nineteenth century were driven by unanimity. For the postcloture Congress, defining the gridlock interval is straightforward, as it is the zone between the filibuster pivot and the veto override pivot. Because Krehbiel's pivotal politics model was developed with the cloture era in mind, we do not report those estimates in the figure.

9. In that period the electoral cycles in the Senate meant that many of the senators in FDR's first term had been elected in 1930.

10. See the methodological challenges made by Chiou and Rothenberg (2008), however.

11. Such a process falls in the "preferences" category, rather than the "parties" chapter because it concerns the parties' preferred governing style. As Grossmann and Hopkins (2016) put it, "The distinct approaches of each party to policymaking are long-standing, reflecting the relatively stable preferences of their representative coalitions" (256).

12. We defined conservative and liberal as a half standard deviation above and below the zero point in Poole's first-dimension NOMINATE score (+.20 and -.20). A moderate is any member within this interval.

13. A one-way analysis of variance test indicates that this is a significance difference ($p < .01$).

14. Liberals sponsor 0.31 repeals, while moderates sponsor 0.35, a difference that is marginally significant ($p = .08$)

15. We start in 1957 because it coincides with the passage of the first civil rights act, which in theory should have increased repeal efforts in the area of civil rights. We use 1994 as the cutoff given that the 104th Congress represented a key point in the realignment of white southern Democrats to the Republican Party. In the 104th Congress, only about one-third of southern lawmakers identified as Democrats.

16. In the model, the number of total bills sponsored has twice as large an effect, but this is a strict control that accounts for a member's baseline sponsorship activity. In other words, it does not tell us much of substance. Likewise, the model indicates that senators sponsor fewer bills than representatives and that this effect is the same size as ideology. But this, too, is included in the model as a control variable and is not substantively important for our purposes. Because the effect of ideology has two significant interaction effects (model 2 in appendix C), we computed the effect sizes in that model.

17. In order to compare the continuous variables, which are on different scales, we standardized each continuous covariate. We defined a strong conservative as a standard deviation above the mean and a strong liberal as a standard deviation below the mean. A moderate is at the mean. Conservatives are expected to sponsor, on average, 0.38 repeal bills per Congress, while a strong liberal is expected to sponsor just 0.23.

18. As we do for ideology, an extremist is defined as a lawmaker with an extremism score a standard deviation above the mean, while a moderate has an extremism score a standard deviation below the mean. Expected value for extremists is .33 repeals per Congress, while a moderate sponsors 0.27 repeals.

19. Because the 115th Congress was not available in the Congressional Bills Project database at the time this was written, to produce a consistent count across Congresses we used the Library of Congress's Congress.gov website. As we did with the Congressional Bills Project database, we searched for the word "repeal" in the bill's title along with "Affordable Care Act" or "Obamacare." As noted previously, while there are inevitably more bills that contain ACA repeals in them, the advantage of this approach is that it identifies bills whose primary purpose is to repeal the ACA. By our count, from the 112th to 114th Congresses, Republican members sponsored an average of 35.3 ACA repeal bills. In the 115th Congress the number dropped to 26.

20. We also include a variable for how extreme the sponsor is, irrespective of its liberalism or conservatism. As we note in appendix C, we log this variable because there are a few very large observations. We do not discuss the variable in the body of the manuscript because it is not central the notion of ideological asymmetries and is insignificant in the model.

21. The exposed space measure is a refinement of the gridlock interval measure used in our 2015 *Political Research Quarterly* paper. The only difference is that while our previous measure for *any* movement to the left or the right for each interval (thus including both contraction and expansion), the current measure only accounts for contraction: that is when the conservative interval becomes more liberal or the liberal interval becomes more conservative.

22. While there are some advantages to Binder's (2003) measure of bicameral distance—which relied on chamber voting on conference committee reports—given the scope of our analysis, the conference vote measure is infeasible.

23. As noted earlier, we also tested a variable for the extremism of the bill's sponsor, irrespective of the direction of his or her ideology. Although this does not bear directly on party asymmetries, there are intuitive reasons why bills sponsored by extremists would be targeted for repeal. However, we find an insignificant effect.

24. It is important to note that the impetus for levying taxes for most of the nation's history, including in this period, was to pay for war efforts. Such was the case during the Civil War, with the adoption of the first income tax, as it was during World War I and World War II with the enactment of large tax increases. It is also important to note that conservative Republicans voted *for* the Sixteenth Amendment for strategic reasons, not ideological or problem-solving reasons. On the one hand, conservative Republicans hoped to head off passage of a separate income tax bill. On the other hand, conservatives miscalculated in their belief that the Sixteenth Amendment would be voted down by the states (Howard 1999, 51–53).

25. While the broader deductions for state and local taxes were enacted in the original Revenue Act of 1913, the deductibility of state sales taxes was not added to the tax code until the Revenue Act of 1942. In this time period the deductibility of state sales taxes was a big deal given that a number of states, mostly in the Midwest and Northeast, didn't have a state income tax, just a sales tax. For a brief period from 2004 to 2014 the deductibility of state sales taxes was reinstated by Congress. Eliminating all state and local tax deductions was hotly debated in 1986 but never made it into the final bill. Republicans finally succeeded in repealing these deductions in 2017.

26. As quoted in Stathis (2003), 263.

27. We use the Revenue Act of 1962 as the targeted law because it created the investment tax credit. We note that the investment tax credit was tweaked numerous times from 1962 to 1986, including its suspension in 1966, restoration in 1967, repeal in 1969, and reenactment in 1971.

28. An article in the *New York Times* from 1986 noted how negotiation among lawmakers with different preferences led to the final product: "Few other measures have been shaped and reshaped by so many conflicts and by so much cooperation. Few have reflected so many political trade-offs by so many politicians with such different styles and viewpoints." See David Rosenbaum, "The Tax Reform Act of 1986: How The Measure Came Together," *New York Times*, October 23, 1986.

CHAPTER SIX

1. Conservative columnist George Will criticized the Affordable Care Act as a "travesty of constitutional lawmaking" that was full of "grotesque provisions" in his op-ed "Government by the 'Experts,'" which appeared in the *Washington Post* on June 10, 2011.

2. Stuart M. Butler, "Assuring Affordable Health Care for All Americans," Heritage Foundation Report, October 1 1989, https://www.heritage.org/social-security/report/assuring-affordable-health-care-all-americans.

3. Norm Ornstein, "The Real Story of Obamacare's Birth," *Atlantic*, July 6 2015; Ezra Klein, "The Unpopular Mandate," *New Yorker*, July 25, 2012.

4. In the Senate vote on HR 3762, the "Restoring Americans' Healthcare Freedom Reconciliation Act of 2015," John McCain (R-AZ) and Lisa Murkowski (R-AK) voted yes. Susan Collins (R-ME) voted no.

5. See Juliet Eilperin, Sean Sullivan, and Ed O'Keefe, "Senate Republicans' Effort to 'Repeal and Replace' Obamacare All but Collapses," *Washington Post*, July 18, 2017.

6. See Brian Faler, "GOP Unity (for Now) on House Tax Plan," *Politico*, November 2, 2017.

7. See David Brooks, "The G.O.P. Rejects Conservatism," *New York Times*, June 27, 2017.

8. See Robert Reich, "Democrats Once Represented the Working Class. Not Any More," *Guardian* November 10, 2016.

9. Frank (2016).

10. See Chuck Schumer, "A Better Deal for American Workers," *New York Times*, July 24, 2017.

11. In the House, 68% of Democrats and 69% of Republicans voted for the Eighteenth Amendment. See House vote no. 61 on S. J. Res. 17 (December 18, 1917). In the Senate, an earlier resolution passed with the support of 75% of Democrats and 78% of Republicans. See Senate vote no. 121 on S. J. Res. 17 (August 1, 1917).

12. "Leaders Here Hail Move for Repeal," *New York Times*, February 17, 1933, 34.

13. John Malcom, "Consideration of a Convention to Propose Amendments under Article V of the U.S. Constitution," Heritage Foundation Report, February 19, 2016.

14. Excluding war laws, which are expressly temporary and thus unique.

APPENDIX A

1. We obtained this variable from the Congressional Bills Project database.
2. For each of these measures, we used Keith Poole's (1997) DW-NOMINATE scores.
3. We divided both variables by one thousand in the analysis.
4. We divided this variable by one thousand in the analysis.
5. We obtained these data from the Policy Agendas Project database.
6. In the model restricted to bills with a high chance of passage, two variables are significant and the opposite direction: *chamber median distance* in the Senate bills model and *congress workload* in the all bills model. In the full analysis of all bills in table A2, however, these variables are in the correct direction and statistically significant.

APPENDIX B

1. We defined "at the time of its repeal" as six months before the date of the repeal and six months after. We searched multiple terms associated with the repealed law. In some cases, this was simply the name of the enacting law. In other cases, we needed to search for the specific provision or statute that was repealed. Finally, in some cases we needed to include the word "repeal" to ensure the count did not inflate the number

of stories. For example, searching for "gold standard" in 1933 produced hundreds of stories that were simply critical of the gold standard as well as stories that focused on FDR's executive actions. By adding the term "repeal" to our search, we ensured that the stories focused on Congress's efforts to undo the law.

APPENDIX C

1. In a Poisson count model, the dispersion parameter, alpha, is significantly greater than zero, indicating our data are indeed overdispersed.
2. Data are available at http://stimson.web.unc.edu/data/.
3. On their website, Adler and Wilkerson write: "The incentive to sponsor bills for position-taking purposes was stronger prior to these reforms and, not surprisingly, sponsorship activity declines after these reforms, while success rates for legislation increases." See http://www.congressionalbills.org/trends.html.

APPENDIX D

1. In our 2015 article, the population consisted of repealed laws only, not all laws in the top 10%. For this reason, we have a slightly different sample size of repeals in this book. As we noted in the 2015 article, we took steps to validate that the results were not biased by the exclusion of nonrepealed laws. We believe similarity of the results in this book support that claim.
2. The log-normal model had an Akaike information criterion (AIC) of 720 and a Bayesian information criterion (BIC) of 1067. The log-logistic model had an AIC of 732 and a BIC of 1079. The Weibull model had an AIC of 738 and a BIC of 1085.
3. The Cox model had an AIC of 1048 and a BIC of 1376.
4. We obtained the final passage votes from two sources. For the period from the 85th to 112th Congresses (1957–2013), we use the PIPC Roll-Call Database compiled by Crespin, Roberts, and Rohde. In this database all recorded votes are classified according to their type: final passage, amendment, motion to table, etc. If a vote had multiple final passage votes, or a final passage vote and then a vote on a conference report, we use the last vote in the sequence. For the period from the 45th Congress to the 84th Congress, no comparable data set is available. Our only option is the Swift et al. (2009) database that identifies all recorded votes from the 1st to the 101st Congresses. Unfortunately, these votes have not been classified according to their type. We made a good faith effort to identify the final passage vote by culling the database to identify the final vote on a bill (using the date variable) and using only votes that had a majority. While votes other than final passage votes are no doubt included in our analysis, because the PIPC and Swift et al. databases overlap from the 85th to 101st Congresses, we can assess the suitability of this approach. Fortunately, the PIPC final passage votes and the final passage votes we identify in the Swift et al. database correlate at 0.94.
5. We see two limitations with the keyword approach. First, some words may not appear in the Policy Agendas Project descriptions. Although the examples provided by Policy Agendas Project are quite extensive, they are certainly not exhaustive. Second,

because the Policy Agendas Project database was created for the post–World War II era, some period-specific keywords may not be included for the period 1877–1945. Our supervised machine-learning algorithm is designed to address these issues.

6. For defense and fatalities in conflict, we restricted the analysis to periods when the number of deaths is greater than zero (i.e., there was at least some conflict overseas). For bank failures, we restricted the analysis to when the number of bank failures was greater than one hundred (i.e., a nontrivial number of bank failures). On both refinements, we would expect periods of relative calm to have little relationship and periods of at least moderate problems in each domain to be when Congress acts. For the debt-to-GDP ratio, we restricted it to when the number of deaths in war is less than ten thousand. On this final restriction, we wanted to remove periods of major war when debt spikes for reasons that are not directly tied to a poor economy.

7. Our data on congressional hearings came from the Policy Agendas Project database. In the model, the effect of hearings is per every one hundred hearings.

8. Jones and Baumgartner (2004) note that during the McCarthy era, Congress dedicated a significant number of hearings to issues that *suppressed* civil rights and liberties. As they put it, this is "an important reminder that attention congruence does not guarantee positional agreement" (9). We suspect that an additional issue may be causing the negative correlation in our analysis: the challenges of passing civil rights legislation in the 1950s and 1960s. Simply put, though issue attention spiked in this period, Democrats struggled to overcome resistance from their southern constituents.

9. We find in the data that the number of hearings in defense is nearly constant across the postwar era. We believe this reflects the fact that defense requires constant "maintenance" in the absence of a major world war. Besides, we are comforted by the fact that our measure of defense issue attention correlates so strongly with the number of deaths in war.

10. Michael H. Crespin and David Rohde, Political Institutions and Public Choice Roll-Call Database," https://ou.edu/carlalbertcenter/research/pipc-votes/.

11. Jason Roberts, David Rohde, and Michael H. Crespin, Political Institutions and Public Choice Senate Roll-Call Database, https://ou.edu/carlalbertcenter/research/pipc-votes/

12. Because of the already limited sample size, we treated any unrecorded vote (for example, voice votes) as unanimous.

13. In other words, the effect of time and coalition degradation are not collinear as one might expect. For example, our data show that for the 45th Congress (1877–79), just 10% of lawmakers remained in power by the fifth subsequent Congress. By the 104th Congress (1995–97), 47% of lawmakers remained in power by the fifth subsequent Congress.

REFERENCES

Abramowitz, Alan I., and Steven W. Webster. 2016. "The Rise of Negative Partisanship and the Nationalization of U.S. Elections in the 21st Century." *Electoral Studies* 41(2): 12–22.

———. 2018. "Negative Partisanship: Why Americans Dislike Parties but Behave Like Rabid Partisans." *Political Psychology* 39(1): 119–35.

Abramson, Paul, John Aldrich, and David Rohde. 2002. *Continuity and Change in the 2000 Elections*. Washington, DC: CQ Press.

Adler, E. Scott, and John D. Wilkerson. 2012. *Congress and the Politics of Problem Solving*. Cambridge: Cambridge University Press.

Aldrich, John H. 1995. *Why Parties? The Origin and Transformation of Political Parties in America*. Chicago: University of Chicago Press.

Aldrich, John H., Mark M. Berger, and David W. Rohde. 2002. "The Historical Variability in Conditional Party Government, 1877–1994." In *Party, Process, and Political Change in Congress*, edited by David W. Brady and Mathew D. McCubbins, 17–35. Stanford, CA: Stanford University Press.

Aldrich, John H., and David W. Rohde. 1997. "The Transition to Republican Rule in the House: Implications for Theories of Congressional Politics." *Political Science Quarterly* 112(4): 541–67.

———. 2001. "The Logic of Conditional Party Government: Revisiting the Electoral Connection." In *Congress Reconsidered*, 7th ed., edited by Lawrence C. Dodd and Bruce I. Oppenheimer, 269–93. Washington, DC: Congressional Quarterly.

American Political Science Association, Committee on Political Parties. 1950. "Toward a More Responsible Two-Party System." New York: Rinehart.

Ansolabehere, Stephen, James M. Snyder, and Charles Stewart. 2001. "Candidate Positioning in U.S. House Elections." *American Journal of Political Science* 45(1): 136–59.

Asher, Herbert B., and Herbert F. Weisberg. 1978. "Voting Change in Congress: Some Dynamic Perspectives on an Evolutionary Process." *American Journal of Political Science* 22(2): 391–425.

Austen-Smith, David. 1990. "Information Transmission in Debate." *American Journal of Political Science* 34(1): 124–52.

Austen-Smith, David, and William H. Riker. 1987. "Asymmetric Information and the Coherence of Legislation." *American Political Science Review* 81(3): 897–918.

Azari, Julia R. 2014. *Delivering the People's Message: The Changing Politics of the Presidential Mandate*. Ithaca, NY: Cornell University Press.

Baker, Frank B. 1992. *Item Response Theory: Parameter Estimation Techniques*. New York: Marcel Dekker.

Baker, Ross K. 2008. *House and Senate*. 4th ed. New York: W. W. Norton.

Barnes, Tiffany, and Timothy O'Neill. 2006. "Learning to Govern: The Texas Experience." *Journal of Political Science* 34(1): 1–36.

Baumgartner, Frank R. and Bryan. D. Jones. 1991. "Agenda Dynamics and Policy Subsystems." *Journal of Politics* 53(4): 1044–74.

———. 1993. *Agendas and Instability in American Politics*. Chicago: University of Chicago Press.

———. 2015. *The Politics of Information: Problem Definition and the Course of Public Policy in America*. Chicago: University of Chicago Press.

Bawn, Kathleen, Martin Cohen, David Karol, Seth Masket, Hans Noel, and John Zaller. 2012. "A Theory of Political Parties: Groups, Policy Demands and Nominations in American Politics." *Perspectives on Politics* 10(3): 571–97.

Bendix, William. 2016. "Neglect, Inattention, and Legislative Deficiencies: The Consequences of One-Party Deliberations in the US House." *Congress & the Presidency* 43(1): 82–102.

Bensel, Richard. 2000. *The Political Economy of American Industrialization, 1877–1900*. New York: Cambridge University Press.

Berry, Christopher R., Barry C. Burden, and William G. Howell. 2010. "The President and the Distribution of Federal Spending." *American Political Science Review* 104(4): 783–99.

Berry, William D., Richard C. Fording, Evan J. Ringquist, Russell L. Hanson, and Carl E. Klarner. 2010. "Measuring Citizen and Government Ideology in the US States: A Re-appraisal." *State Politics & Policy Quarterly* 10(2): 117–35.

Beth, Loren. 1971. *The Development of the American Constitution, 1877–1917*. New York: Harper and Row.

Bianco, William T. 1994. *Trust: Representatives and Constituents*. Ann Arbor: University of Michigan Press.

Bianco, William T., Ivan Jeliazkov, and Itai Sened. 2004. "The Uncovered Set and the Limits of Majority Rule." *Political Analysis* 12(3): 256–76.

Binder, Sarah A. 1997. *Minority Rights, Majority Rule: Partisanship and the Development of Congress*. New York: Cambridge University Press.

———. 1999. "The Dynamics of Legislative Gridlock, 1947–96." *American Political Science Review* 93(3): 519–33.

———. 2003. *Stalemate: Causes and Consequences of Legislative Gridlock*. Washington, DC: Brookings Institution Press.

———. 2017. "Four Lessons from the GOP Failure to Repeal Obamacare." Monkey Cage (*Washington Post* blog). July 28, 2017.

Birkhead, Nathaniel A. 2015. "The Role of Ideology in State Legislative Elections." *Legislative Studies Quarterly* 40(1): 55–82.

———. 2016. "State Budgetary Delays in an Era of Party Polarization." *State and Local Government Review* 48(4): 259–69.

Blocker, Jack S., Jr. 2006. "Did Prohibition Really Work? Alcohol Prohibition as a Public Health Innovation." *American Journal of Public Health* 96(2): 233–43.

Blossfeld, Hans-Peter, Katrin Golsch, and Götz Rohwer. 2007. *Event History Analysis with Stata*. London: Lawrence Erlbaum Associates Publishers.

Bond, Jon R., and Richard Fleisher. 1990. *The President in the Legislative Arena*. Chicago: University of Chicago Press.

Bower-Bir, Jacob, William T. Bianco, Nicholas D'Amico, Christopher Kam, Itai Sened, and Regina Smyth. 2015. "Predicting Majority Rule: Evaluating the Uncovered Set and the Strong Point." *Journal of Theoretical Politics* 27(4): 650–72.

Box-Steffensmeier, Janet M., and Bradford S. Jones. 2004. *Event History Modeling: A Guide for Social Scientists*. New York: Cambridge University Press.

Boyack, Andrea. 2011. "Laudable Goals and Unintended Consequences: The Role and Control of Fannie Mae and Freddie Mac." *American University Law Review* 60(5): 1489–1561.

Brady, David W. 1988. *Critical Elections and Congressional Policy Making*. Vol. 1. Palo Alto, CA: Stanford University Press.

Brady, David W., and Craig Volden. 2005. *Revolving Gridlock: Politics and Policy from Jimmy Carter to George W. Bush*. Boulder, CO: Westview.

Brambor, Thomas, William Roberts Clark, and Matt Golder. 2006. "Understanding Interaction Models: Improving Empirical Analyses." *Political Analysis* 14(1): 63–82.

Brodsky, Alyn. 2000. *Grover Cleveland: A Study in Character*. New York: St. Martin's.

Broockman, David E., and Daniel M. Butler. 2017. "The Causal Effects of Elite Position-Taking on Voter Attitudes: Field Experiments with Elite Communication." *American Journal of Political Science* 61(1): 208–21.

Bucci, Laura. 2018. "Organized Labor's Check on Rising Economic Inequality in the U.S. States." *State Politics and Policy Quarterly* 18(2): 148–73.

Buchanan, James M., and Gordon Tullock. 1962. *The Calculus of Consent: Logical Foundations of Constitutional Democracy*. Ann Arbor: University of Michigan Press.

Buchanan, Russell A. 1964. *The United States and World War II*. 2 vols. New York: Harper and Row.

Burke, Edmund. 1996. "Speech at the Conclusion of the Poll, 3 November 1774." In *The Writings and Speeches of Edmund Burke*, vol. 3, *Party, Parliament and the American War, 1774–80*, edited by V. M. Elofson and J. A. Woods, 68–70. Oxford: Clarendon.

Burnham, Walter Dean. 1970. *Critical Elections and the Mainsprings of American Politics*. New York, NY: W. W. Norton.

Burns, James MacGregor. 1963. *The Deadlock of Democracy: Four-Party Politics in America*. Englewood Cliffs, NJ: Prentice Hall.

Butler, Daniel M., and Eleanor Neff Powell. 2014. "Understanding the Party Brand: Experimental Evidence on the Role of Valence." *Journal of Politics* 76(2): 492–505.

Cameron, Charles. 2000. *Veto Bargaining: Presidents and the Politics of Negative Power.* New York: Columbia University Press.

Campbell, Angus, Philip E. Converse, Warren E. Miller, and Donald E. Stokes. 1960. *The American Voter.* Chicago: University of Chicago Press.

Carpenter, Daniel P., and David E. Lewis. 2004. "Political Learning from Rare Events: Poisson Inference, Fiscal Constraints, and the Lifetime of Bureaus." *Political Analysis* 12(3): 201–32.

Carsey, Thomas M., and Geoffrey C. Layman. 2006. "Changing Sides or Changing Minds? Party Identification and Policy Preferences in the American Electorate." *American Journal of Political Science* 50(2): 464–77.

Caughey, Devin, and Christopher Warshaw. 2016. "The Dynamics of State Policy Liberalism, 1936–2012." *American Journal of Political Science* 60(4): 899–913.

Chamberlain, Lawrence Henry. 1967. *The President, Congress and Legislation.* Columbia Studies in the Social Sciences no. 523. New York: AMS.

Chiou, Fang-Yi, and Lawrence S. Rothenberg. 2008. "Comparing Legislators and Legislatures: The Dynamics of Legislative Gridlock Reconsidered." *Political Analysis* 16(2): 197–212.

Clarke, Andrew J. (n.d.). "Congressional Capacity and the Abolition of Legislative Service Organizations." *Journal of Public Policy* 1–22.doi:10.1017/S0143814X1800034X

Cleves, Mario A., William W. Gould, and Yulia V. Marchenko. 2016. *An Introduction to Survival Analysis Using Stata.* Rev. 3rd ed. College Station, TX: Stata.

Clinton, Joshua D. 2012. "Congress, Lawmaking and the Fair Labor Standards Act, 1971–2000." *American Journal of Political Science* 56(2):355–72.

Clinton, Joshua D., Simon Jackman, and Douglas Rivers. 2004. "The Statistical Analysis of Roll Call Data." *American Political Science Review* 98(2): 355–70.

Clinton, Joshua D., and John Lapinski. 2006. "Measuring Legislative Accomplishment, 1877-1994." *American Journal of Political Science* 50(1): 232-249.

Coburn, Tom. 2017. *Smashing the DC Monopoly: Using Article V to Restore Freedom and Stop America's Runaway Government.* Nashville: WND Books.

Cohen, Jacob. 1988. *Statistical Power Analysis for the Behavioral Sciences.* 2nd ed. Hillsdale, NJ: Erlbaum.

Cohen, Marty, David Karol, Hans Noel, and John Zaller. 2008. *The Party Decides: Presidential Nominations Before and after Reform.* Chicago: University of Chicago Press.

Cohen, Michael D., James G. March, and Johan P. Olsen. 1972. "A Garbage Can Model of Organizational Choice." *Administrative Science Quarterly* 17(1): 1–25.

Coleman, John J. 1999. "Unified Government, Divided Government, and Party Responsiveness." *American Political Science Review* 93(4): 821–35.

Collingwood, Loren, and John Wilkerson. 2012. "Tradeoffs in Accuracy and Efficiency in Supervised Learning Methods." *Journal of Information Technology & Politics* 9(3): 298–318.

Conley, Patricia Heidotting. 2001. *Presidential Mandates: How Elections Shape the National Agenda.* Chicago: University of Chicago Press.

Cooper, Joseph, and David W. Brady. 1981. "Institutional Context and Leadership Style: The House from Cannon to Rayburn." *American Political Science Review* 75(2): 411–25.

Corder, J. Kevin. 2004. "Are Federal Programs Immortal? Estimating the Hazard of Program Termination." *American Politics Research* 32(1): 3–25.
Cox, Gary W., and Mathew D. McCubbins. 1993. *Legislative Leviathan: Party Government in the House*. California Series on Social Choice and Political Economy, 23. Berkeley: University of California Press.
———. 2005. *Setting the Agenda: Responsible Party Government in the US House of Representatives*. Cambridge: Cambridge University Press.
———. 2007. *Legislative Leviathan: Party Government in the House*. Cambridge: Cambridge University Press.
Crespin, Michael H., and David Rohde. 2018. Political Institutions and Public Choice Roll-Call Database. https://ou.edu/carlalbertcenter/research/pipc-votes/.
Critchlow, Donald T., and Philip R. VanderMeer. 2012. *The Oxford Encyclopedia of American Political and Legal History*. Vol. 1. Oxford: Oxford University Press.
Cross, Frank B., and Stefanie Lindquist. 2009. "Judging the Judges." *Duke Law Journal* 58(7): 1383–1437.
Curry, James M. 2015. *Legislation in the Dark: Information and Power in the House of Representatives*. Chicago: University of Chicago Press.
Cutler, Lloyd N. 1988. "Some Reflections about Divided Government." *Presidential Studies Quarterly* 18(30):485–92.
Davis, Kenneth S. 1986. *FDR: The New Deal Years*. New York: Random House.
Deering, Christopher J., and Steven S. Smith. 1997. *Committees in Congress*. 3rd ed. Washington, DC: CQ Press.
Dinan, John. 2011. "Contemporary Assertions of State Sovereignty and the Safeguards of American Federalism." *Albany Law Review* 74(4): 1637–69.
Dodd, Lawrence C. 1986a. "The Cycles of Legislative Change." In *Political Science: The Science of Politics*, edited by Herbert Weisberg, 82–104. New York: Agathon.
———. 1986b. "A Theory of Congressional Cycles: Solving the Puzzle of Change." In *Congress and Policy Change*, edited by Gerald Wright, Leroy Rieselbach and Lawrence C. Dodd, 3–44. New York: Agathon.
———. 2015. *Coalitions in Parliamentary Government*. Princeton, NJ: Princeton University Press.
Doherty, David. 2015. "How Policy and Procedure Shape Citizens' Evaluations of Senators." *Legislative Studies Quarterly* 40(2): 241–72.
Döring, Herbert, ed. 1995. *Parliaments and Majority Rule in Western Europe*. Frankfurt: Campus.
Dulles, Foster Rhea. 1955. *America's Rise to World Power, 1898–1954*. New York: Harper andBrothers.
Dupont, Brandon. 2014. "'Henceforth, I Must Have No Friends': Evaluating the Economic Policies of Grover Cleveland." *Independent Review* 18(4): 559–79.
Durr, Robert H., John B. Gilmour, and Christina Wolbrecht. 1997. "Explaining Congressional Approval." *American Journal of Political Science* 41(1): 175–207.
Edwards, George C., III, Andrew Barrett, and Jeffrey Peake. 1997. "The Legislative Impact of Divided Government." *American Journal of Political Science* 41(2): 545–63.
Erikson, Robert S., Michael B. MacKuen, and James A. Stimson. 2002. *The Macro Polity*. Cambridge: Cambridge University Press.

Erikson, Robert S., and Gerald C. Wright. 2009. "Voters, Candidates, and Issues in Congressional Elections." In *Congress Reconsidered*, edited by Lawrence C. Dodd and Bruce I. Oppenheimer, 71–95. Washington, DC: CQ.

Erikson, Robert S., Gerald C. Wright, and John P. McIver. 1993. *Statehouse Democracy: Public Opinion and Policy in the American States*. New York: Cambridge University Press.

Eskridge, William N., and Philip P. Frickey. 1994. "The Making of 'The Legal Process.'" *Harvard Law Review* 107(8): 2031–55.

Faulkner, Howard U. 1959. *Politics, Reform and Expansion, 1890–1900*. New York: Harper and Row.

Feigenbaum, James, Alexander Hertel-Fernandez, and Vanessa Williamson. 2018. *From the Bargaining Table to the Ballot Box: Political Effects of Right to Work Laws*. Cambridge, MA: National Bureau of Economic Research.

Fenno, Richard F. 1973. *Congressmen in Committees*. Boston: Little, Brown.

———. 1997. *Learning to Govern: An Institutional View of the 104th Congress*. Washington, DC: Brookings Institution Press.

Ferrell, Robert H. 1985. *Woodrow Wilson and World War I, 1917–1921*. New York: Harper and Row.

Finocchiaro, Charles J., and David W. Rohde. 2008. "War for the Floor: Partisan Theory and Agenda Control in the US House of Representatives." *Legislative Studies Quarterly* 33(1): 35–61.

Fiorina, Morris P. 1980. "The Decline of Collective Responsibility in American Politics." *Daedalus* 109(3): 25–45.

Flynn, D. J., and Laurel Harbridge. 2016. "How Partisan Conflict in Congress Affects Public Opinion: Strategies, Outcomes, and Issue Differences." *American Politics Research* 44(5): 875–902.

Frank, Thomas. 2016. *Listen, Liberal; or, What Ever Happened to the Party of the People*. New York: Metropolitan Books.

Frieden, Jeffry. 1997. "Monetary Populism in Nineteenth-Century America: An Open Economy Interpretation." *Journal of Economic History* 57(2): 367–95.

Friedman, Lee S., Donald Hedeker, and Elihu D. Richter. 2009. "Long-Term Effects of Repealing the National Maximum Speed Limit in the United States." *American Journal of Public Health* 99(9): 1626–31.

Friedman, Milton. 1990. "Bimetallism Revisited." *Journal of Economic Perspectives* 4(4): 85–104.

Friedman, Milton, and Anna Jacobson Schwartz. 1963. *A Monetary History of the United States, 1867–1960*. Princeton, NJ: Princeton University Press.

Foner, Eric. 2010. *A Short History of Reconstruction*. New York: HarperCollins.

Fuller, Wayne E. 1964. *RFD: The Changing Face of Rural America*. Bloomington: Indiana University Press.

Garraty, John A. 1968. *The New Commonwealth, 1887–1890*. New York: Harper and Row.

Gilens, Martin. 1996. "Race and Poverty in America: Public Misperceptions and the American News Media." *Public Opinion Quarterly* 60(4): 515–41.

———. 1999. *Why Americans Hate Welfare: Race, Media, and the Politics of Antipoverty Policy*. Chicago: University of Chicago Press.

Givel, Michael. 2006. "Punctuated Equilibrium in Limbo: The Tobacco Lobby and US State Policymaking from 1990 to 2003." *Policy Studies Journal* 34(3): 405–18.

Glennon, Michael J. 1990. *Constitutional Diplomacy*. Princeton, NJ: Princeton University Press.

Goldman, Eric F. 1960. *The Crucial Decade and After: America, 1945–1960*. New York: Random House.

Goldwater, Barry Morris. 1960. *The Conscience of a Conservative*. Shepherdsville, KY: Victor.

Gordon, Robert J. 2016. *The Rise and Fall of American Growth: The U.S. Standard of Living since the Civil War*. Princeton, NJ: Princeton University Press.

Grant, Adam M., and Barry Schwartz. 2011. "Too Much of a Good Thing: The Challenge and Opportunity of the Inverted U." *Perspectives on Psychological Science* 6(1): 61–76.

Grantham, Dewey W., and Thomas Maxwell-Long. 2011. *Recent America: The United States since 1945*. 3rd ed. Wheeling, IL : Harlan Davidson.

Green, Donald P., Bradley Palmquist, and Eric Schickler. 2004. *Partisan Hearts and Minds: Political Parties and the Social Identities of Voters*. New Haven, CT: Yale University Press.

Greenstone, J. David. 1969. *Labor in American Politics*. New York: Knopf.

Grofman, Bernard, Robert Griffin, and Gregory Berry. 1995. "House Members Who Become Senators: Learning from a Natural Experiment in Representation." *Legislative Studies Quarterly* 20(4): 513–29.

Grossmann, Matt, and David A. Hopkins. 2016. *Asymmetric Politics: Ideological Republicans and Group Interest Democrats*. Oxford: Oxford University Press.

Hacker, Jacob S. 2004. "Privatizing Risk without Privatizing the Welfare State: The Hidden Politics of Social Policy Retrenchment in the United States." *American Political Science Review* 98(2): 243–60.

Hacker, Jacob S., and Paul Pierson. 2005. *Off Center: The Republican Revolution and Erosion of American Democracy*. New Haven, CT: Yale University Press

———. 2011. *Winner Take All Politics: How Washington Made the Rich Richer—and Turned Its Back on the Middle Class*. New York: Simon and Schuster.

Harden, Jeffrey J. 2015. *Multidimensional Democracy: A Supply and Demand Theory of Representation in the American States*. New York: Cambridge University Press.

Harvey, Charles M. 1896. *History of the Republican Party Together with the Proceedings of the Republican National Convention*. St. Louis: Haas.

Haskins, Ron. 2007. *Work over Welfare: The Inside Story of the 1996 Welfare Reform Law*. Washington, DC: Brookings Institution Press.

Haynes, Stan M. 2015. *President-Making in the Gilded Age: The Nominating Conventions of 1876–1900*. Jefferson, NC: McFarland.

Heitshusen, Valerie, and Garry Young. 2006."Macro-Politics and Changes in the U.S. Code: Testing Competing Theories of Policy Production, 1874–1946." In *The Macro-Politics of Congress*, edited by E. Scott Adler and John Lapinski, 129–50. Princeton, NJ: Princeton University Press.

Hershey, Marjorie. 2005. *Party Politics in America*. 11th ed. New York: Pearson-Longman.

Hibbing, John R., and Elizabeth Theiss-Morse. 1995. *Congress as Public Enemy: Public Attitudes toward American Political Institutions.* New York: Cambridge University Press.

———. 1998. "Too Much of a Good Thing: More Representative Is Not Necessarily Better." *PS: Political Science & Politics* 31(1): 28–31.

———. 2002. *Stealth Democracy: Americans' Beliefs about How Government Should Work.* New York: Cambridge University Press

Hicks, John D., 1960. *Republican Ascendency, 1921–1933* New York: Harper & Row

Himelfarb, Richard. 1995. *Catastrophic Politics: The Rise and Fall of the Medicare Catastrophic Coverage Act of 1988.* State College: Pennsylvania State University Press.

Horn, Murray J., and Kenneth A. Shepsle. 1989. "'Commentary on Administrative Arrangements and the Political Control of Agencies': Administrative Process and Organizational Form as Legislative Responses to Agency Costs." *Virginia Law Review* 75(2): 499–508.

Hounshell, David A. 1985. *From the American System to Mass Production, 1800–1932: The Development of Manufacturing Technology in the United States.* Baltimore: Johns Hopkins University Press.

Howard, Christopher. 1999. *The Hidden Welfare State: Tax Expenditures and Social Policy in the United States.* Princeton, NJ: Princeton University Press.

Howell, William, Scott Adler, Charles Cameron, and Charles Riemann. 2000. "Divided Government and the Legislative Productivity of Congress, 1945–94." *Legislative Studies Quarterly* 25(2): 285–312.

Hoxie, Robert F. 1893. "The Silver Debate of 1890." *Journal of Political Economy* 1(4): 535–87.

Huddy, Leonie, Lilliana Mason, and Lene Aarøe. 2015. "Expressive Partisanship: Campaign Involvement, Political Emotion, and Partisan Identity." *American Political Science Review* 109(1): 1–17.

Huder, Joshua, Jordan Michael Ragusa, and Daniel A. Smith. 2011. "Shirking the Initiative? The Effects of Statewide Ballot Measures on Congressional Roll Call Behavior." *American Politics Research* 39(3): 582–10.

Hughes, Tyler, and Deven Carlson. 2015. "Divided Government and Delay in the Legislative Process: Evidence from Important Bills, 1949–2010." *American Politics Research* 43(5): 771-792.

Huret, Romain. 2014. *American Tax Resisters.* Cambridge, MA: Harvard University Press.

Iaryczower, Matias, Gabriel Katz, and Sebastian Saiegh. 2012. "Voting in the Bicameral Congress: Large Majorities as a Signal of Quality." *The Journal of Law, Economics, & Organization* 29(5): 957-991.

Jaffee, Dwight. 2008. "The U.S. Subprime Mortgage Crisis: Issues Raised and Lessons Learned." Commission on Growth and Development Working Paper no. 28.

Jenkins, Jeffery A., and Timothy P. Nokken. 2008. "Partisanship, the Electoral Connection, and Lame-Duck Sessions of Congress, 1877–2006." *Journal of Politics* 70(2): 450–65.

Jervis, Robert. 1992. "Political Implications of Loss Aversion." *Political Psychology* 13(2): 187–204.

Jones, Bryan D., and Frank R. Baumgartner. 2004. "Representation and Agenda Setting." *Policy Studies Journal* 32(1): 1-24.
———. 2005. *The Politics of Attention: How Government Prioritizes Problems*. Chicago: University of Chicago Press.
Jones, Bryan D., Tracy Sulkin, and Heather A. Larsen. 2003. "Policy Punctuations in American Political Institutions." *American Political Science Review* 97(1): 151–69.
Jones, Bryan D., Sean Theriault, and Michelle Whyman. 2019. *The Great Broadening: How the Vast Expansion of the Policymaking Agenda Transformed American Politics*. Chicago: University of Chicago Press.
Jones, David R. 2001. "Party Polarization and Legislative Gridlock." *Political Research Quarterly* 54(1): 125–41.
Karp, Jeffrey A. 1995. "Explaining Public Support for Legislative Term Limits." *Public Opinion Quarterly* 59(3): 373–91.
Kelly, Sean Q. 1993. "Divided We Govern? A Reassessment." *Polity* 25(3): 475–84.
Kemmerer, Edwin Walter. 1944. *Gold and the Gold Standard: The Story of Gold Money, Past, Present, and Future*. Auburn, AL: Ludwig von Mises Institute.
Kent, James. 1826. "Of Reports on Judicial Decisions." In *Commentaries on American Law*, 439–51. New York: O. Halsted.
Key, V. O. 1955. "A Theory of Critical Elections." *Journal of Politics* 17(1): 3–18.
———. 1964. *Politics, Parties, and Pressure Groups*. 5th ed. New York: Thomas Y. Crowell.
Kingdon, John W. 1984. *Agendas, Alternatives and Public Policies*. Boston: Little, Brown.
———. 1994. "Agendas, Ideas, and Policy Change." in *New Perspectives on American Politics*, edited by Lawrence C. Dodd and Calvin Jillson, 215–29. Washington, DC: Congressional Quarterly Press.
———. 1995. "Agenda Setting." In *Public Policy: The Essential Readings*, edited by Stella Z. Theodoulou, Matthew A. Cahn, 105–13. Englewood Cliffs, NJ: Prentice Hall.
Klar, Samara, and Yanna Krupnikov. 2016. *Independent Politics: How American Disdain for Parties Leads to Political Inaction*. Cambridge: Cambridge University Press.
Koger, Gregory. 2010. *Filibustering: A Political History of Obstruction in the House and Senate*. Chicago: University of Chicago Press.
Koger, Gregory, and Matthew J. Lebo. 2017. *Strategic Party Government: Why Winning Trumps Ideology*. Chicago: University of Chicago Press.
Krehbiel, Keith. 1992. *Information and Legislative Organization*. Ann Arbor: University of Michigan Press.
———. 1993. "Where's the Party?" *British Journal of Political Science* 23(2): 235–66.
———. 1998. *Pivotal Politics: A Theory of US Lawmaking*. Chicago: University of Chicago Press.
Landis, John D., and Kirk McClure. 2010. "Rethinking Federal Housing Policy." *Journal of the American Planning Association* 76(3): 319–48.
Landsberg, Brian K. 2003. *Major Acts of Congress*. New York: Macmillan Reference.
Lapinski, John S. 2008. "Reviving Policy Substance: Studying Policy Issues, Legislative

Significance, and Lawmaking in American Politics, 1877–1994." *American Journal of Political Science* 52(2): 235–251.

LaPira, Timothy M., and Hershel F. Thomas. 2017. *Revolving Door Lobbying: Public Service, Private Influence and the Unequal Representation of Interests*. Lawrence: University Press of Kansas.

La Raja, Ray J., and Brian F. Schaffner. 2015. *Campaign Finance and Political Polarization: Why Purists Prevail*. Ann Arbor: University of Michigan Press.

Lascher, Edward L., Jr. 1996. "Assessing Legislative Deliberation: A Preface to Empirical Analysis." *Legislative Studies Quarterly* 21(4): 501–19.

Lax, Jeffrey R., and Justin H. Phillips. 2012. "The Democratic Deficit in the States." *American Journal of Political Science* 56(1): 148–66.

Layman, Geoffrey C., and Thomas M. Carsey. 2002. "Party Polarization and Party Structuring of Policy Attitudes: A Comparison of Three NES Panel Studies." *Political Behavior* 24(3): 199–236.

Lebo, Matthew J., and Andrew J. O'Green. 2011. "The President's Role in the Partisan Congressional Arena." *Journal of Politics* 73(3): 718–34.

Lee, Frances E. 2009. *Beyond Ideology: Politics, Principles, and Partisanship in the US Senate*. Chicago: University of Chicago Press.

———. 2016. *Insecure Majorities: Congress and the Perpetual Campaign*. Chicago: University of Chicago Press.

Leighton, Wayne A., and Edward J. López. 2012. *Madmen, Intellectuals, and Academic Scribblers: The Economic Engine of Political Change*. Stanford, CA: Stanford University Press.

Leuchtenburg, William. 1963. *Franklin D. Roosevelt and the New Deal*. New York: Harper and Row.

Levi, Margaret. 1997. "A Model, a Method, and a Map: Rational Choice in Comparative and Historical Analysis." In *Comparative Politics: Rationality, Culture, and Structure*, edited by Mark Lichbach and Alan Zuckerman, 19–41. Cambridge: Cambridge University Press.

Lewis, David E. 2002. "The Politics of Agency Termination: Confronting the Myth of Agency Immortality." *Journal of Politics* 64(1): 89–107.

Lewis-Beck, Michael S. 1988. "Economics and the American Voter: Past, Present, Future." *Political Behavior* 10(1): 5–21.

Light, Paul. 2002. *Government's Greatest Achievements: From Civil Rights to Homeland Defense*. Washington, DC: Brookings Institution Press.

Link, Arthur Stanley. 1954. *Woodrow Wilson and the Progressive Era, 1910–1917*. New York: Harper.

Long, J. Scott, and Jeremy Freese. 2005. *Regression Models for Categorical Outcomes Using Stata*. College Station, TX: Stata Press.

Lord, Frederic M. 1980. *Application of Item Response Theory to Practical Testing Problems*. Hillsdale, NJ: Lawrence Erbaum Associates.

Lott, John R., and Stephen G. Bronars. 1993. "Time Series Evidence on Shirking in the US House of Representatives." *Public Choice* 76(1–2): 125–49.

MacLeod, Laurie, Darrel Montero, and Alan Speer. 1999. "America's Changing Attitudes Toward Welfare and Welfare Recipients, 1938–1995." *Journal of Sociology & Social Welfare* 26(2):175–86.

Madison, James. 1787. "Vices of the Political System of the United States, April 1787." Founders Online, National Archives. https://founders.archives.gov/documents/Madison/01-09-02-0187.

———. 1788. Federalist No. 62. In *The Federalist Papers*, edited by Clinton Rossiter, 347–50. New York: New American Library, 1961.

Maltzman, Forrest, and Charles R. Shipan. 2008. "Change, Continuity, and the Evolution of the Law." *American Journal of Political Science* 52(2): 252–67.

Mann, Thomas E. 1990. "Thinking about the Reagan Years." In *Looking Back on the Reagan Presidency*, edited by Larry Berman, 18–33. Baltimore: Johns Hopkins University Press.

Mann, Thomas E., and Norman J. Ornstein. 2012. *It's Even Worse Than It Looks: How the American Constitutional System Collided with the New Politics of Extremism*. New York: Basic Books.

Martin, Andrew D., and Kevin M. Quinn. 2002. "Dynamic Ideal Point Estimation via Markov Chain Monte Carlo for the U.S. Supreme Court, 1953–1999." *Political Analysis* 10(2): 134–53.

Masket, Seth. 2016. *The Inevitable Party: Why Attempts to Kill the Party System Fail and How They Weaken Democracy*. Oxford: Oxford University Press.

Mason, Lilliana. 2015. "'I Disrespectfully Agree': The Differential Effects of Partisan Sorting on Social and Issue Polarization." *American Journal of Political Science* 59(1): 128–45.

Matusow, Allen J. 1984. *The Unraveling of America: A History of Liberalism in the 1960s*. New York: Harper and Row.

Mayhew, David R. 1974. *Congress: The Electoral Connection*. New Haven, CT: Yale University Press.

———. 1991. *Divided We Govern: Party Control, Lawmaking and Investigations, 1946–1990*. New Haven, CT: Yale University Press.

———. 2005. *Divided We Govern: Party Control, Lawmaking and Investigations, 1946–2002*. 2nd ed. New Haven, CT: Yale University Press.

McCarty, Nolan, Keith T. Poole, and Howard Rosenthal. 2001. "The Hunt for Party Discipline in Congress." *American Political Science Review* 95(3): 673-687.

———. 2006. *Polarized America: The Dance of Ideology and Unequal Riches*. Cambridge, MA: MIT Press.

McGraw, Kathleen M., Samuel Best, and Richard Timpone. 1995. "'What They Say or What They Do?': The Impact of Elite Explanation and Policy Outcomes on Public Opinion." *American Journal of Political Science* 39(1): 53–74.

McKelvey, Richard D. 1976. "Intransitivities in Multi-dimensional Voting Models and Some Implications for Agenda Control." *Journal of Economic Theory* 12(3): 472–82.

———. 1986. "Covering, Dominance, and Institution Free Properties of Social Choice." *American Journal of Political Science* 30(2): 283–14.

McKelvey, Richard D., and Norman Schofield. 1987. "Generalized Symmetry Conditions at a Core." *Econometrica* 55(4): 923–33.

Miller, Susan M., and L. Marvin Overby. 2014. "Discharge Petitions and the Conditional Nature of Agenda Control in the US House of Representatives." *Party Politics* 20(3): 444–55.

Mowry, George Edwin. 1958. *The Era of Theodore Roosevelt, 1900–1912*. New York: Harper and Row.

Murphy, Paul L. *The Constitution in Crisis Times, 1918–1969*. 1972. New York: Harper and Row.

Niskanen, William A. 2003. "A Case for Divided Government." Cato Policy Institute Report 2.

Noah, Timothy. 2017. "Does Labor Have a Death Wish?" *Politico*, November 7, 2017.

Noel, Hans. 2013. *Political Ideologies and Political Parties in America*. New York: Cambridge University Press.

Nyhan, Brendan, Eric McGhee, John Sides, Seth Masket, and Steven Greene. 2012. "One Vote Out of Step? The Effects of Salient Roll Call Votes in the 2010 Election." *American Politics Research* 40(5): 844–79.

Olson, Adam, Timothy Callaghan, and Andrew Karch. 2017. "Return of the 'Rightful Remedy': Partisan Federalism, Resource Availability, and Nullification Legislation in the American States." *Publius: The Journal of Federalism*. 48(3):495–22.

Olson, Mancur. 1965. *Logic of Collective Action: Public Goods and the Theory of Groups*. Cambridge, MA: Harvard University Press.

Page, Benjamin I., and Robert Y. Shapiro. 1983. "Effects of Public Opinion on Policy." *American Political Science Review* 77(1): 175–90.

Page, Scott E. 2007. "Making the Difference: Applying a Logic of Diversity." *Academy of Management Perspectives* 21(4): 6–20

Patashnik, Eric M. 2003. "After the Public Interest Prevails: The Political Sustainability of Policy Reform." *Governance* 16(2): 203–34.

———. 2008. *Reforms at Risk: What Happens after Major Policy Changes Are Enacted*. Princeton, NJ: Princeton University Press.

Patashnik, Eric M., and Julian E. Zelizer. 2013. "The Struggle to Remake Politics: Liberal Reform and the Limits of Policy Feedback in the Contemporary American State." *Perspectives on Politics* 11(4): 1071–87.

Perry, Rick. 2010. *Fed Up! Our Fight to Save America from Washington*. New York: Little, Brown.

Petrocik, John R. 1996. "Issue Ownership in Presidential Elections, with a 1980 Case Study." *American Journal of Political Science* 40(3): 825–50.

Pierson, Paul. 1994. *Dismantling the Welfare State? Reagan, Thatcher and the Politics of Retrenchment*. New York: Cambridge University Press.

———. 2000. "Increasing Returns, Path Dependence, and the Study of Politics." *American Political Science Review* 94(2):251–67.

———. 2004. *Politics in Time: History, Institutions, and Social Analysis*. Princeton, NJ: Princeton University Press.

Polsby, Nelson W. 1968. "The Institutionalization of the US House of Representatives." *American Political Science Review* 62(1): 144-168.

Poole, Keith T. 1998. "Recovering a Basic Space from a Set of Issue Scales." *American Journal of Political Science* 42(3): 954-993

———. 2007. "Changing Minds? Not in Congress!" *Public Choice* 131(3–4): 435–51.
Poole, Keith T., and Howard Rosenthal. 1997. *Congress: A Political-Economic History of Roll Call Voting*. Oxford: Oxford University Press.
Pope, Jeremy C., and Jonathan Woon. 2009. "Investigating the Dynamics of Party Reputations, 1939–2004." *Political Research Quarterly* 62(4):653–61.
Quinn, Kevin M., Burt L. Monroe, Michael Colaresi, Michael H. Crespin, and Dragomir R. Radev. 2010. "How to Analyze Political Attention with Minimal Assumptions and Costs." *American Journal of Political Science* 54(1):209–28.
Quirk, Paul J. 1993. "Structures and Performance: An Evaluation." In *The Post-Reform Congress*, edited by Roger Davidson, 303–24. New York: St. Martin's.
Ragusa, Jordan M. 2010. "The Lifecycle of Public Policy: An Event History Analysis of Repeals to Landmark Legislative Enactments, 1951–2006." *American Politics Research* 38(6): 1015–51.
———. 2017. "An Examination of Congressional Efforts to Repeal the Affordable Care Act." In *Congress Reconsidered*, 11th ed., edited by Bruce I. Oppenheimer, 237–58. Thousand Oaks, CA: CQ Press.
Ragusa, Jordan M., and Nathaniel A. Birkhead. 2015. "Parties, Preferences, and Congressional Organization: Explaining Repeals in Congress from 1877 to 2012." *Political Research Quarterly* 68(4): 745–59.
Ragusa, Jordan M., and Anthony Gaspar. 2016. "Where's the Tea Party? An Examination of the Tea Party's Voting Behavior in the House of Representatives." *Political Research Quarterly* 69(2): 361–72.
Rainey, Carlisle. 2014. "Arguing for a Negligible Effect." *American Journal of Political Science* 58(4): 1083–91.
Ranney, Austin. 1962. *The Doctrine of Responsible Party Government: Its Origins and Present State*. Urbana: University of Illinois Press.
Richman, Jesse. 2011. "Parties, Pivots, and Policy: The Status Quo Test." *American Political Science Review* 105(1): 151–65.
Riddell, Craig W. 1981. "Bargaining under Uncertainty." *American Economic Review* 71(4): 579–90.
Roberts, Gareth, and Jeffrey Rosenthal. 2001. "Optimal Scaling for Various Metropolis-Hastings Algorithms." *Statistical Science* 16(4): 351–67.
Roberts, Jason, David Rohde, and Michael H. Crespin. 2018. Political Institutions and Public Choice Senate Roll-Call Database. https://ou.edu/carlalbertcenter/research/pipc-votes/.
Robertson, Andrew, Michael A. Morrison, William G. Shade, Robert Johnston, Robert Zieger, Thomas Langston, and Richard Valelly. 2010. *Encyclopedia of US Political History*. Washington, DC: CQ Press.
Rockoff, Hugh. 1990. "The 'Wizard of Oz' as a Monetary Allegory." *Journal of Political Economy* 98(4): 739–60.
Rogers, Steven. 2017. "Electoral Accountability for State Legislative Roll Calls and Ideological Representation." *American Political Science Review* 111(3): 555–71.
Rogowski, Jon C. 2017. "Electoral Institutions and Legislative Particularism." *Legislative Studies Quarterly* 42(3): 355–85.

Rohde, David W. 1991. *Parties and Leaders in the Postreform House.* Chicago: University of Chicago Press.

Rohde, David W., Edward H. Stiglitz, Barry R. Weingast. 2013. "Dynamic Theory of Congressional Organization." Unpublished manuscript.

Roof, Tracy. 2013. *American Labor, Congress, and the Welfare State, 1935–2010.* Baltimore: Johns Hopkins University Press.

Ryan, Josh M. 2011. "The Disappearing Conference Committee: The Use of Procedures by Minority Coalitions to Prevent Conferencing." *Congress & the Presidency* 38(1): 101–25.

———. 2018. *The Congressional Endgame: Interchamber Bargaining and Compromise.* Chicago: University of Chicago Press.

Saldin, Robert P. 2017. *When Bad Policy Makes Good Politics: Running the Numbers on Health Reform.* Oxford: Oxford University Press.

Sartori, Giovanni. 1968. "Representational Systems." In *International Encyclopedia of the Social Sciences*, 13:470–75. New York: Macmillan.

Schattschneider, E. E. 1935. *Politics, Pressures and the Tariff.* New York: Prentice-Hall.

———. 1942. *Party Government: American Government in Action.* Piscataway, NJ: Transaction.

Scheibehenne, Benjamin, Rainer Greifeneder, and Peter M. Todd. 2010. "Can There Ever Be Too Many Options? A Meta-Analytic Review of Choice Overload." *Journal of Consumer Research* 37(3): 409–25.

Schofield, Norman. 1978. "Instability of Simple Dynamic Games." *Review of Economic Studies* 45(3): 575–94.

Schram, Sanford, Joe Soss, and Richard C. Fording. 2003. *Race and the Politics of Welfare Reform.* Ann Arbor: University of Michigan Press.

Sheffer, Lior, and Peter Loewen. 2019. "Electoral Confidence, Overconfidence, and Risky Behavior: Evidence from a Study with Elected Politicians." *Political Behavior* 41(1): 31–51.

Sheffer, Lior, Peter Lowen, Stuart Soroka, Stefaan Walgrave, and Tamir Sheafe. 2018. "Non-Representative Representatives: An Experimental Study of the Decision Making Traits of Elected Politicians." *American Political Science Review* 112(2): 302–21.

Shepsle, Kenneth A. 1979. "Institutional Arrangements and Equilibrium in Multidimensional Voting Models." *American Journal of Political Science* 23 (1): 23–57.

———. 1992. "Bureaucratic Drift, Coalitional Drift, and Time Consistency: A Comment on Macey." *Journal of Law, Economics and Organization* 8(1):111–19.

Shor, Boris, and Nolan McCarty. 2011. "The Ideological Mapping of American Legislatures." *American Political Science Review* 105(3): 530–51.

Sides, John. 2006. "The Origins of Campaign Agendas." *British Journal of Politics* 36 (3): 407–36.

Sigelman, Lee, Carol K. Sigelman, and Barbara J. Walkosz. 1992. "The Public and the Paradox of Leadership: An Experimental Analysis." *American Journal of Political Science* 36(2): 366–85.

Sinclair, Barbara. 1999. "Transformational Leader or Faithful Agent? Principal-Agent

Theory and House Majority Party Leadership." *Legislative Studies Quarterly* 24(3): 421–49.

———. 2002. "The '60-Vote Senate': Strategies, Process and Outcomes." In *US Senate Exceptionalism*, edited by Bruce Oppenheimer, 241–56. Columbus: Ohio State University Press.

———. 2008. "Spoiling the Sausages? How a Polarized Congress Deliberates and Legislates." In *Red and Blue Nation? Consequences and Corrections of America's Polarized Politics*, edited by Pietro S. Nivola and David W. Brady.55–88. Washington, DC: Brookings Institution Press.

———. 2012. "Doing Big Things: Obama and the 111th Congress." In *The Obama Presidency: Appraisals and Prospects*, edited by Bert A. Rockman, Andrew Rudalevige, and Colin Campbell, 198–222. Washington, DC: CQ Press.

Sinkey, Joseph F. 2001. "A New Era for Banking." In "The Clinton Regulatory Legacy," edited by William Niskanen, special issue, *Regulation* 24(2): 53–55.

Skocpol, Theda. 2010. "The Political Challenges That May Undermine Health Reform." *Health Affairs* 29(7): 1288–92.

Skocpol, Theda, Kenneth Finegold, and Michael Goldfield. 1990. "Explaining New Deal Labor Policy." *American Political Science Review* 84(4): 1297–1315.

Snyder, James M., Jr., and Michael M. Ting. 2002. "An Informational Rationale for Political Parties." *American Journal of Political Science* 40(2): 90–110.

Solomon, Gerald B. H., and Donald. R. Wolfensberger. 1994. "The Decline of Deliberative Democracy in the House and Proposals for Reform." *Harvard Journal on Legislation* 31(2): 321–70.

Soss, Joe. 2000. *Unwanted Claims: The Politics of Participation in the U.S. Welfare System*. Ann Arbor: University of Michigan Press.

Stathis, Stephen W. 2003. *Landmark Legislation 1774-2002: Major U.S. Acts and Treaties*. Washington, DC: CQ Press.

Stevens, John Paul. 2014. *Six Amendments: How and Why We Should Change the Constitution*. New York: Little, Brown.

Stiglitz, Joseph E. 2009. "The Anatomy of a Murder: Who Killed America's Economy?" *Critical Review: A Journal of Politics and Society* 21(2–3): 329–39.

Stimson, James A. 1999. *Public Opinion in America: Moods, Cycles, and Swings*. 2nd ed. Boulder, CO: Westview.

Streible, Dan. 2008. *Fight Pictures: A History of Boxing and Early Cinema*. Berkeley: University of California Press.

Sulkin, Tracy 2009. "Campaign Appeals and Legislative Action." *Journal of Politics* 71(3):1093–1108.

Sundquist, James L. 1983. *Dynamics of the Party System: Alignment and Realignment of Political Parties in the United States*. Washington, DC: Brookings Institution.

———. 1988. "Needed: A Political Theory for the New Era of Coalition Government in the United States." *Political Science Quarterly* 103(4): 613–35.

Sunstein, Cass R. 2005. "Group Judgments: Statistical Means, Deliberation, and Information Markets." *NYU Law Review* 80(3): 962–1059.

Swift, Elaine K., Robert G. Brookshire, David T. Canon, Evelyn C. Fink, John R.Hibbing

———, Brian D. Humes, Michael J. Malbin, and Kenneth C. Martis. 2009. Database of [United States] Congressional Historical Statistics, 1789–1989. Ann Arbor, MI: Interuniversity Consortium for Political and Social Research. https://doi.org/10.3886/ICPSR03371.v2

Theiss-Morse, E., D.-G. Barton, and M. W. Wagner. 2015. "Political Trust in Polarized Times." In *Motivating Cooperation and Compliance with Authority*, edited by B. H. Bornstein and A. J. Tomkins, 167–90. New York: Springer.

Theriault, Sean M. 2006. "Party Polarization in the US Congress: Member Replacement and Member Adaptation." *Party Politics* 12(4): 483–03.

———. 2013. *The Gingrich Senators: The Roots of Partisan Warfare in Congress*. Oxford: Oxford University Press.

Theriault, Sean M., and David W. Rohde. 2011. "The Gingrich Senators and Party Polarization in the U.S. Senate." *Journal of Politics* 73(4):: 1011–24.

Thomsen, Danielle M. 2017. *Opting Out of Congress: Partisan Polarization and the Decline of Moderate Candidates*. Cambridge: Cambridge University Press.

Thorson, Gregory R. 1998. "Divided Government and the Passage of Partisan Legislation, 1947–1990." *Political Research Quarterly* 51(3): 751–64.

Thrasher, Christopher David. 2015. *Fight Sports and American Masculinity: Salvation in Violence from 1607 to the Present*. Jefferson, NC: McFarland.

Thrower, Sharece. 2017. "To Revoke or Not Revoke? The Political Determinants of Executive Order Longevity." *American Journal of Political Science* 61(3): 642–56.

Tocqueville, Alexis de. 1838. *Democracy in America*. New York: G. Dearborn.

Tomz, Michael, and Robert P. Van Houweling. 2010. "Candidate Inconsistency and Voter Choice." Presented at the Experimental Political Science Conference, New York University.

Tullock, Gordon. 1981."Why So Much Stability." *Public Choice* 37(2): 189–204.

Tversky, Amos, and Daniel Kahneman. 1991. "Loss Aversion in Riskless Choice: A Reference-Dependent Model." *Quarterly Journal of Economics* 106(4): 1039–61.

Volden, Craig, and Alan E. Wiseman. 2014. *Legislative Effectiveness in the United States Congress: The Lawmakers*. Cambridge: Cambridge University Press.

Walker, Jack L. 1977. "Setting the Agenda in the US Senate: A Theory of Problem Selection." *British Journal of Political Science* 7(4): 423–45.

Weatherford, M. Stephen. 1994. "Responsiveness and Deliberation in Divided Government: Presidential Leadership in Tax Policy Making." *British Journal of Political Science* 24(1): 1–31.

Weaver, R. Kent. 2000. *Ending Welfare as We Know It*. Washington, DC: Brookings Institution Press.

Weiner, Bernard. 1985. *Attributional Theory of Motivation and Emotion*. New York: Springer.

Weingast, Barry R., and William J. Marshall. 1988. "The Industrial Organization of Congress; Or, Why Legislatures, Like Firms, Are Not Organized as Markets." *Journal of Political Economy* 96(1): 132–63.

Wildavsky, Aaron B. 1964. *Politics of the Budgetary Process*. New York: Little, Brown.

Wilson, Woodrow. 1885. *Congressional Government: A Study in American Politics*. Boston: Houghton, Mifflin.

Windett, Jason H., Jeffrey J. Harden, and Matthew E. K. Hall. 2015. "Estimating Dynamic Ideal Points for State Supreme Courts." *Political Analysis* 23(3): 461–69.

Wlezien, Christopher. 1995. "The Public as Thermostat: Dynamics of Preferences for Spending." *American Journal of Political Science* 39(4): 981–1000.

Woon, Jonathan. 2008. "Bill Sponsorship in Congress: The Moderating Effect of Agenda Positions on Legislative Proposals." *Journal of Politics* 70(1): 201–16.

Zahariadis, Nikolaos. 1999. "Ambiguity, Time, and Multiple Streams." In *Theories of the Policy Process*, edited by Paul Sabatier, 73–93. Boulder, CO: Westview.

INDEX

AFDC. *See* Aid to Families with Dependent Children (AFDC)
Affordable Care Act: passage, 1–2, 70, 114, 132; repeal effort, 1–2, 8, 69–70, 114, 129–33, 136, 149, 185, 188, 192, 194
Agricultural Adjustment Act, 38
agriculture, 155–56, 167, 172
Aid to Families with Dependent Children (AFDC), 2–3, 7, 14, 34, 43, 47, 49, 95–97
amendments: floor, 16, 42, 170, 195; statutory, 5–6, 10–11, 14–15, 18–20, 28, 41, 55, 68, 75, 126, 144–47, 154–57, 185–86
American Political Science Association (APSA), 72, 134, 150
appropriation, 10, 18–19, 154–56, 186
ascendant majority. *See* campaigns and elections
asymmetric politics: and repeals, 20, 24, 105, 109, 111, 115, 118, 122, 131, 138, 140, 143; theory of, 68, 84, 100, 105, 108–9, 183, 191. *See also* polarization

banking and commerce: bank failures, 23, 58, 61, 68, 144, 175–76, 188, 196; issue attention, 58, 61, 168, 172, 175–76, 188; issue domain, 155–56; regulation, 25, 34, 52, 102–3
Barbour Fight Film Act, 41
Bayesian Item Response Model, 33, 159–60
bicameral distance: effect of, 120–21, 155–56, 167, 173–74, 177–78, 181–82; hypothesis, 101, 108; measure, 117–18, 154, 171, 193
bill complexity, 167, 169, 173, 175, 177–78, 180–82

bill introduction. *See* bill sponsorship
bill passage: correlates of, 93, 109, 146, 176; model of, 17, 154–56, 186; post-passage history, 4, 14, 36, 38–39, 43, 46, 48, 64, 75, 85, 92, 115–19, 124, 129, 143, 182–84, 190, 196; probability of passage, 13, 16–20, 127, 154, 157, 194
bill quality, 94, 169, 171
bill significance, 32, 167, 173, 175, 177–78, 180–82
bill sponsorship: data on, 17, 57, 83, 154, 163, 186; frequency, 154, 161–63, 192, 195; ideology of sponsor, 116, 118, 154, 163, 180–81, 183, 193; party of sponsor, 156–57, 163. *See also* repeal sponsorship
bill titles, 18, 146, 153–54, 172, 192
bimetallism: debates over, 5, 11, 65–67; free silver, 67, 189; gold standard, 3, 11, 34, 41–42, 56, 65–66, 195; silver coinage, 11, 34, 65–67. *See also* Sherman Silver Purchase Act
bipartisan legislation. *See* bill passage
Bland-Allison, 34. *See also* Sherman Silver Purchase Act
block grant, 34, 96
Brooks, David, 136, 194
Bryan, William Jennings, 67, 81, 88
Bush, George W., 81
Bush, George H. W., 107

campaigns and elections: ascendant majority, 22–23, 42, 48, 52, 71, 79–84, 86–91, 98, 107, 125, 129, 162, 167, 173–74, 177–78, 181–82, 190; congressional elections,

215

campaigns and elections (*continued*)
48, 101, 141; entrenched majority, 71, 79–80, 86–92, 98, 128; party cycles, 79–81, 86–88, 108, 128, 138, 140, 146; party seat change, 48, 79, 83, 86, 94, 110, 167, 173–74, 177–78, 180–82, 191; party strategy, 73; presidential elections, 1–2, 9, 30, 67–68, 81, 88, 95, 104, 141, 147, 188; repeal platform, 47, 80, 124, 134
Cannon, Joe, 78
cataloging repeals, 27–33, 146, 153, 159
Cato Institute, 102–3, 191
CBO. *See* Congressional Budget Office
China, 35, 43, 189
Chinese Exclusion Acts, 3, 35, 41, 43, 187–88
civil rights: issue attention, 155–56, 168, 172, 176, 196; passage, 116, 192; repeal efforts, 112–13, 144, 192
Civil Service Reform Act, 122
Clean Water Act, 122
Cleveland, Grover, 26, 41–42, 65–67, 188–89
Clinton, Bill, 41: financial regulation, 41, 102–3, 191; healthcare, 136; welfare reform, 2, 41, 43, 95–96, 98
cloture: effect of, 119–20, 124, 167, 173–74, 177–78, 181–82; hypothesis, 104, 106; measure, 191; and repeal efforts, 121. *See also* filibuster
coalition degradation. *See* coalition drift
coalition drift: effect of, 24, 45, 119, 167, 173–74, 177–78, 181–84, 196; hypothesis, 10, 24, 46, 101, 103, 109–10, 183; measure, 116, 119, 184, 196
Collins, Susan, 132, 194
committees: and bill passage, 95, 98, 153; campaign, 139; chairperson, 43, 132–33, 154–56, 162–63, 170; and committee reform efforts, 139–40 (*see also* Congress: reforms); hearings, 51, 57–58, 63, 109, 154, 170, 176, 178, 196; markup, 170
compromise, 4, 91, 115, 119, 131, 139
concentrated benefits and diffuse costs, 14–15, 132, 186
conditional party government: effect of, 88, 167, 173–74, 177–78, 181–82; measure, 78, 85, 190; theory, 4, 21, 23, 31, 43, 71–73, 76, 82, 85, 89, 91, 96, 98, 143, 154, 190. *See also* parties in Congress
Congress: agenda, 23, 49, 53–54, 79, 96, 125, 128, 133, 136, 138–40 (*see also* parties in Congress); approval, 24, 48, 137–39; do nothing, 25; legislative capacity, 4, 21–22, 24, 31, 68, 71, 76, 78–79, 86, 134–35, 139–40, 154; productivity, 4, 7, 11, 23, 25, 38, 43, 48, 72, 121; reforms, 36, 49, 78, 139–40, 195; repeal activity, 22–23, 25–28, 31, 33, 36–37, 39–45, 47–49, 89, 127; rules and procedures, 3–4, 11, 42, 49, 70, 76, 78, 96, 104, 106, 119–21, 124, 139–40, 145, 167, 170, 173–74, 177–78, 181–82, 191; textbook era, 78; workload, 154–56, 194
Congressional Bills Project, 17–18, 151, 161, 171–72, 192, 194
Congressional Budget Office, 51, 130, 188
Congressional Quarterly, 28–29, 166
Congressional Record, 30, 191
constituents: effect on repeal sponsorship, 83–84, 124, 134–37, 143; and issue ownership, 17; opposition to repeals, 13–15, 48, 126, 186; and party conflict, 138–39; and problem solving, 13, 51, 54, 66. *See also* public mood
Constitution: amendment convention, 141–42, 194; amendment repeal, 24, 140–42; Eighteenth Amendment, 140–41, 194; Fifteenth Amendment, 39, 52; Founding Fathers, 4, 170; Fourteenth Amendment, 141; and repeals, 3, 11, 46, 126, 142, 145; Sixteenth amendment, 122, 141, 193; Twenty-First Amendment, 141; war powers, 51
Consumer Pricing Act, 43
"Contract with America," 36, 42, 96
cosponsorship, 4, 18, 154, 157, 163, 186
crime. *See* law and crime

deaths in war. *See* defense
debt-to-GDP ratio, 58, 61, 144, 175–76, 188, 196
defense: and deaths in war, 58, 61, 63, 68, 175–76, 188, 196; issue attention, 155–56, 167, 172, 174, 176, 196
deliberation, 75–76, 170–71
democracy, 12, 71, 126, 137
Democratic Party. *See* parties
depressions. *See* economic downturns
de Tocqueville, Alexis, 4, 12, 126
divided government. *See* party control of Congress
Dodd-Frank Act, 147
Don't Ask, Don't Tell, 7, 35
doomed statutes: defined, 22, 26, 36; and

party control, 22, 40, 48; patterns, 37, 48; and productivity, 38–39, 43, 187

economic downturns: depression of 1893–97, 65–66; Great Depression of 1929–39, 5, 25, 37, 57, 59, 101, 103, 141; Great Recession of 2007–9, 26, 34, 52, 57, 59, 102; and problem solving, 23, 50, 53, 61, 68, 176; stagflation in 1970s, 57, 59. *See also* macroeconomics
education, 122, 155–56, 172
Eisenhower, Dwight, 88, 103
elections. *See* campaigns and elections
Emergency Railroad Transportation Act, 41
enacting: Congress, 26, 36–38, 48, 85, 116, 118–19, 129, 137, 184; laws, 4, 13, 30, 34, 84, 91, 94, 101, 137, 159, 165, 186–87, 194
energy, 57–60, 63, 155–56, 167, 172
entrenched majority. *See* campaigns and elections
environment, 13, 64, 80, 97, 155–56, 167, 172
Equal Pay Act, 116
event history analysis. *See* survival analysis
exposed space. *See* gridlock interval

Family and Medical Leave Act (FMLA), 96
Family Assistance Plan, 95, 190
Federal Deposit Insurance Corporation (FDIC), 101
Federal Election Laws. *See* Force Acts
Federal Reserve System, 102
filibuster, 1–2, 104–6, 119–21, 124, 136, 191. *See also* cloture
final passage. *See* bill passage
financial services, 25, 34, 41, 101–3, 147, 191. *See also* Glass-Steagall
Food Quality Protection Act, 41
Food Stamp Act, 116
Force Acts, 5, 30, 39–41, 52
foreign policy, 7, 35, 50. *See also* foreign trade
foreign trade, 155–56, 167, 172
Freedom Caucus, 131–32
free silver. *See* bimetallism
Friedman, Milton, 65–66, 95

General Land Revision Act, 41
Gingrich, Newt, 42–43, 89, 95–96, 140
Glass-Steagall: and the Great Recession, 26, 102, 191; law, 25, 101–2, 106, 191; repeal of, 2–3, 22, 25–26, 33–34, 47–49, 52, 101–3, 187–88, 191

gold. *See* bimetallism
Goldwater, Barry, 21, 24, 97, 100
Gramm-Leach-Bliley Act, 34, 41, 187, 191
Great Society, 136
Greenspan, Allan, 103
gridlock, 74, 134, 138, 154
gridlock interval: effect of, 24, 119–25, 129, 167, 173–74, 177–78, 181–82; hypothesis, 24, 104–6, 116–18; measure, 106–7, 116–18, 122, 191–92
Gulf of Tonkin Resolution: passage, 50–51, 116, 188–89; repeal, 3, 35, 41, 47, 50–51, 61, 65, 127

health care: issue domain, 155–56, 171–72; reform, 1–2, 9, 69–70, 129, 131–32, 135, 189, 193; Republican divisions on, 132–33. *See also* Affordable Care Act
hearings. *See* committees
Heritage Foundation, 141, 189, 193–94
historical minority status: effect of, 42, 48, 52, 84, 88–91, 98, 125, 129, 162, 167, 173–74, 177–78, 181–82, 190; hypothesis, 22–23, 71, 79–80, 82–83, 86, 89; measure, 81, 86–87, 190
Huckabee, Mike, 141

immigration, 35, 136, 168, 172, 186
impeachment, 26
individual mandate, 70, 131, 133, 194. *See also* Affordable Care Act
interest groups, 13–15, 126
international affairs, 155–56, 167, 172, 188
issue attention: effect of, 59–60, 63, 68, 127, 155–56, 167, 173–74, 177–78, 180–82, 187, 196; hypothesis, 4, 50, 52–56; measure, 23, 56–58, 63, 68, 154, 169, 171–72, 176, 188. *See also* problem solving

Japan, 43, 189
Javits, Jacob, 51, 61
Jim Crow, 52
Johnson, Andrew, 26, 35
Johnson, Jack, 62
Johnson, Lyndon, 47, 50–51, 189

Kennedy, John Fitzgerald, 123
killer congresses: defined, 26, 36, 39; and party control, 22, 40, 42, 48–49; patterns, 39–41, 43; and productivity, 43, 49
Ku Klux Klan, 39, 52

Labrador, Raul, 69, 130
landmark laws: and amendments, 55; database of, 56, 85, 118, 143, 151, 165, 188; measurement of, 30–31, 33; and repeals, 8, 15, 25–26, 36–39, 43, 46, 52, 76, 89, 92, 94, 124, 127, 133, 136–37, 147, 151, 169; and repeal significance, 102, 159; and unified vs. divided government, 38, 72, 74, 104, 109. *See also* Congress
law and crime, 96, 141, 155–56, 167, 172, 188
law creation: compared to repeal, 1–4, 6–7, 11–14, 25, 38, 43–44, 48–49, 55, 68, 71, 74, 80, 93, 126–28, 135, 139, 143, 145–47, 163; and parties, 4, 84, 86, 89, 91–92, 94, 137; and preferences, 100–101, 109, 122, 124; probability of passage, 18–19, 23; and problem solving, 49, 59, 68, 130, 137
legislative capacity. *See* Congress

macroeconomics: issue attention, 56–61, 144, 172, 175–76, 188–89; issue domain, 5, 56, 58, 63–64, 89, 93, 144, 155–56, 168
Madison, James, 4, 11, 126, 171
MCCA. *See* Medicare Catastrophic Coverage Act (MCCA)
McCain, John, 69–70, 130–31, 194
McConnell, Mitch, 132
McKinley Tariff, 41, 87, 187
Medicaid, 129
Medicare, 171
Medicare Catastrophic Coverage Act (MCCA), 9, 18, 35, 47, 50, 119, 127, 188
middle class, 122, 136
Miller-Tydings Act, 38
monetary policy, 3, 11, 56, 65–67, 144. *See also* bimetallism
Motor Voter Act, 96
Murkowski, Lisa, 131–32, 194

Nader, Ralph, 36
National Labor Relations Act, 121
National Maximum Speed Law: passage, 26, 36, 60–61; repeal effort, 2, 6, 22, 25–26, 33, 36, 48, 60–61, 65, 68, 187
Navy Promotions Act, 41
Neutrality Acts: passage, 7, 56, 187; repeal effort, 6–7, 34, 37, 41, 43, 127
New Deal: era, 106, 118, 180–81, 183; laws enacted, 42, 101; repeal efforts, 3, 34, 96, 102–3; and repeals, 42, 49
new law. *See* law creation

New York Times: articles, 123, 136, 187–88, 191, 193–94; and cataloging repeals, 28–30, 32; and measuring repeal significance, 32, 36, 159; repeal media attention, 185
Nixon, Richard, 41, 51, 95, 189
North American Free Trade Agreement (NAFTA), 96
nullification, 140, 142

Obama, Barack, 1–2, 8, 129, 131, 136, 147, 185, 188
Obamacare. *See* Affordable Care Act
oil, 26, 57
O'Neill, Tip, 15

Panama Canal Treaty, 136
parties: Democratic, 1–2, 8, 37, 39, 42–43, 48, 52, 65–70, 77, 80–81, 84, 87–88, 95–97, 99, 101–2, 105, 108–9, 111–13, 121–22, 129–30, 132–33, 135–37, 142, 149, 192, 194, 196; Republican, 1–3, 8, 24–25, 29, 39, 42–43, 48–49, 51, 61, 66–70, 81, 84, 87–88, 92, 95–97, 102, 105, 108–9, 111–14, 117, 119, 121–22, 129–33, 135–36, 140–42, 147, 149, 154, 190, 192–94
parties in Congress: agenda setting, 21–22, 42, 44, 71–73, 76, 78, 82, 84, 86, 91, 97, 134–35, 139, 169, 191; enacting party, 1, 4, 17, 85, 94, 108, 110, 127, 139, 145; party cohesion, 21, 42, 71, 73, 76–78, 81–93, 95–96, 98, 108, 111–12, 121–22, 125, 128–29, 132–33, 139, 146, 162, 190 (*see also* conditional party government); party leaders, 1, 15–16, 21–23, 42, 50–51, 70–73, 76, 78, 80, 82, 84, 96–98, 130, 132–33, 135, 137, 139–40, 146, 169, 194; party seat change (*see* campaigns and elections)
party control of Congress: ascendant majority (*see* campaigns and elections); divided government, 3, 31, 37, 72, 74–76, 85, 93, 104, 108; entrenched majority (*see* campaigns and elections); party cycles (*see* campaigns and elections); unified government, 2–3, 22–23, 31, 37–40, 42, 48–49, 61, 72, 74–76, 81, 83–85, 89, 92–95, 98, 104–5, 113, 128–29, 131, 133, 162, 167, 173–74, 177–78, 180–82
party organizations: party brands, 11, 13, 16–17, 20–21, 73, 91, 108, 127, 145; party platforms, 47, 80, 124, 134–35

party theory: cartel theory, 16, 71–73, 76, 82, 89, 96, 98; conditional party government (*see* conditional party government); electoral competition, 16–17, 21–23, 47, 69, 71–73, 79–80, 82, 85, 89, 91, 98–99, 115, 119, 131, 138, 142–143, 146; responsible parties, 4, 24, 30, 71, 134–35
path dependency, 14–15, 45–46, 48, 64
Patriot Act, 188
Pelosi, Nancy, 137
Perry, Rick, 141
Personal Responsibility and Work Opportunity Reconciliation Act (PRWORA), 41, 50, 95
PIPC. *See* Political Institutions and Public Choice (PIPC) program
plenary time, 21, 82, 96
polarization: asymmetries in, 109, 111 (*see also* asymmetric politics); historic patterns, 78, 88; and legislative productivity, 54, 108, 109, 113; measure of, 110–11, 154, 163, 170; and repeals, 111, 113–14, 154–56, 162
Policy Agendas Project: bill data, 17, 166, 187; database, 151, 186–87, 194; hearings data, 58, 172, 196; policy domains, 57, 62, 171, 195–96
policy problems. *See* problem solving
Political Institutions and Public Choice (PIPC) program, 151, 168, 179, 195–96
preferences, 20–21, 23–24, 32, 53–54, 56, 66, 68, 70–71, 73–74, 79, 83, 85, 99–101, 103–5, 107–11, 113–15, 117, 119, 121, 123–25, 127–32, 140, 143, 151, 168–69, 174, 191, 193
presidents, 2, 13, 23, 26, 29, 31, 39–40, 42, 46, 49, 51, 70, 72, 74–75, 83, 85, 87–88, 92, 97–98, 101, 110, 136, 189
problem solving: effect of, 46, 52, 59–63, 65–68, 97, 99, 128, 130, 141, 144, 169, 173–74, 176, 179, 193; measure, 54–59, 62, 83, 169–70, 176, 196; theory, 20, 23, 49–54, 63, 69, 71, 93, 100, 103, 105, 127, 130, 168. *See also* issue attention
Progressive Era, 29
prohibition, 141
public mood, 162

Railroad Unemployment Insurance Act, 41
Reagan, Ronald: and the gridlock interval, 106–7, 117; and legislative capacity, 68, 140; repeal efforts, 42, 52, 97, 102, 123

reauthorizations: probability of passage, 18–20, 146, 154–56, 186; and statutory revision, 5, 10, 28, 144
recessions. *See* economic downturns
Reed, Thomas Brackett, 42, 49, 78
Reed Rules, 42, 49, 78
repeal sponsorship: data, 28, 71, 82–83, 103, 109–10, 115, 143, 161; historic patterns, 111; hypotheses, 83–84, 111–12, 115, 142, 163; model of, 157, 161–63; results, 84–85, 111–14, 123–24, 128, 143, 163, 192
Republican Party. *See* parties
Republican Revolution, 49, 81, 102
Revenue Act of 1913, 193
Revenue Act of 1942, 123, 193
Revenue Act of 1943, 41
Revenue Act of 1962, 123, 193
"right-to-work" laws, 5, 121, 136–37
Roosevelt, Franklin D., 29, 41, 81, 102, 123, 183, 191, 195
Roosevelt, Theodore, 29
Rubin, Richard, 102, 191
Ryan, Paul, 1, 51, 130, 188

Schumer, Chuck, 137, 194
science and technology, 61, 155–56, 167, 172, 177
Sherman, John, 65. *See also* Sherman Silver Purchase Act
Sherman Silver Purchase Act: passage, 34, 41, 65–66, 189; repeal of, 34, 39, 41–42, 49, 65–67, 87, 127, 189
silver. *See* bimetallisim
social policy: durability, 15, 55, 64, 89, 93, 127, 132–33; issue attention, 64, 89, 93, 132–33, 155, 167, 172
Social Security, 8, 15, 95, 171. *See also* social policy
Southern Democrats, 42, 112–113, 121, 192
Speaker of the House. *See* parties in Congress
Stiglitz, Joseph, 26, 52, 188
sunsets, 9–10, 187
survival analysis: model of repeal, 46, 56, 85, 118, 165, 168, 173, 175, 177–78, 180–81, 183, 195; parametric vs. semiparametric, 166, 188

Taft-Hartley, 5–6, 88, 93, 121–22, 124, 136, 147
TANF. *See* Temporary Assistance for Needy Families (TANF)

taxes: Affordable Care Act, 2–3, 8, 70, 129, 131–33, 194; Civil War income tax, 63, 122, 193; excise taxes, 6, 87–88; gift and capital-stock taxes, 5; negative income tax, 95; Revenue Act of 1913, 193; Revenue Act of 1962, 123, 193; Sixteenth Amendment, 122, 141, 193; Tax Rate Extension Act of 1958, 41; Tax Reduction Act of 1975, 41; Tax Reform Act of 1986, 10, 41, 43, 121–23, 188, 193; Tax Reform Act of 2017, 5, 147, 185, 194

Tea Party, 131

technological advancement: effect of, 63, 68, 176–77, 189; measure, 62

Temporary Assistance for Needy Families (TANF), 7, 14, 34, 96

Tenure of Office Act, 3, 22, 25–26, 33, 35, 48

Texas Seed Bill, 67

transportation, 62–63, 155–56, 168, 172, 187

Trump, Donald, 2, 8, 129, 137, 141, 185

unified at enactment. *See* party control of Congress

unified at subsequent. *See* party control of Congress

unified government. *See* party control of Congress

US Code, 6–8, 25, 27–28, 30, 169, 185

Volstead Act, 5. *See also* Constitution: Eighteenth Amendment

voters. *See* constituents

Wall Street, 101, 136

Wall Street Journal, 191

War Powers Resolution, 35, 51, 61. *See also* Gulf of Tonkin Resolution

wars: Civil War, 39, 42, 63, 80, 87, 89, 122, 193; Cold War, 97; and policy productivity, 53, 62, 107; and repeals, 23, 50, 188; Spanish-American War, 87–88, 92, 189; Vietnam War, 35, 47, 50–51, 61, 189; war laws, 56, 63, 88, 92, 168, 189, 194; war taxes, 30, 56, 63, 87, 189, 193; World War I, 29, 34, 56, 63, 189; World War II, 7, 29, 35, 37, 43, 59, 62–63, 74, 81–82, 88, 104, 112, 122, 144, 147, 189, 193, 196

Washington Post, 28–30, 32, 36, 193–94

welfare: AFDC repeal, 2–3, 6–7, 14, 34, 41, 43, 47, 49, 95–98; durability of, 15, 55, 64, 89, 93; issue domain, 155–56, 172; and preferences, 100, 122; and problem solving, 50

Wheeler-Lea Transportation Act, 41

Wilson, Woodrow, 4, 29, 74, 81

working class, 124, 136–37, 147, 194

www.ingramcontent.com/pod-product-compliance
Lightning Source LLC
Chambersburg PA
CBHW051356290426
44108CB00015B/2041